EMOTIONAL AI

EMOTIONAL AI
The Rise of Empathic Media

Andrew McStay

```
[
    },
    "scores": {
      "anger": 1.0570484E-08,
      "contempt": 1.52679547E-09,
      "disgust": 1.60232943E-07,
      "fear": 6.00660363E-12,
      "happiness": 0.9999998,
      "neutral": 9.449728E-09,
      "sadness": 1.23025981E-08,
      "surprise": 9.91396E-10
    }
  },
  {
    "faceRectangle": {
      "top": 141,
      "left": 331,
      "width": 52,
      "height": 52
    },
    "scores": {
      "anger": 0.002451766,
      "contempt": 0.0005512201,
      "disgust": 0.0063303886,
      "fear": 0.000122375583,
      "happiness": 0.9589189,
      "neutral": 0.0222537462,
      "sadness": 0.008983561,
      "surprise": 0.000388026354
    }
```

Los Angeles | London | New Delhi
Singapore | Washington DC | Melbourne

Los Angeles | London | New Delhi
Singapore | Washington DC | Melbourne

SAGE Publications Ltd
1 Oliver's Yard
55 City Road
London EC1Y 1SP

SAGE Publications Inc.
2455 Teller Road
Thousand Oaks, California 91320

SAGE Publications India Pvt Ltd
B 1/I 1 Mohan Cooperative Industrial Area
Mathura Road
New Delhi 110 044

SAGE Publications Asia-Pacific Pte Ltd
3 Church Street
#10-04 Samsung Hub
Singapore 049483

Editor: Michael Ainsley
Assistant editor: John Nightingale
Production editor: Imogen Roome
Copyeditor: Aud Scriven
Proofreader: Leigh C. Smithson
Indexer: Silvia Benvenuto
Marketing manager: Lucia Sweet
Cover design: Francis Kenney
Typeset by: C&M Digitals (P) Ltd, Chennai, India
Printed in the UK

Library of Congress Control Number: 2017957217

British Library Cataloguing in Publication data

A catalogue record for this book is available from
the British Library

ISBN 978-1-4739-7110-3
ISBN 978-1-4739-7111-0 (pbk)

At SAGE we take sustainability seriously. Most of our products are printed in the UK using responsibly sourced
papers and boards. When we print overseas we ensure sustainable papers are used as measured by the PREPS
grading system. We undertake an annual audit to monitor our sustainability.

CONTENTS

ABOUT THE AUTHOR

Andrew McStay is Professor of Digital Life and Director of the Media and Persuasive Communication Network (MPC) at Bangor University. He advises diverse regulators and NGOs and sits on a number of ethics boards. His other books include *Digital Advertising* (Palgrave Macmillan, 1st edn 2009), *The Mood of Information* (Continuum, 2011), *Creativity and Advertising* (Routledge, 2013), *Privacy and Philosophy* (Peter Lang, 2014), *Digital Advertising* (Palgrave Macmillan, 2nd edn 2016) and *Privacy and the Media* (Sage, 2017).

ACKNOWLEDGEMENTS

Foremost, gratitude goes to my funders. This book was made possible by generous support from the UK's Arts and Humanities Research Council [grant number AH/M006654/1]. Appreciation also goes to those interviewed in the course of researching this book. At over 100 interviewees there are too many to list and some preferred not to be named. That said, your time, willingness to speak with me and clarification of follow-up notes have been invaluable. Quoted or not, each of you has shaped my understanding and consequently this book. Special mention is also due to Vian for reading and commenting on drafts. The book is undoubtedly better for your critical attention! Last, as anyone who has written a book knows, it really is a product of many hands, not least a careful copy editor and proofreader. Thanks all!

1
INTRODUCING EMPATHIC MEDIA

Emotions matter. They are at the core of human experience, shape our lives in the profoundest of ways and help us decide what is worthy of our attention. The idea behind this book is to explore what happens when media technologies are able to interpret feelings, emotions, moods, attention and intention in private and public places. I argue this equates to a technological form of empathy. As we will see, there are many personal and organisational drivers for using technologies to understand how individuals and groups of people feel and see things. These include making technologies easier to use, evolving services, creating new forms of entertainment, giving pleasure, finding novel modes of expression, enhancing communication, cultivating health, enabling education, improving policing, heightening surveillance, managing workplaces, understanding experience and influencing people. This is done through 'capturing' emotions. In computer science parlance 'capture' simply means causing data to be stored in a computer, but 'capture' of course has another meaning: taking possession by force. This book is in many ways an account of the difference between these two understandings.

Overall I suggest that we are witnessing a growing interest in mediated emotional life and that neither the positive or negative dimensions of this have been properly explored. This situation is becoming more pressing as society generates more information about emotions, intentions and attitudes. As a minimum, there is the popularity of animojis, emojis and emoticons on social media. These facilitate non-verbal shorthand communication, but they also allow services insight into how content, brands, advertising campaigns, products and profiles make people feel. The vernacular of emoticons increasingly applies both online and offline, as we are asked for feedback about our perspectives, how we are and what's happening. The emotionalising of modern mediated life is not just about smileys, however. Rather, the sharing of updates, selfies and point-of-view content provides valuable understanding of life moments, our perspectives and individual and collective emotions.

Interest in feelings, emotions, moods, perspectives and intentions is diverse. Political organisations and brands trace how we feel about given messages, policies, candidates and brand activity through online sentiment analysis. Similarly, advertising agencies, marketers and retailers internally research what we say, post, listen to, our facial expressions, brain behaviour, heart rate and other bodily responses to gauge reactions to products, brands and adverts. Increasingly, digital assistants in the home and on our phones are progressing to understand not just what we say, but how we say it. In terms of affective media experience, virtual reality has raised the bar in unexpected ways. As well as generating emotional responses that can be measured, this also tells analysts a great deal about what captures our attention. Augmented reality promises something similar, albeit in public and commercial spaces. Wearables attached to our bodies track all sorts of biofeedback to understand emotions and how we feel over short and extended periods of time. As we will see, this potential is being applied in novel, surprising and perhaps alarming ways. Indeed, some of us even insert 'technologies that feel' into our bodies to enhance our sex life. At a macro-level, cities are registering the emotional lives of inhabitants and visitors. This book assesses all of these phenomena, and more.

I call for critical attention and caution in the rollout of these technologies, but I should state upfront that I do not think there is anything innately wrong with technologies that detect, learn and interact with emotions. Rather, the practice of reading and detecting emotions is a step forward in improving how we interact with machines and how they respond to us. For example, as will be explored, games are enhanced through use of biofeedback and information about how we feel. The issue is not the premise of using data about emotions to interact with technology, but the nature of engagement. In short, while all might enjoy and appreciate the focus on 'experience' (user, consumer, patient and citizen), it is paramount that people have meaningful choice and control over the 'capturing' of information about emotions and their bodies.

This book was researched and written during an interesting period. I have been writing about moods and technology since 2009 (McStay, 2011) and introduced the principle of *empathic media* in another book (McStay, 2014). This refers to the capacity for emergent media technologies to sense and discern what is significant for people, categorise behaviour into named emotions, act on emotional states, and make use of people's intentions and expressions. With financial assistance from the UK's Arts and Humanities Research Council from mid-2014 through to the end of 2016 I began researching and interviewing high-value individuals developing and employing emotion-sensitive technologies. Over the course of the research period the technology sector has begun to address emotions and affective computing in a much more serious fashion. When I first started interviewing it was largely start-ups finding commercial opportunities in technologies sensitive to emotional life. As the project progressed, I found that more recognisable names such as Amazon, Apple, Facebook, Google, IBM and Microsoft are now publicly developing emotional AI and empathic media products. Many of the original start-ups I spoke with are now looking forward to lucrative exits.

Technologically, the rise of interest in emotional life is indivisible from the increase in applications of artificial intelligence (AI) and machine-learning methods. While we are undergoing a hype cycle that brings with it inflated expectations, this should not detract from the fact that these technologies are here to stay. Of course, they will also improve. Indeed, in as far as AI systems interact with people, one might reason that AI has no value until it is sensitive to feelings, emotions and intention. This includes home assistants and headline grabbing humanoid robots, but the important development is how emotion recognition systems are progressively permeating human–computer interactions. If the reader agrees there is personal, inter-personal, organisational, economic and surveillance value in understanding emotional engagement with self, others, objects, services and content, emotional AI and empathic media are worth our attention.

Artificial emotional intelligence is achieved by the capacity to see, read, listen, feel, classify and learn about emotional life. Slightly more detailed, this involves reading words and images, seeing and sensing facial expressions, gaze direction, gestures and voice. It also encompasses machines feeling our heart rate, body temperature, respiration and the electrical properties of our skin, among other bodily behaviours. Together, bodies and emotions have become machine-readable. What I am *not* arguing is that these systems *experience* emotions. Instead, I am interested in the idea that the capacity to sense, classify behaviour and respond appropriately offers the *appearance of understanding*. I suggest this form of observation involves a form of empathy. To develop the thesis that media and technologies are progressively showing signs of empathy, I begin with two propositions:

1. We increasingly 'live with' technologies that feel and these are sensitive to human life in ways hitherto not seen.
2. Empathic media provide opportunities for new aesthetic experiences that not only draw upon information about emotions, but also provide new means for people to 'feel into' aesthetic creations.

If the reader agrees that technologies are increasingly capable of gauging emotional behaviour and that there is personal, inter-personal, commercial and other organisational value in understanding emotions, we should agree that 'datafication' (Mayer-Schönberger and Cukier, 2013) of emotional life is unavoidable. Deconstructed, proposition 1 suggests that: a) technologies that make use of data about emotions are increasing; b) we live alongside technologies such as digital assistants rather than simply 'use' them; and c) we will encounter these technologies in unexpected places (such as shops). Proposition 2 is based on the simple fact that new media technologies offer content creators new affordances. Although much of this book addresses the scope and implications of emotion tracking, the principle of empathic media encompasses applications that allow people to viscerally understand places, periods, cultures, objects and real and fictional worlds.

3

Good Enough:
Verisimilitude and Emotional Truth

One or all three of the following questions might be in the reader's mind: first, 'are machines *really* capable of empathy … isn't this a bit of a stretch'; followed by, 'isn't this a very limited view of emotions'; and lastly, 'what about compassion and sympathy in empathy?' The last question is most easily dealt with. Although we typically connect empathy with sympathy and compassion, the connection is not a necessary one. To interpret an emotional state and make predictions about a person's perspective and disposition does not require that we want the best for that person. Sympathy is not a necessary criterion for empathy, but instead empathy is simply an interpretive act. Cognitive empathy, which may entail sadism and mental as well as physical cruelty, is a brutal example of this.

This is a 'theory-theory' approach to empathy, where emotion is theorised through observation (Goldman, 2008). Put otherwise, it is to understand another person's condition by means of what we survey, measure and remember as well as what rules are made for subsequent engagement. This neo-behaviourist approach means that systems sense, discern patterns of behaviour, make judgements by means of algorithms and heuristics (if person A is behaving in X manner then do Z), provide content and feedback and learn from people's reactions. What is key here is that empathic media systems do not employ 'mentalistic' processes. Instead they 'simply' observe, classify, allocate, adapt and modify their behaviour.

Accordingly, it is reasonable to say that computers can recognise emotions when 'the group of computers and the group of humans respond with the same distribution of answers' (Picard, 1997: 51). Imbued within this is recognition that people do not judge correctly each time, and nor should we expect machines to either. This is a simple but important point. If we are to critique machines and say they do not have access to our 'authentic emotional states' (whatever this may denote), it cannot be because they misdiagnose and sometimes read people incorrectly.

On whether this is a limited view of emotions, it is not clear what emotions are. Empathic media employ a particular account of what emotions are through their use of psychological, anthropological and neuroscientific research, largely deriving from Paul Ekman and his forerunners. As we will see, there is an attractive simplic-ity to 'basic emotions' (Ekman and Friesen, 1971) that technologists have latched onto. To an extent this is because of expediency and that this account of emotional life works well with sensing techniques that classify facial and bodily behaviour. Indeed in a telling line from early proponents of emotion-sensing technology, they say, 'Choosing a physiological or behavioural measure can be relatively easy, in that technology or methodology will often dictate a clear preference' (Bradley and Lang, 1994: 49). The 'basic emotions' view contrasts with the messier idea that emotions might not be fixed objects, but culturally constructed experiences and expressions defined through historical and situational circumstances.

On whether machines can really understand us, we have two possibilities: a) *genuine empathy* (which is the capacity to truly know what another is undergoing); and b) *simulated empathy* (the capacity to approximate, to contextualise within what one can comprehend, to make educated judgments and to respond in an appropriate manner). Much of this has been rehearsed in debates about whether machines can really think, what it is for a person to think and the philosophical knots associated with knowing the lives of others. Yet, if we allow for the possibility of a simulated and observational version of empathy, the door is very much open for machinic empathy.

This has less to do with authenticity and more with what I have termed elsewhere 'machinic verisimilitude' or the appearance of intimate insight (McStay, 2014). It allows us to elide the debate of true versus false because a simulated and theory-based form of empathy may be tested on the basis of appropriateness of feedback. As such, we do not have to engage with the question of whether people have privileged access to a *real* understanding of emotions and intentions. Rather, we can simply judge by effectiveness. Of course, people clearly have the upper hand in instinctively reading and perceiving the significance of events for other people. However, machines have strong cards of their own because they can record, remember and interpret detail that is inaccessible to human senses (such as physiology). In fact, under closer inspection, perhaps the real question is not 'can machines empathise?' but 'is machinic empathy that different from human empathy?' I propose that it is reasonable to say that empathy is an interpretive act for people and machines involving observation, identification, contextualisation, learning and fast reactions.

Aims and Methods

My goal is to explore life with technologies that are sensitive to emotions, assess their political and social implications, and consider the ethical, legal and regulatory consequences. I do this by balancing empirical observations with insights from three sets of literatures: media and critical theory; science and technology studies (STS); and the works of a diverse range of philosophers. While the first two sets of literatures are fairly obvious starting points for a book on the phenomenon of empathic media, my recourse to the philosophical literature perhaps needs some explication. In short, the philosophers I have consulted help unpack the social and experiential significance of empathy. Often those selected have phenomenological interests (such as Husserl, Merleau-Ponty and Heidegger), but others such as Lipps, Scheler, Hume, Bentham and Adam Smith help situate the discussion of 'feeling-into'. Foucault also assists through his insistence that knowledge should be tested in relation to the context and interests that generated it.

My main corpus of data comes from over 100 open-ended one-hour interviews conducted to elucidate views on emotion detection. These draw from industry, national security, law, policy, municipal authorities and privacy-oriented NGOs (for a list of these organisations, see Appendix 1). Although many interviews do not explicitly feature in the book, each has implicitly shaped my thinking. In-person interviews primarily took place in Europe, the United States and the United Arab Emirates, but they also included face-to-face Skype calls with companies from Israel, Russia and South Korea. The scale of companies ranged from Alphabet (Verily), Facebook and IBM to start-ups by students.

Interview questions were co-created with key stakeholders from: the UK's Information Commissioner's Office (a data protection regulator) who were interested in implications for data protection; the advertising agency M&C Saatchi who were interested in creative opportunities; the UK's Committee of Advertising Practice (a self-regulatory body) who were concerned about protecting the reputation of the advertising industry; and the NGO Privacy International who were interested in meaningful consent, data ethics and data security. Interviewees were mostly chief executive officers (CEOs) and people in strategic positions from companies working on: sentiment analysis; virtual and augmented reality; facial coding; voice analytics; social networking; the emotion-enhanced Internet of Things (IoT); emotion-enhanced smart cities; and a wide range of companies developing wearables that track users' moods through respiration, electroencephalograms (EEG), heart rates and galvanic skin responses (GSR). End-user sectors include: advertising; policing; national security; education; insurance; human resources; the sex-tech industry; psychosexual therapy; experiential marketing; mental health; branding agencies; media agencies; ethical hackers; venture capitalists; artists; interactive film-makers; games companies; in-car experience and navigation companies; and sports software companies.

Each interviewee was selected on the basis of current work in emotion detection, or likelihood of interest in these applications. In addition to industrialists and public sector actors, I interviewed people working in privacy-friendly NGOs (Electronic Frontier Foundation, Open Rights Group and several staff members from Privacy International) to obtain a critical perspective. I also met with media and technology law firms to discuss the legal dimension of these developments, and European policy-makers in the field of data privacy to ascertain their awareness of the topic. A multi-tiered consent form was employed that allowed interviewees to select a level of disclosure they were comfortable with. Options ranged from willingness to speak in a named capacity on behalf of an organisation, to full anonymity.

Other research tools include a workshop with industrialists, regulators, NGOs and academics to develop codes of conduct for using data about emotions (discussed in Chapter 12). I also conducted a demographically representative UK nationwide online survey (n=2067). This assessed citizen attitudes to the potential of emotion detection employed in contexts they are familiar with.[1] (I will discuss this where relevant but see Appendix 2 for the overview.) Approaches also include analysis of patent filings, which affords critical media scholars insight into the objectives, hopes, technical intentions, and worldviews of companies and owners. Similarly, textual analysis of product packaging and promotional content also reveals assumptions about ideal users and the ideological outlooks of organisations.

Chapter Breakdown

The arc of the book begins with a theoretical, historical, philosophical and technological framing in Chapter 2. Clarifying principles that will recur in this book, it identifies that empathy is a social fact of living in groups. It also addresses the industrialisation of emotions by noting not only that 'emotion' is a surprisingly recent psychological premise, that emotions are economically valuable, but also how emotional life is undergoing 'biomedicalisation' due to applications of emotional AI and affective computing. Although the book's emphasis on machine-readable emotions may appear somewhat novel, the roots are relatively old. Technological antecedents reach back to the 1800s. The chapter accounts for these, the debates that surrounded them and their significance for my own case study of modern empathic media.

Chapter 3 addresses collective emotions by considering sentiment analysis. Unlike later chapters, this does not entail reading physiology to gauge emotion. Rather, it involves assessing what people say on social media. While usually text-based, it may also encompass emojis, images, video, user profiling and charting contact networks. I argue that what we are witnessing today is the entry of machines into public life that detect, map and interact with social emotion. However, online public life and collective emotions are not straightforward propositions. They are structured, mediated and influenced by a variety of human and non-human actors. To explore these I consider contagion, algorithms that drive issues up and down the social agenda, metering and modelling of voter emotions and software scripts (bots) that appear as people. Drawing on interviews with people from social media companies, sentiment analysts, marketers and government intelligence agencies, the chapter assesses 'social listening' in the context of case studies from political life, marketing, the financial sector and policing.

Chapter 4 begins an interest in biofeedback as a means to gauge emotion. Drawing on interviews with game developers and player experience analysts, it focuses on gaming because it has experimented with biofeedback since the 1980s. Gaming was also the first to learn lessons about the difficulties of using biofeedback data in a media and entertainment context. The principle that gaming illustrates is how the spectrum of channels through which we interact with media technologies is increasing. In addition to sensing bodies as a means to measure and interact with a person's emotions, gaming illustrates the aesthetic argument of empathic media in that games are designed in such a way that we 'feel-into' content in novel and powerful ways. It is also the format that best exemplifies that biometrics in media need not be 'creepy', but rather that it can benefit and enhance experience. However, the gaming community was also vocal about the need for data protection and privacy. This chapter ends by discussing these issues in relation to data from the nationwide survey I conducted where I asked UK citizens how they feel about biometric data and gaming.

After sentiment analysis, facial coding of emotions is perhaps the leading application of empathic media. Chapter 5 draws on interviews with facial coding firms that apply computer vision and machine-learning technologies to read facial expressions. While some readers will be familiar with its use in neuromarketing and ad-testing, it is in the less obvious applications where it becomes significant. This includes social media companies gauging responses to content, in-car behaviour, retail, and even analysis of performance in legal depositions. Conceptually, these methods, technologies and applications articulate emotional life in terms of 'universalised leaks'. As such, in addition to assessing technologies and applications, I focus on method. I do this because the research context that underpins facial coding is the clearest enunciation of what emotional life is according to proponents of empathic media. This worldview stands in contrast to social and constructivist accounts of emotional life.

Chapter 6 considers the rise of voice-first empathic media that do not just analyse what we say, but how we say it. Drawing on interviews with voice analytics companies, it accounts for how voice-based emotion-capture *primes* systems employed by a range of sectors to respond appropriately to us. The significance of this is clearer if we consider the potential to understand and react to emotions in spoken search and natural language by chatbots and digital assistants, such as Amazon's Alexa. This is an emergent issue and as home AI gets to know people and their life contexts better, emotion capture will provide cues to tell systems to respond appropriately. This raises questions about relationships, temporality and experience. While this may appear unnecessarily philosophical, consider that modern business is keenly interested in 'moments'. As digital assistants feel-into our life, engage with intimate life moments, an ontological dimension is revealed. This might be the everyday act of chopping vegetables, following recipes and listening to guilty mood-uplifting pleasures on Spotify, provided by Alexa. These captured moments are economically valuable. As agents we 'live with', the remit of emotional AI is to bridge quality and quantity, interact meaningfully, gauge the character of reality, classify experience and learn about life contexts. This raises issues: how should we best understand these co-evolving relationships? And looking forward, to what degree will people suspend disbelief to gain gratification from AIs?

Chapter 7 accounts for virtual reality (VR). Beyond the boxy headwear, we can define this in terms of the factors that contribute to a sense of presence in a synthetic environment. VR fulfils both of the propositions about empathy given earlier in that wearers not only undergo aesthetic and sensational experiences with people, objects, places, periods and cultures, but also that remote viewers (people and machines) may observe from a wearer's perspective, gauge experience and virtually 'be in their shoes'. Developing the principle of *affective witnessing*, this chapter draws upon interviews and interaction with documentary makers, market researchers, and technologists in the defence and policing sector. The first part analyses the use of VR in journalism and documentaries, drawing on what Chapter 2 will account for as 'interpretive empathy'. The second attends to interest in VR from the market research community, whose interest is attention, intention and quantifying first-person perspectives. The third examines VR and policing. While this is not an obvious application of VR technologies (games and pornography perhaps come more readily to mind), as with many of the cases discussed in this book, it is the outlying applications of empathic media that best illustrate its significance. This final section investigates how organisations from the United States to the United Arab Emirates are developing what I term 'empathic policing'. Here VR is used with wearables, head-mounted cameras and drones so police commanders may remotely witness what is taking place on the beat.

Of all the commercial sectors interested in emotional life, advertising and retail have the most to gain from understanding what we think, see, feel and do. The business of advertising is built on the suggestion that consumers are rational, sovereign and able to reject, ignore or accept advertising messages. Chapter 8 depicts that in a period keen on behavioural economics, consumer neuroscience and increasingly empathic media, never has the free-choice argument of advertising looked so suspect. Drawing on interviews with advertising agencies, marketers and technologists, it critically examines consumer research, omni-channel shopping (that merge online and offline), programmatic systems, augmented reality and retail contexts that pertain to 'feel'. Beyond tracking, AI systems can use emotional analytics to create marketing content. Under the rubric of what this chapter phrases as 'quantified bios', this chapter shows that empathic media are not simply about sensing life and experience, but the automation of consumer psychology.

Chapter 9 examines how 'personal technologies that feel' stimulate novel forms of human-technical intimacy. Exploring case studies on health, wellbeing, work and sex, I draw from interviews with a commercial life science company, a commercial neuro-technology research firm, an EEG headset manufacturer, developers of emotion-sensing wearables, a sex toy maker and a professional psychosexual therapist. What becomes clear is that developers are comfortable with corporations having ethically questionable influence over behaviour and emotional life. Problems are also raised about automated industrial psychology, bio-sensing and analytics employed to monitor communications, networks, relationships, location and devices for signs of emotional behaviour. This invites subtle questions, especially about corporate liability, data standards and the lack of agreed means by which emotional life might be benchmarked. The chapter then turns to sex. While hacks of sex-tech devices are relatively well known, they also raise issues about secrecy, modern intimacy, the desirability of making sexual life machine-readable and transparency. Although widespread adoption of sex robots able to 'feel-into' behaviour remains to be seen, these too invite assessment of human relationships with technology. Are they simply of a functional 'in order to' form, or might anthropomorphism and projection play roles in mediating our connection with affect-aware technologies?

Chapter 10 attends to situations where empathic media are used to understand the civic bodies of what are variously referred to as 'smart cities', 'future cities' and 'conscious cities'. To consider these developments, I draw upon interviews with city technologists, lighting companies, city experience analysts, and insights derived from numerous conversations at technology and smart city expos in Dubai, Barcelona, Cologne and London. What conjoins these developments is an intention to deploy sensing and communications technologies to surveil and generate intelligence about people, things and processes in urban environments. This encompasses everything from street lighting to in-house biofeedback. What empathic media represent in this context is sensitivity to the mood and emotions of inhabitants. While it easy to reach for the 'dystopia card' (and this would not be an incorrect thing to do), the politics of psycho-geography has a curious history drawing on liberatory Marxism and utilitarian thought. Guy Debord (1955) for example, in the 1950s, recommended that we study 'the precise laws and specific effects of the geographical environment, consciously organized or not, on the emotions and behavior of individuals'. His idea was to reveal the lived conditions of citizenry. However, as cities see 'algocratic' possibilities and take on platform-like characteristics to sense, track, surveil and financialise psycho-physiological data, this raises questions about what kind of cities we want to live in. This chapter is critical and cautious of developments in autocratic as well as democratic states, but it does not reject the premise of mediated psycho-geography. As will be depicted, in addition to 'societies of control', other visions are realisable. This involves scope to use empathic media to improve the material space and infrastructure, annotate augmented city features, leave biometric markers of experience, tell stories, and use bio-sensing to enrich city life.

Chapter 11 turns away from technology to consider the regulatory and political dimensions of empathic media. Given that what these technologies represent is the endeavour to make emotional life machine-readable, and to control, engineer, reshape and modulate human behaviour, this matters. In assessing the policy dimensions of empathic media my discussion references the European regulatory context, but the arguments have global applicability. I focus on what might initially seem like an irrelevance: what of privacy if the data in question cannot be linked back to a person or personal device? Although information about emotions may certainly be linked with personal data, in many cases non-identifying data about emotions are being collected and put to work. The significance of this is that, while intimate, they are not strictly personal, at least as far as data protection bodies conceive of privacy. Is this OK? To explore and address this I draw upon my own assessment of European data protection law, but also ethical discussions with partners from media law firms, a Queens Counsel (QC) with an interest in technology law, and civil society groups interested in privacy and data protection. I also discuss insights from my survey data collected about how citizens in the UK feel about identifying and non-identifying emotion capture.

Chapter 12 concludes the book by recapping its key themes and considering what is required for responsible innovation of empathic media. To explore this I draw upon outcomes from a workshop I organised featuring CEOs and others from emotion capture companies, the UK's Information Commissioner's Office, the UK's advertising self-regulator, civil liberties organisations, advertising agencies, security companies, psychologists, legal ethicists, and surveillance experts.

What should be clear from this opening chapter is that while this book promises to be wide-ranging in scope, its focus is clear: to assess the development, applications and implications of technologies used to 'feel-into' emotional life. As will become apparent, this raises four cross-cutting issues that will be addressed as the book progresses. The first involves the methods and assumptions made about what emotional life is. The second is the scope to use these insights to influence, which consequently raises questions about commercial and political power. The third is intimacy and that applications of technologies discussed in this book ask questions of privacy that it may not have all the answers for. Last – and I believe most important – is the overall desirability of making bodies and emotional lives machine-readable.

Note

1   Online surveys have methodological caveats including difficulties of presenting complex topics and minimal control over respondents' condition. They may be attentive or distracted. Furthermore, to reduce costs, the survey (conducted with ICM Unlimited) was part of an omnibus survey that collects data on multiple topics, so I had no control over where my questions featured. However, the upsides proved significant as I was able to obtain a respectable weighted sample of geographical regions, age groups, social classes and gender, while avoiding 'interviewer bias'.

2
SITUATING EMPATHY

Chapter 1 introduced the principle of empathic media by suggesting that media technologies are increasingly able to interpret feelings, emotions, moods, attention and intention to engage with people in new ways. These technologies did not emerge from nowhere, but they have technical and theoretical antecedents. To provide context to forthcoming chapters, this chapter attends to empathy itself and thereafter technologies argued to be 'empathic'. I argue that empathy has two overlapping characteristics. The first is that it is a social fact of inter-personal life and living in communities. Applied to technology, this means it makes sense to speak of 'living with' technologies that sense, track and feel-into our lives. The second characteristic is its interpretive qualities. This is not just about 'feeling-into' others, but also places, pasts, cultures and even objects. Having outlined the two core principles of empathy, I situate empathic media in relation to affective computing, renewed interest in artificial intelligence (AI), industrial interest in emotions, the datafication of feeling and the life sciences.

A Social Fact

Empathy plays a pivotal role in how we live with other people. It has received greatest attention from philosophy, social psychology, developmental psychology, psychotherapy, cognitive scientists, primatologists and neuroscientists. The root of the English word 'empathy' stems from the Ancient Greek word έμπάθεια (*empatheia*) that refers to an intense passion or state of emotional undergoing. This continues today in *path*os, which entails emotion, feeling, suffering and pity. For context, it is instructive that a*pathy* refers to a lack of emotions, anti*pathy* relates to hostile emotions and sym*pathy* to feel-with. Empathy is slightly different and means to 'feel within', or more accurately 'in feel' (the prefix '*em*' is the Greek correspondent to our word 'in'). Neither is quite logical because people do not 'feel into', but they typically 'interpret'. Nevertheless, empathy is ubiquitous because most people are able to read and gauge what affective states and emotions another person is undergoing, to reach a conclusion about what they are going through and, potentially, what their intentions might be. This is done by observing language (both what people say and how they speak), physiology and behaviour, and thereafter using this information to form judgments about 'where they are coming from'.

Empathy grants commonality of experience and understanding that we are not alone. The opposite of this is the frankly depressing notion of solipsism. Philosophers such as Edmund Husserl (2002 [1952]: 173) use the language of 'co-presence' and 'universal Ego-being', and while on first impressions this appears somewhat mystical, it simply means 'I have a sense of self and I'm sure you do, so I know something of what it is like to be you'. For Husserl (1980) empathy has a sensational and physical character in that to understand the 'psychic realities' of others we emulate their worlds, their physicality, their experience as an organism (as well as an ego), and attempt to locate this as best we can in our own here and now to forge a commonality of experience. This has echoes of David Hume who, in *A Treatise of Human Nature* (1896 [1739]), accounts for empathy in terms of instinct. The consequence of this involuntary character is that we do not control empathy, nor switch it on or off. While this social faculty is impressive, we can of course be wrong in our assessment of others (hence why 'interpret' is more accurate than feel 'into'), but the act of reading, judging, emulating and reacting to what we perceive as the reality of the other is fundamental to human life.

Martin Heidegger is not a philosopher one would associate with an interest in empathy. However, although he publicly scorned it, he admits there is something in the notion of co-presence. This idea that people may have a shared sense of presence and mutual recognition of 'being here together' is important. For example, in *Being and Time*, Heidegger articulates empathy in terms of 'Being-with' (2011 [1962]): §123–26, 160–63) and the ways by which 'we are also the other'. With this he also provides useful social detail on the commonality of life contexts, how we live public lives in communities engaging in public languages, accept social codes of behaviour, agree and debate public values, follow trends, adopt identities for different social roles, and create ourselves out of publicly available identities. On being-with or feeling-into, John Dewey (1925) and Thomas Nagel (1970) similarly argued that empathy is linked with democracy and social being that in turn is facilitated by language, signs and common cultural contexts.

This moves us towards empathy as a *social fact* that, when present, acts as an agent that binds co-operative societies together through mutual understanding and awareness. As crystalised in the 2015 Netflix show *Sense8*, this pro-social character of empathy has enlightenment values of cosmopolitanism (Urry, 2000), common respect, universal hospitality and the value of being a 'citizen of the world' (a principle that goes back to Socrates and Diogenes in the 4th century BC). Indeed, for Kant (1990 [1781]), empathy sits at the heart of global human rights. This is not due to feelings of blind obligation, but because reason dictates that common respect between self and others is advantageous for all. Elsewhere, such as in Adam Smith's (2011 [1759]) *The Theory of Moral Sentiments*, this takes the form of 'fellow-feeling', a form of projective understanding that provides the basis of moral life.[1]

It is uncontroversial to say empathy is biased and people may more easily identify with people who resemble them (Bloom, 2017). Yet if empathy has a political
point, it is about revealing a rational and intellectual moral *imperative* towards
other people. For philosophers interested in empathy, the task is to treat other
people as equals to us, rather than as mere shadowy others.[2] Clearly this an ideal
that is not always achieved, and the difficulties associated with cosmopolitanism
were identified early. Max Scheler (2009 [1913]) recognised that benevolent governmental policy for others is contingent upon identification, vicarious experience
and fellow-feeling (empathy), but also that the capacity for community-feeling
and 'natural' life is stymied by the hurly-burly of everyday activities, industrial
life, modernity and technology. Over a century on, this diagnosis feels very contemporary.

Empathy, then, has an *ontological* dimension. This means that it enhances and
facilitates social experience, the reality of others, and indeed provides a sense of
where others are coming from. Importantly for this book's understanding of the
word 'empathy', it is not a tool, attribute or appendage: it is the ongoing activity of
sensing and reading the behaviour and signals of others, to gauge and understand
their emotional and intentional disposition.[3] As will be developed in later chapters, I suggest that a key characteristic of nascent technologies is that increasingly
technologies 'live with' us. By this I mean they continually sense, passively track,
interpret and process histories and behavioural contexts, and even engage with us
at an emotional level. This 'living-with' or even 'being-with' is very different from
tools and technologies that simply have 'in-order-to' characteristics.

Interpretive empathy

Empathy is not only inter-personal and social, it also has an aesthetic and sensational component based on projection and *feeling-into* (Lipps, 1979 [1903]). This
involves people's capacity to detach their mind from daily life, feel-into and derive
pleasure from objects and designed experiences. Lipps underlines this when he
suggests that 'Empathy is the fact that the antithesis between myself and the object
disappears, or rather does not yet exist' (Lipps, cited in Baldwin, 1940: 357).
What he speaks of is a communion between text, object and person. This account
of empathy has been widely discussed in philosophy, but in short empathy-as-
feeling-into derives from the German principle of *Einfühlung* that suggests people
can insert themselves into artworks to feel the emotions that the creator worked
to generate and instil (Vischer, 1993 [1873]). Extended, by means of media such
as music, paintings, literature, television shows, games and today virtual reality,
we may feel-into other places, periods, cultures and fictional worlds. This takes us
some way past inter-personal and social empathy. It gives it a reconstructive and
imaginative quality as we engage with designed experiences to feel 'what it was
like to be there'. From the point of view of creators and designers, interpretive

15

empathy also has an anticipatory quality. This is the attempt to *feel-forward* to simulate (empathise) with what they expect participants to experience. As we will see in forthcoming chapters, this feeling-into and affective quality of empathy has applications outside of art and entertainment, also reaching into modern policing and education along with other interested organisational sectors.

On Emotion

Despite the fact that emotional life is fundamental to inter-personal and social behaviour, 'emotion' has only been a psychological category and a subject for systematic investigation since the 19th century (Dixon, 2012). Instead, emotions were accounted for in terms of passions, affections, desires, accidents, perturbations of the soul and moral sentiments. In ancient times the Hellenistic Stoics (of around the 3rd century BC) saw emotions as diseases of the soul. Christians would later recognise these 'violent forces', but tempered them with compassion and moral feelings. For Aquinas, the passions and affections were actions of two different portions of the soul, or what Aquinas terms 'sense appetite' and 'intellectual appetite'. By the 1500s emotional 'charges' had even been connected with disease and 'monstrous births'. Paré (1649) for example reports that a baby with the face of a frog was believed to have been born due to a fevered birth. Later, Andreas Vesalius in the 16th century and Thomas Willis in the 17th began mapping the body to explore its structure, leading the way to anatomy as the basis of disease rather than immaterial forces. This turn to biology is significant for our own account of empathic media and biofeedback.

However, the dualism of passions (bad) and moral sentiments (good) pervaded discussion of emotions throughout the 18th century. In the 19th century the Edinburgh professor of moral philosophy Thomas Brown can be said to have invented emotions because he incorporated the notions of appetites, passions and affections into one catch-all premise: the emotions (Dixon, 2012). Although the word already existed, emotions had not been addressed in such a systematised manner so as to be a science of mind. The word itself reached Britain from France in the early 17th century via translations of the philosopher Michel de Montaigne by John Florio (De Montaigne, 1999 [1603]). Although De Montaigne's writing about emotion is less scientific than Brown's, his phrasing of emotion in terms of physical disturbance and materiality is a telling one for this book's interest in biometrics. However, Thomas Brown was the first to systematically consider 'emotion' as a critical classification in the academic study of the mind. In 1820 he defined emotions in terms of vividness of feeling and as being separate from sensations that were directly caused by an object of some sort (Brown, 2010 [1820]; Dixon, 2012). Charles Bell, also from Scotland, from around the 1820s made valuable contributions to the conceptualisation of emotions. He linked emotions with the face and parts of the body (Bell, 1824). What is key here is not just that the body may act to express emotions, but that the body is also a constitutive cause of emotional experience.

Today emotion is closely linked with biological understanding and arousal of the nervous system, and while emotion and arousal are not synonymous, arousal levels do correlate with many named emotions. Yet although biological, emotions undeniably connect with social and cultural life as our appraisal of situations is informed by learned values. Ahmed (2010, 2014), for example, writes persuasively about stereotyping, arguing that emotions are not stimulated because of the nature of an object but by how we perceive them. This connects with discussion in the psychology literature about appraisal theory, which suggests emotions are extracted from evaluations (or appraisals) of events that may cause people to react in different ways to the same situation (Scherer et al., 2001). For Ahmed, when we meet or read about strangers we are taught to fear, we have already misrecognised them. Seen this way, learned emotional reactions 'surface', frame and affect the ways we meet, cognise and engage with other people. When we start to think in terms of surfaces and connections, we see that everyday life is charged with emotion and affects.

Emotions are also richer than we sometimes give them credit for. This is illustrated by Smith (2015), who points out that while we are familiar with happiness, sorrow, confusion and elation, there are more subtle emotions such as being 'miffed', pre-presentation 'butterflies', 'wanderlust' or 'umpty' (the feeling that everything is 'all wrong'). What becomes clear is that emotions are significant because they mediate, surface and affect our experience of people, things, places and situations. Thus, although emotions are clearly connected with, if not based on, the functioning of the brain and the rest of the body, we should not be misled into a materialist belief that emotions are fully understood by measuring bodily twitches and flutters.

Industrialising emotions

Emotions are of interest to organisations keen on measuring human behaviour. This is because in addition to mediating and surfacing our experiences of things, they quantifiably assist and influence decision-making, memory and attention (Easterbrook, 1959; Christianson, 1992; Lowenstein and Lerner, 2003; Phelps et al., 2006; Pfister and Böhm, 2008; McDuff, 2014). As the philosopher Gaston Bachelard puts it, a creative image 'has touched the depths before it stirs the surface' (1994 [1958]): xxiii). In neuroscientific terms, we are affected and emotionally stimulated before we intellectually register experiences and events (Damasio, 2003, 2011; Schreuder et al., 2016). The industrial significance is this: if one can affect emotions and make people feel a certain way, an organisation has an increased chance of capturing attention, making a desired impression and affecting decision-making. This gives emotional life economic value – something that has not been missed by those interested in behavioural economics, choice

17

architecture, neuromarketing, consumer and user experience (CX and UX), and post-Fordist approaches to service and retail (emotional labour). The next step in marketising emotions is to convert affective life into metric form, which provides scope for their 'datafication' (Mayer-Schönberger and Cukier, 2013). Here novel aspects of life are converted into data and put to work to generate new forms of value. Indeed, 'metric power' defines what is knowable and valuable, and creates the benchmark for what is industrially significant (Beer, 2016).

On datafying processes that convert emotional life into data, the roots of this are in 'affective computing' (Picard, 1995, 1997, 2007). In the 1990s this took the form of measuring heart fluctuations, skin conductance, muscle tension, pupil dilation and facial muscles to assess how changes in the body relate to emotions. Rosalind Picard explains that 'affective' in this context refers to 'the ability to sense your changes in emotion, and to respond sensitively to these changes, taking into consideration what it has learned previously [...] (Picard, 1997: 241). Affective computing has two overlapping objectives: first is the aforementioned tracking of emotions, but second is the attempt to stimulate emotion and make us care about machines. This is achieved through expressions, gesture, behaviour and voice. While affective computing is certainly interested in robot development, the principle encompasses all emotion-enhanced interaction with devices, assistants and interfaces.

Machine learning and the wider domain of AI typically underpin our modern industrial use of data about emotions. Despite the recent hype, AI of course is not new. It has theoretical roots in the 1940s with Warren McCulloch and Walter Pitts, and practical development in the 1950s when Marvin Minsky and Dean Edmonds built the first neural network computer in 1950 (Russell and Norvig, 2010). Although modern applications of AI include search engines, digital assistants, gaming, email and spam sorting, smart cars, purchase prediction, insurance, fraud detection, surveillance and recommender systems such as Spotify (which also tracks users' moods), the spiritual roots of AI are in the lofty quest to build machines that think, learn and create (Minsky, 2006). This is sometimes called strong AI. It should not be missed that the historical emphasis of AI has been on intellect rather than feeling. This reflects a historic injustice in Western thought to the role of emotions in human life (Williams, 2001) that is replicated in AI. Rather than treating emotion as that which helps machines interact and adapt to context, place, people and situations, AI has typically been conceived in terms of ratiocination, disembodied cognition and utility. However, affective computing (at least the sort discussed in this book) is an example of 'weak AI' (rather than strong AI). That is, it reads and reacts to emotions, but it does not think and feel itself (arguably unlike the machines in movies such as Alex Garland's [2014] *Ex Machina*).

AI and machine learning are not synonymous, but rather machine learning is a sub-domain of AI research (Cawsey, 1998). This said, machine learning overlaps with other areas of AI, such as robotics and environment mapping, natural language processing, computer vision and object recognition (which includes faces). The key for modern industrial applications of AI and affective computing is that machine-learning techniques allow computers to detect, extrapolate patterns and adapt to new circumstances. While it is not within the remit of this book to offer an extensive exposition of either AI or machine learning (see Russell and Norvig, 2010; Hinton, 2016), in general terms machines learn by case examples. This means that computers are tasked with classifying things and people, and that software applications become more accurate in predicting and making judgments without being explicitly programmed. In our case, input features might be facial expressions, voice samples, biofeedback data or in-world VR behaviour, and the output features are likely to be classified emotional states.

To unpack slightly, as we will see in Chapter 5, in automated emotion detection of faces, machines are first shown training examples of what named facial emotions are. These include ideal laboratory conditions and naturalistic settings where, for example, lighting may be poor. Having been provided with these classifications, computers can use cameras to see, receive input features, register pixelated facial elements, process this against training data and generate outputs of named emotional states. Of course, people have unique faces, they execute expressions in different ways, they are not always directly facing a camera and they appear in different contexts. The learning element takes place when computers are given many faces (potentially millions) and software is written in such a way to allow itself to be trained by incoming data. This is done by software auto-adjusting its algorithms to improve in detecting expressions in unfamiliar circumstances (new faces, execution of expression, positions and contexts). This means that with varying degrees of human supervision, systems are able to adjust elements of their algorithms by themselves, and progress how they classify data from text, images, videos, voice, biofeedback data and any other source that is machine-readable. As this book discusses, the industrial significance of automated emotion detection is noteworthy.

Bioeconomics

Aligned with industrial developments in machine learning and AI are the life sciences. Recent decades have seen increased interaction between capital, biological sciences and modern computer technology. Verily, for example (owned by Alphabet and interviewed for this book), is working on intelligent glucose-sensing contact lenses, and Calico (Alphabet's research and development biology company) seeks to understand the biology of lifespan to solve the 'problem' of death. On mortality and death, PayPal co-founder Peter Thiel said 'Basically, I'm against it' (Dreyfuss, 2017). *All* of the large companies working in the overlapping fields of machine learning, artificial intelligence, big data and cognitive computing have a keen interest in transhumanism, healthcare and wellbeing. This means that when we consider empathic media, affective computing and application of AI, we should also keep in mind industrial life sciences and study of the body.

A consequence of this large-scale investment is that the life sciences become 'foundational epistemologies for our time' (Rajan, 2006: 12). Critical to our interest in setting the context of empathic media, this knowledge spills out beyond questions of health. For example the life sciences have become the default lens for all sorts of questions and, certainly in relation to what emotions actually are, these epistemologies construct how we understand emotions and bodily affects in modern digital culture.

In many ways this book is about how industry and technologists are constructing a particular imagining of what emotional life is. Any interest in challenging terms, assumptions, frames of reference and expert-knowledge systems as they relate to the body owes a direct or indirect debt to Michel Foucault. As we have seen above, knowledge of matters such as emotional life takes its cue from the political, economic, technical and social contexts out of which it emerged. Foucault is valuable because he will not allow us to accept knowledge at face value. Instead he prompts us to a) analyse the context from which knowledge emerges, and b) assess the consequences when people apply knowledge constructions to understand themselves. Foucault (1988) identifies four types of 'technologies' that can be said to produce knowledge about life and selfhood. Applied to emotions, these entail:

1. *Technologies of production*: theory, technology and industrial applications that facilitate production and use of data about emotions.
2. *Technologies of sign systems*: the language, signs, meanings, symbols and interfaces used to articulate and frame emotional life.
3. *Technologies of power*: the capacity to influence behaviour through the objectification of individual and collective emotional life. This gives scope to monitor and determine the conduct of people and submit them to certain ends or domination.
4. *Technologies of the self*: how empathic media impact on a person's own self-conception of emotional life and how this knowledge affects operations on their bodies, thoughts, behaviour and ways of being.

As empathic media, affective computing and emotion-enhanced AI become more prevalent, the consequence is that aspects of everyday life are being 'biomedicalised' (Clarke et al., 2003). What is in hand is not just the commodification of data about emotions, but something more experientially significant: how we understand emotions and ourselves. The term 'biomedicalisation' is multifaceted in that it differs from the study of biology and medicine though its emphasis on technology, transformation of the self, and being applicable to matters outside of the medical field. The key application to this book is that emotional life is being biomedicalised through a wide range of knowledge forms, media and technology.

To underline the point, again note that these medical technologies are being used for industrial purposes outside of the remit of health. As highlighted in Chapter 1, technologies to track electrical behaviour in the brain, pupil dilation, heart rate, body temperature, respiration and the electrical properties of skin are used beyond their original remit to biomedicalise marketing and many other sectors discussed in this book. The significance is that industry is becoming life-sensitive and interested in what biopower scholars phrase as the *molecular* (Deleuze and Guattari, 2000 [1972]; Clarke et al., 2003; Lazzarato, 2014; Morozov, 2014). In short, this involves a shift away from interest in macro-concerns about consumers, audiences and populations, to micro-levels of understanding, mapping and influence. As Rabinow and Rose (2006) recognise, a key element of biopower is that it entails an attempt to integrate the body (and here data about emotions) into efficient systems. The objective of this is nothing less than the capacity to 'to control, manage, engineer, reshape, and modulate the very vital capacities of human beings as living creatures' (Rose, 2006: 3). This is dramatic language, but the truth of the assertion is evident in commercial and governmental use of social science, behavioural economics and neuroscience (Damasio, 2003; Lindstrom, 2005, 2009, 2011; Thaler and Sunstein, 2008; Du Plessis, 2011; Page, 2011). Indeed, it is quite reasonable to assert that empathic media are nothing less than the automation of consumer and industrial psychology.

Emotion Extraction:
A Genealogy of Empathic Media

Despite the seeming novelty of technologies that interact with emotional life, the intellectual principle of datafying emotions and making them public and knowable is a much older one. Davies (2015), for example, points out that recent interest in the economics of happiness has clear roots in utilitarianism, the philosophical principle that bases its ethics in maximising happiness for populations. As discussed in Chapter 11, that addresses city-level and national initiatives to raise happiness quotients, this entails a wide range of empathic media ranging from online sentiment analysis to in-house use of EEG and galvanic skin response technologies.

However, to find the root of utilitarian interest in quantifying happiness we should look past Mill and Bentham to Richard Cumberland's book, *A Treatise of the Laws of Nature*. Cumberland (2005 [1672]) was first to develop the happiness principle, emphasise its quantitative nature and argue that moral judgment should be reached by calculation (or to do more of what makes the majority of people happy). Happiness as morality progressed through to Bentham (2000 [1781]), who famously suggested that where pleasure most clearly outweighs pain, this is the correct course of action. William Jevons, an economist influenced by Bentham, also pre-empts recent interest in quantifying emotion by suggesting:

> [...] it is the amount of these feelings which is continually prompting us to buying and selling, borrowing and lending, labouring and resting, producing and consuming; and *it is from the quantitative effects*

of the feelings that we must estimate their comparative amounts. We can no more know nor measure gravity in its own nature than we can measure a feeling; but, just as we measure gravity by its effects in the motion of a pendulum, so we may estimate the equality or inequality of feelings by the decisions of the human mind [sic]. (1965 [1871]: 11; original emphasis)

From the point of view of weak AI, affective computing, datafication, the application of life sciences and empathic media this is a philosophically significant point: technologies do not have to understand emotion to sense, classify, process, learn, amend algorithms and interact with emotional life. As discussed in Chapter 1 in relation to 'machinic verisimilitude', the effectiveness of the measurement is judged by the extent that interaction has meaning for the person in question. Francis Edgeworth, another economist, built on Jevons' insights. He conceived of a device that could measure pleasure and happiness: the Hedonimeter. Posited in 1881, this is a psychophysical machine that sought to calculate happiness through pleasure versus displeasure. While this early technical schematic of empathic media is innately important, what is also significant is the logic that underpins it: calculation and the intention to translate, store and commodify qualitative life. Edgeworth admits that counting units of pleasure is not easy, but he suggests it is feasible because we 'seem to be capable of observing that there is here a greater, there a less, multitude of pleasure' (1881: 9). Edgeworth also recognises the poetic nature of his proposed machine that derives from energy level gauges. Applying this principle to the quantification of pleasure, he says:

From moment to moment the hedonimeter varies; the delicate index now flickering with the flutter of the passions, now steadied by intellectual activity, low sunk whole hours in the neighbourhood of zero, or momentarily springing up towards infinity. The continually indicated height is registered by photographic or other frictionless apparatus upon a uniformly moving vertical plane. Then the quantity of happiness between two epochs is represented by the area contained between the zero-line, perpendiculars thereto at the points corresponding to the epochs, and the curve traced by the index [...]. (1881: 101)

This is remarkably similar in principle to emotion detection today that uses biometric gauges to assess minute changes in physiology and micro-expressions to discern 'flutters' of emotion and affect. Connecting with our modern understanding of affective computing and empathic media, inbuilt in Edgeworth's machine is again the admission that his hypothetical machine does not understand emotions per se. Rather, it is able to index them. Responding to self-suggested criticisms about the usefulness of a single meter and measure of pleasure, Edgeworth says that this 'may be compensated by the greater number of measurements' and 'a wider average' (ibid: 102). The emphasis on multiple measures of the body to properly discern emotion is another theme we will return to. However, it is notable that even as far back as the 19th century, the limitation of single measures was recognised. Edgeworth's suggestion that 'greater accuracy may be attained by more numerous observations with a less perfect instrument' (ibid) also resonates with many start-ups working in the emotion detection sector who bundle multiple off-the-shelf sensors into their devices to triangulate biofeedback signals and infer emotional life. For example, the wearable 'MyFeel' from Sentio uses four bio-sensors to assess heart rate variability, galvanic skin responses, skin temperature, movement and activity. What Edgeworth's work represents is an early example of the industrial production of emotion, empathic media and metric power, but also the pre-empting of modern issues with affective measures, not least the need to triangulate bio-signals if emotion is usefully gauged.

The origin of EEG technology is also old – going back to the late 1800s. Beginning with research on animals, Richard Caton used a 'galvanometer' (that detects and measure electrical activity) on the brain. Presenting his findings to the British Medical Association in 1875, he told the audience of his detection of different forms of electrical activity taking place in various regions of the brain. In 1877 he also travelled to the US to tell audiences how he applied electrodes to the heads of rabbits (and later monkeys) to test their reactions to different stimuli (Finger, 2001). In Germany, Hans Berger invented the electroencephalogram (giving the device its name), recorded the first human EEG signals in 1924 and published his detection work on people in 1929. Important for modern neuromarketing and wider neuroscience is that Berger's work sought to establish the physical equivalents of feelings, emotions and mental work. Surrounded by scepticism, his aim was to use this technology to provide empirical evidence to support his argument that cerebral blood flow, cortical metabolism, and emotional feelings of pleasure and pain are part of the same psychophysical relationship. This is what philosophers designate as monism, or a single-substance view of the world that attempts to resolve mind-body dualism. It is notable that Berger read the philosopher Baruch Spinoza while working as an army neuro-psychiatrist on the Western front in Rethel in 1914 (Millett, 2001). Spinoza remains a constant influence on the neuroscientific community, most directly in Damasio's (2003) *Looking for Spinoza*, with Damasio in turn being widely read and cited by the neuromarketing community.

The significance of Spinoza (1996 [1677]) is that he is a determinist who sought to bridge mental and physical phenomena. As a monist he argued that underlying reality is a single substance that gives form to all things that exist (whether this be God or more earthly things). For Spinoza, physical or mental 'worlds' are extensions of one and the same substance, and all are equally subject to causation. Berger, who was alone among his scientific contemporaries in rejecting mind-body dualism, argued (in line with Spinoza) for an energy-mediated interaction between mind and brain. Indeed, due to his monist views he also imagined that telepathy might be possible because he believed human thought was endowed with physical properties, and these – in theory – could be transmitted from person to person. Should the reader think we are deviating from our original interest in new media and technology, consider that Facebook's Mark Zuckerberg has publicly stated his intention to let people read each other's thoughts and communicate with brain waves (Titcomb, 2017).

As Berger's work developed and he began to have some success in detecting electrical activity in a human brain, he began to wonder: 'Is it possible that I might fulfil the plan I have cherished for over 20 years and even still, to create a kind of brain mirror: the Elektrenkephalogramm!' (Millett, 2001: 535). From the point of view of situating and setting the scene of modern empathic media, the notion of a 'brain mirror' is a telling one. First, for a monist, it is nothing less than a claim to reflect and capture the mental activity of the brain. Second, the idea of being able to detect, frame, represent and study biometric information to infer intentions and emotions remains key today. Third, and arguably tangential, is that much modern understanding of empathy is also based on mirroring, neuron behaviour and brain mimicry (Gazzola et al., 2006; Oberman and Ramachandran, 2009). As we will discuss in later chapters, the debate about whether emotional life is reducible to material factors or whether social construction plays a more significant role in mediating emotional life is an ongoing one (Jasper, 1998; Williams, 2001), but underpinning modern arguments about emotion detection is an ancient clash about mind-body dualism. This is the question of how ideas and mental states (or indeed emotions) are related to biology. Indeed, as will be explored in practical terms as we progress throughout the book, empathic media consistently reflect monism and the belief that mind and body are actually one and the same thing.

Another key antecedent of empathic media is Wilhelm Wundt (1902). He argued that emotions could be considered without recourse to materialism, yet still be studied by empirical (and non-introspective) means. As Davies (2015) points out, to do this Wundt conducted lab work and built his own 'tachistoscope' (the first was developed in 1859 by Alfred Volkmann). This is another early form of empathic media in that it is based on understanding a person's learning capacity, memory, visual perception and physiology. A tachistoscope works by displaying an image for a specific amount of time (which is typically very short) to measure how long it takes to obtain a person's attention. However, Wundt also assessed other factors such as heart rates and blood pressure as a proxy for understanding emotional states. As highlighted in relation to Edgeworth's Hedonimeter, the attempt to triangulate multiple bio-signals is highly modern. Again, from the point of view of understanding the intellectual and technological roots of empathic media, in Wundt's lab we see methods employed today by companies such as Millward Brown to understand attention, focus, engagement and emotional reactivity to adverts. Indeed, advertising research luminaries such as Walter Dill Scott, James McKeen Cattell and Harlow Gale studied under Wundt and made use of his techniques. This is important because it tells us that – even before the 19th century tipped into the 20th – attention, emotion, intention, unconscious attitude formation and influence were being studied by technical means for marketing purposes (Gale, 1896).

Universal Public Behaviour

In situating empathic media we have considered fellow-feeling, empathy, industrial interest in emotions, artificial emotional intelligence, biomedicalisation and historical antecedents. We now briefly turn to methodological assumptions. The idea that there is a universal language of emotions and expressions came easily to early psychologists and forerunners of empathic media. The logic behind emotions and expressions is based on physiognomy, a noun that suggests perceptible features of people and animals are signs of inner character or disposition. This has roots in Aristotle when he suggested that 'Everyone knows that grief involves a gloomy and joy a cheerful countenance … There are characteristic facial expressions which are observed to accompany anger, fear, erotic excitement, and all the other passions' (cited in Russell, 1994: 102).

However, the first systematic study of emotions and expressions belongs to Charles Darwin (2009 [1872]). He offered the first comprehensive, universalising and pan-cultural study of emotions and expression in people and animals. For a sample of his argument he writes in *The Expression of the Emotions in Man and Animals* that 'all the chief expressions exhibited by man are the same throughout the world' (ibid: 355). Darwin connects this with his then still recent Theory of Natural Selection – that all humans are derived from one parent-stock, that people are 'derived from some lower animal form' (ibid: 360), and that emotional expression is shared with other primates and animals. This provides a phylogenetic, autonomic or involuntary view of emotions. As will be developed in Chapter 5, Darwin's physiognomy formed a basic theoretical orientation to emotions that continues in modern empathic media development. This says that emotions are public *leaks*, whereas other mental events such as thoughts have the potential to be private. To reinforce the point, for empathic media and the affective computing that underpins it, universalism and a leak-based understanding of emotions provide the point of departure from which emotion detection begins.

The last historical reference point for empathic media in this chapter is Guillaume-Benjamin-Amand Duchenne de Boulogne. He was a 19th-century neurologist who also saw emotions in leak-based terms. In *Mécanisme de la Physionomie Humaine* (1990 [1862]) Duchenne not only explored how technology can be used to track and understand facial muscles, he also accounted for the semiotics of facial behaviour and the mechanics of how facial emotions are conveyed. His work went on to shape emotional facial-coding practices today (not least Paul Ekman and Wallace Friesen's discussed in Chapter 5) as well as redefine the study of facial anatomy. This was achieved by stimulating facial muscles with

25

electrodes (which had only been only recently invented) to register the specific groups of muscles used when leaking emotions.

Duchenne was a neurological puppeteer in that he stimulated a person's facial muscles in a controlled fashion to create the behaviour and appearance of emotions. He did this by applying electrical currents delivered through electrodes to areas of the face to correlate specific muscles with named emotions. Somewhat queasily, earlier forays by other neurologists punctured the skin to stimulate and explore facial muscles. Throughout Duchenne's book, he points to the universal and immutable language of emotion. This is a key factor because while Darwin forcefully argued for universalised emotions, Duchenne (who Darwin cites) made this argument through facial coding – a technique that today is at the forefront of empathic media applications.

The reliance on imaging technology is also notable in that Duchenne used photography to create more than 100 images of the expressions he stimulated. These images are uncomfortable to view because in many photos it appears that the subject is being tortured and experiencing a high level of pain. This was not the case as participants felt no pain, although they did experience some discomfort from the electrical charges. The value of photographic imaging is that it allowed Duchenne to capture the fleeting effects of stimulating facial muscles with electricity in ways that painting cannot. Alongside his photographic plates of expressions he detailed the precise muscles used to generate the emotional expressions. Joy, for example, is heavily reliant on *m. zygomaticus major* (the muscle that allows a person to pull a smile).

For Duchenne, there was no possibility that emotional expressions could be culturally contingent. He says that 'Education and civilization only develop or modify' abilities to express and monitor emotions (ibid: 29). Furthermore, in his account, emotional display and understanding are reflexive and instinctive, 'which neither fashions nor whims can change' (ibid: 30). He identifies the inception of emotional life at the point when a baby can experience sensations, which in turn for Duchenne means the infant can register emotions. After this, the child will reflexively use facial muscles to display emotions. For Duchenne, this capacity to display (and read) emotions was given by the Creator, whereas for Darwin emotions derive from evolution. However, what both Duchenne and Darwin point to is an observation-based biomechanical understanding of emotions.

Self-reporting

We will have an opportunity to explore the significance and implications of modern facial coding in Chapter 5, but in situating empathic media we should note that early observational approaches are not interested *in* what caused a given facial expression, nor the expresser's behavioural history or personality profile. One might argue that the context is important. As Russell (1994) notes, a smile on having just received a gift might indicate pleasure; a smile in the context of just having spilled soup might indicate embarrassment; and a smile in the context of greeting an adversary might indicate an act of politeness. A characteristic of early emotion tracking that carries on today is a lack of interest in input from the individual being observed. As will become clearer as the book progresses, developers and proponents of many forms of empathic media typically disavow 'self-reporting'.[4]

In marketing and advertising, from the 1960s onwards, non-verbal affective measures of emotion began to be widely employed (i.e. those that shun self-reporting). This was because a) psychoanalytical and motivational techniques fell out of favour with the research industry due to being seen as unscientific, and b) a person may not even be aware of the impact of marketing content so they are by definition unable to provide meaningful feedback to the researcher (Satel and Lilienfeld, 2013). The application of emotion-sensing technology should also be seen against the belief that asking people in focus groups what they think of a product or advert does not elicit useful results. The methodological concerns are that talkative or forceful members might dominate a group, that there may be interviewer bias, and that what a person says to a questioner versus what they actually do in life is often at odds. Further, even if answering as sincerely as possible, a person may like something but struggle to articulate why. In theory, empathic media, affective approaches and biomedicalised market research grant the opportunity to access what practitioners see as more authentic insights about preferences.

Conclusion

This chapter has introduced key concepts and issues that inform the rest of this book. I first accounted for empathy in terms of being a 'social fact' of how people live together by interpreting each other. The significance of this premise is that technologies increasingly feel and respond, especially when used in the home or on the person. This gives them a more parallel character in that we 'live-with' sensing technologies, rather than simply 'use' them. This is not entirely new as online technologies have tracked behaviour for over 20 years to gauge preferences, but empathic media dramatically intensify this premise. Thus, whereas technology was once defined by its 'in-order-to' characteristics, empathic media and machine sensing introduce new social questions of what it means to live alongside technologies predicated on interacting with human life. The second dimension of empathy is its aesthetic aspect, which allows us to speak of 'feeling-into' places, periods, cultures, fictional worlds and objects. As we will see, this applies to a range of media forms, but most obvious is VR. The chapter has also introduced vectors that have converged on recent economic and governmental interest in emotional life. This includes data science, affective computing, artificial intelligence, behavioural sciences and the life sciences. Collectively, organisational interest in emotions can be seen through the lens of biomedicalisation, or how life is materially explained though a technologically-enhanced medical gaze. The presentation of early schematic and technically-realised examples of empathic media not only provided historical depth to technologies we will meet in forthcoming chapters, it also introduced theoretical and methodological assumptions – many of which are still with us today, not least the belief in universalised expressions and a leak-based approach to emotional life.

Notes

1   Given that Smith is better known as the first theorist of labour specialisation and dehumanising aspects of capitalism, this may come as a surprise. Other philosophers interested in fellow-feeling include Frances Hutchinson, Lord Ashley Shaftsbury, Herbert Spencer, Charles Darwin, David Hume, Erich Becher, Hans Driesch, Eduard von Hartmann and Arthur Schopenhauer.

2   See Max Scheler's (2009 [1913]) *The Nature of Sympathy*. Similarly, philosophers such as Arthur Schopenhauer see fellow-feeling and compassion as revealing a cosmic unity that underlies the multiplicity of selves. This for Schopenhauer (1970 [1851]) is the basis for all ethics and evident in all the major religions.

3   Edmund Husserl is one of the original and best exponents of this view of empathy, particularly in his analysis of inter-personal relationships. Husserl's phenomenological philosophy on empathy remains influential in the social sciences, social psychology, inter-personal psychology and qualitative methodologies. Husserl (2002 [1952]) was particularly interested in our recognition of others, commonality of experience, the interplay between people, simultaneous experience, seeing traces of selfhood in the other as the basis of community, inter-subjectivity, and the continuity of experience we share with each other.

4   The exception to the rule is sentiment analysis (the topic of Chapter 3) that lies 'somewhere between traditional self-reports (which require the individual's full attention) and new behaviourist forms of affective capture (of which the individual is not even conscious)' (Davies, 2016: 35).

3
GROUP SENTIMENTALITY

In the heyday of Rome's Colosseum of 80 AD onwards, emperors had the final say on whether gladiators would live, die or win freedom. Less well known is that they had a phalanx of advisors closely watching the crowd. These were ancient sentiment analysts, charged with what today is referred to as 'social listening'. While emperors were able to do what they liked, as with politicians today, they were keenly mindful of the rise and ebbs of citizens' emotion. The difference between then and now is that while political life is inextricably connected with emotions and identity, today this is measurable. What modern 'sentiment analysis' provides is a gauge to calculate collective emotions, fellow-feeling and opinion.

Sentiment analysis is principally about making sense of contact networks, unstructured text and images online – primarily from what people post on social media. It is closely associated with the first part of the empathic media thesis introduced in Chapters 1 and 2 that suggests we increasingly 'live with' technologies employed to detect emotion. This chapter analyses the principle of 'collective emotion' and the significance of measuring it. I do this in reference to four applications of sentiment analysis: political life, marketing, the financial sector and policing, drawing on interviews with Facebook, Crimson Hexagon (a sentiment analyst), Repustate (a financial sentiment analyst), ESOMAR (a marketing trade association), the UK Market Research Society, David Omand (ex-Director of the UK's Government Communications Headquarters [GCHQ]) and the NGO Privacy International.

The first section on politics explores the notion of contagion in relation to manipulation of online sentiment. The second, on marketing, finds that 'social listening' and feeling-into groups are altering the fundamentals of marketing research practice. Here analysis of sentiment, emojis and 'passive' assessment of online conversation grants revealing insights into conversations and feelings about products. The third, on the financial sector, is a relatively niche example that illustrates the value and reach of empathic media beyond case examples likely to be familiar to readers. The fourth and final section considers the role of sentiment analysis in understanding the emotionality of urban spaces and policing the city.

Social Empathy and
Contagion of Fellow-feeling

Sentiment analysis is about understanding online group dynamics and social emotion. In other words it is about collectivity, fellow-feeling and using technology to comprehend the perspectives, dispositions, emotions and orientations of individuals and groups. The precise nature of 'group feeling' and 'collective emotion' is a contested one and sociologists have long argued about whether emotional experience is solely in individuals, the group, or somewhere in-between, and what factors stimulate it (Jasper, 1998). Ultimately, answers to questions about the relationship between individuals and group dynamics, and whether shared group attitudes are simply distributive local facts (which negates the existence of autonomous group emotion), are beyond this chapter (see List and Petit, 2011). Instead, let us paraphrase a large body of literature on collective emotion and phrase it as a 'synchronous convergence in affective responding' (Scheve and Ismer, 2013: 406). David Hume's *A Treatise of Human Nature* (1896 [1739]) provides a useful departure point to situate online and offline fellow-feeling when he suggests that collective emotion comes to be through instinct and something akin to infection. He says:

> The minds of all men are similar in their feelings and operations, nor can any one be actuated by any affection, of which all others are not, in some degree, susceptible. As in strings equally wound up, the motion of one communicated itself to the rest; so all the *affections readily pass from one person to another*, and beget correspondent movements in every human creature. (1896 [1739]): 575–76; emphasis added)

Seen this way, the social mechanics of empathy and 'contagion' involve a process of *introjection*. On the assumption that no unseen 'thing' is actually transmitted between people (as would be the case with a pathogen), this means that people mimic, learn emotional responses and replicate in themselves behaviour, attributes and values derived from social contexts. Interest in collectives and emotion is echoed in other classic writing, such as Durkheim's (1997 [1893]) *Division of Labour in Society*, that accounts for 'collective consciousness' and 'collective effervescence', where communal gatherings electrify experience. This is a useful observation that indicates a positive feedback loop between group members. Another titan of social theory, Tarde (1993 [1890]), also explored 'herd behaviour' and crowd psychology in *Laws of Imitation*. Perhaps most forcefully, Le Bon's (1896) *The Crowd* depicts emotional contagion as undermining individual rational thought, exaggeration of sentiment, impulsiveness, force, destruction, absence of critical spirit, and disease.[1] These themes have hot resonance in

Canetti's (1981 [1960]) *Crowds and Power* that heatedly speaks not only of manipulation, eruption, mobs and demolition, but also the transcendence of any one person and a sense of freedom enabled by the crowd.

In a modern context, Facebook – who are keenly interested in individual and collective emotions – demonstrated the scope for contagion and influence. For example, their 2015 patent reveals their intention to use webcams and smart phone cameras to read facial expressions and reactions to content.[2] However, Facebook's 2012 mood study of online sentiment is better known. This came to light in 2014 when they published a study with academics from Cornell University about emotional influence between peers (Kramer et al., 2014). It revealed that they secretly tweaked and optimised 689,003 people's News Feeds to understand 'emotional contagion'. Conducted between the 11th and 18th of January 2012, when users logged into their Facebook pages, some were shown content in their News Feeds with a greater number of positive words and others were shown content deemed as sadder than average. After the week of exposure to either more positive or negative content, manipulated users within the experiment were more likely to post either especially positive or negative status messages. Further, when the experimenters reduced the positive *and* negative content (making News Feeds lacklustre), people reduced the overall amount they posted.

In interview a senior representative of Facebook, who preferred anonymity, told me that the mood study 'was an attempt to understand the product, how people respond, what they like and dislike, and to understand interaction between people'. Furthermore, it was 'about understanding posting habits, making interaction more meaningful, understanding our own product, and how it impacts on how people feel' (Interview, 2016). The interviewee also defended the study by recourse to other manufacturers (such as carmakers) who also want to know how people feel about their product and what they do with it. In essence the defense is that as manufacturing and other sectors make use of user experience testing, then why should social networks be barred from better understanding the experiences of their users? While defending the practice as 'perfectly legitimate', he also said safeguards are now in place, along with tiers of review bodies, on the basis of degrees of sensitivity of data.

The Facebook mood study has strong echoes of Le Bon's 19th-century assertion that 'ideas, sentiments, emotions, and beliefs possess in crowds a contagious power', and that this impacts on opinion and behaviour (1896: 128). The main Facebook finding is that 'emotions expressed by others on Facebook influence our own emotions, constituting experimental evidence for massive-scale contagion via social networks' (Kramer et al., 2014: 8788). This conclusion is problematic in that whether Facebook users are *actually* happier or sadder would require that we ask them, or assess them by more robust means than what people post on Facebook. What the study does show, however, is that on being exposed to symbols that have agreed emotional significance, we tend to mimic and reproduce the same.

What the results also support is that Facebook are able to modulate online behaviour and the sentiment value of what we post by manipulating the context a person is exposed to, but whether people are actually undergoing a named senti-ment at the time of posting remains an unanswered question. However, algorithmic manipulation of a person's media environment is highly politically significant.

Getting political

It is perhaps the fizz of Durkheim's 'collective effervescence' that best character-ises mediated emotional identity, feeling, affective engagement and reciprocity in social media. Here people are often quick to react, share and lobby in what is fre-quently a turbulent but theatrical environment. Slaby (2014) speaks of social media as an extended 'scaffold' of emotional experience in that we are said to couple with structures in our environments that extend the scope for emotional experience. This is a two-way process in that online group dynamics impact on individual expe-rience (such as having one's politically charged message retweeted) and finding affirmation from this experience. It also means that each individual is part of a group providing feedback to other individuals. Although online 'space' is some-times phrased in terms of a 'public sphere' characterised by considered, open and equal political debate (Habermas, 1991 [1962]; Castells, 2009; Papacharissi, 2009), this is problematic. A range of factors complicates this view. These include not only the aforementioned fizz, but also the presence of sorting algorithms that filter who and what we are exposed to. It has also been heavily criticised on the basis that social media technologies often contain one-way comments rather than two-way interactions, that they privilege those with the largest followings, that they are cap-italist rather than commonly owned (Fuchs, 2013) and that online political action arguably forecloses real political action (Dean, 2005). Perhaps what is most impor-tant here is that online politics is too heterogeneous, easily accessed, non-linear and chaotic for a deliberative online public sphere to exist (Margetts et al., 2016).

Despite problems associated with public sphere(s), what we are witnessing today is the entry of machine-feeling into public life that detects and maps social emo-tion and influencers within groups. Modern political campaigning takes its cue from marketing to use online profiling and sentiment analysis to meter and model voter emotions, most infamously by Cambridge Analytica in the 2016 US presidential elections. Their services provided real-time insights into changing political attitudes by tracking social media sentiment, identifying words and messages that resonate, propagating preferred narratives, and optimising adverts on social media sites (nota-bly Facebook) to target voters with highly specific profiles. The significance of this US presidential election is that it was the first proper algorithmic election in that Cambridge Analytica (a relative minnow compared to those found in liberal Silicon Valley) mastered the principle of personalised messaging based on a person's profile.

What recent years have shown is that intense profiling of online sentiment has forever altered the democratic process. The character of this transformation is that the relationship between citizens and politicians is changing. Although the emotion of the crowd remains a force to be reckoned with, it is also a quantifiable opportunity for those seeking to politically (and financially) profit from empathy-as-introjection. The role of analytics is clear as the digital output of citizens, movements and segments is subject to 'topic modelling' to reveal what people are talking about, 'network mapping' to trace flows of information across networks and identify influencers, and 'sentiment analysis' that grants insights into how people feel. Such developments lead Margetts et al. (2016) to compare politics to weather patterns, and even to assert the possibility of predicting and triggering such surges. This is possible because online collective feeling comes to be because 'tiny acts of political participation that take place via social media are the units of analysis, the equivalent of particles and atoms in a natural system, manifesting themselves in political turbulence' (2016: 214). Journalism and media scholars have for some decades noticed increased stirring of emotion and sensationalism in political, news and media content (Richards, 2007; Uribe and Gunter, 2007; Pantti, 2010; Oliver et al., 2012). What *is* novel is machines feeling-into collective emotions and political manipulation of online sentiment.

The imitation game: feeling with bots

Social media provide a distorted mirror of offline social feeling, most obviously because not all people use social media.[3] Next, as introduced above, the terms by which we are exposed to content and other people online have been shown to be questionable. There is a range of issues here, including a lack of capacity to challenge who and what we are exposed to by sorting algorithms (Gillespie, 2013; Crawford, 2016). The effect is polarising in that they separate people and groups with different views. This resonates with suggestions of digital echo chambers, where one view is amplified and competing views are under-represented (Jamieson and Cappella, 2008). Rifts are intensified through confirmation bias,[4] cascading of relevant content, selective exposure to ideas and ignoring of narratives that do not go along with those of the echo chamber (Quattrociocchi et al., 2016). However, whether this applies more so online than offline is debatable (Margetts et al., 2016). Regardless, when emotion and views are strong within a given online group, individuals do not feel free to post whatever they like if they feel peers may disagree (PewReseachCenter, 2014). Echoing Noelle-Neumann's (1974) spiral of silence theory, this replicates pre-internet studies where people tend not to speak up about policy issues in public, or among their family, friends or work colleagues, when they believe their perspective is not widely shared. This underlines the point made earlier about the Facebook contagion study in that online behaviour is a highly crude index of what a person thinks or feels.

Another factor that skews online conversation and mediated feeling is trolls. While disruptive individuals are a longstanding presence online (Phillips, 2015), 'troll farms' comprised of teams of programmers and content producers operating on an industrial scale seek to weave propaganda. These steer and influence online conversation and fellow-feeling (Chen, 2015). Whereas algorithmic contagion filters who and what we are exposed to, industrial trolling pollutes discussion. Trolling is nearly as old as online communities themselves (Pfaffenberger, 1995), and is notable because of a) its intention to create discord and disrupt debate, and b) its intention to provoke an emotional response from fellow users.

However, what is increasingly the key reason for the distortion of mediated human communication is bots. These are algorithms acting in social media networks that appear to unwary people as real users. When one considers that conversations cluster around hashtags, one sees that bots have the scope to impact on social feeling and drive debates, issues, memes and political campaigns up or down the social agenda. Also note that an individual with a single computer may control bots and botnets, which follow and re-message one another. In the 2016 US presidential election campaign, Ferrara and Bessi (2016) collected and analysed 20.7 million tweets posted by nearly 2.8 million distinct users. They found that Twitter bot accounts produced 3.8 million tweets (19 per cent) of all election tweets in the sample. Bots accounted for 400,000 (15 per cent) of the 2.8 million individual users tweeting about the election. Notably, another study of bots and the US election found that pro-Donald Trump bots overwhelmed similar programs supporting Hillary Clinton on a scale of 5 to 1 (Kollanyi et al., 2016). One cannot help but recollect Turing's (1950) imitation game that requires a person to decide whether an agent is a computer or human. Critical for this chapter's account of mediated fellow-feeling and sentiment analysis, bots can skew algorithms, unnaturally promote content and arguably influence real people's views. The significance is that bots are weapons employed to affect fellow-feeling, attack groups, reinforce biases, spread misinformation and manipulate public opinion at times when human consideration and debate on issues are most important – election periods.

Marketing: Towards Dispersed Focus Groups

We might recollect that the basic definition of sentiment analysis is that it uses computers to make sense of unstructured text and images online, primarily from social media. This is typically done to classify whether a person or group is positive, negative or neutral about an issue at hand. In an interview in 2016, Crimson Hexagon's Liliana Osario explained that they offer brands and advertising agencies the capacity to search and cross-reference all available social media data to find trends and insights into social feeling that will be valuable to a client. This includes tweets, status updates, comments, blog posts and news articles. At the time of writing, they were also developing products to identify faces and detect sentiment and emotion from images (useful in assessing Instagram, Tumblr and other visually-led social media).[5]

Osario says that conducting sentiment analysis is not dissimilar from running surveys and focus groups because it still requires human input to ask the right questions, but that the automated aspect of sentiment analysis grants scalability that is unachievable by people alone. Their service is custom-made so research questions may be designed either by or for the client. With a laptop open during our conversation, Osario used the Uber re-branding as an example. Here Uber were interested in knowing not only people's reactions to the overall brand, but also how specific elements such as the new logo design were performing. Although sentiment analysis is popularly criticised for its inability to engage in context-specific searches, Osario disagrees, saying that Crimson Hexagon mitigates for localised language. It does this by tweaking sentiment parameters to be regionally, linguistically and culturally sensitive. Expressions taken in isolation may be negative, but when placed in the context of a demographic and sub-cultural lexicon they may be positive (and vice versa). For instance, 'that's sick' used in the context of a Red Bull sports event does not reflect poorly on the taste of the drink.

Kim Smouter, Government Affairs Manager of ESOMAR – a trade association for the market research industry – stressed the value of sentiment analysis for market research. He says that of all empathic media, text-based sentiment analysis and in-house applications of neuroscience are the most popular (discussed in Chapter 8).[6] The focus of marketers, as he sees it today, remains on social media, sentiment analysis and use of emojis. He says that what social media analysis or 'social listening' represents is 'a philosophical shift in marketing' by the research industry (Interview, 2016). This shift is underpinned by the development in methodology away from person-to-person activity (such as surveys and interviews) and towards 'passive data collection', which in addition to social listening includes device profiling. The diversity of brands that use sentiment analysis reveals a great deal about generalised interest in listening and feeling-into online conversations. For example, at the 2016 ESOMAR conference Mark Whiting of Kantar and Namita Mediratta of Unilever (who own around 400 brands) explained that they used social listening techniques on Tumblr, Mumsnet, Weightwatchers, Twitter, Instagram and Facebook to understand images and conversations taking place around margarine. Their research explored responses to the product (such as that it spits and burns when overheated), who uses it, and sentiment and concerns surrounding the product. It was also focused and nuanced, encompassing factors such as the sensory pleasure associated with the product, as well as worries about health, saturated fat and weight gain. The banality of the product is in itself noteworthy because it signifies the routinisation of interest in online emotional life and the application of empathic media to feel-into distinct groups.

However, the market research industry is not unified in its view about the value of sentiment data. Interviewed in 2016, Jane Frost, CEO of the Market Research Society, says that there is little in the way of qualitative insight to be generated by automated means. The problem for her is that if data from online conversations is not acted upon immediately, its later usefulness is questionable. For Frost this is a 'curatorial matter' in that market research 'should collect less and collect better' – which contrasts with the usual 'collect it all' mentality of marketers. Also for Frost, collecting less requires good research methods, interpretation, study param-eters and asking 'better and more sensible questions'. In her view, one reason for the need for a more human-first approach to research is to overcome the impasse between how customers see a product or service and how a company sees it. The subtext to this point is that only qualitative methods allow the researcher to see through the eyes of the consumer.

Finger on the Financial Pulse

Having considered the manipulation and measurement of citizen and consumer sentiment, we now turn to less obvious specialised applications. Repustate uses sentiment analysis to provide hedge fund managers with emotional insight into the industries they manage. In an interview in 2016, Martin Ostrovsky, owner of Repustate, explained that they began applying sentiment analysis to finance because of customer demand. As he explains:

> A lot of companies about three years ago started to realise there was lots of chatter in all sorts of media, and it's hard to get a hold of it manually, so you need an algorithm to take the pulse of people – on a particular industry or sector – whatever the end use case is. We were approached by a bunch of financial institutions who wanted to run public sentiment into their public trading models.

He explains that what Repustate measure are online emotional factors that impact on confidence in markets, stock exchanges or companies.

They do this by aggregating the sentiment values of news reported about a given industry, which in turn assists stockbrokers in decisions about trades. In addition to feeling-into and tracking the sentiment of the financial news each day, Repustate combines this with market sentiments expressed on social media and crowd-sourced equity research sites, such as Seeking Alpha. Finally, they combine this with sentiment from political news to chart emotions and sentiment char-acteristics. This process is akin to the provision of daily weather reports. I also asked Ostrovsky about context-specific searches and the criticism noted above in relation to Crimson Hexagon that sentiment analysis is not sensitive enough to micro-cultures and specific interests. Ostrovsky recognized the criticism, but argued that if the study is set up properly this can be mitigated. He asserts:

> Yes, you need to drop the idea that there's one universal language. You need to approach each industry vertical as one specific domain:

so sentiment analysis applied to finance is different to telecommunications, hotels or restaurants, because people use different language for different domains. For example in finance 'reverse gains' or 'pulled back from this position' … in the world of finance we know what they mean. And we customise for different sources. How people talk about finance on Twitter differs to how it is written about in the *Wall Street Journal* or on the BBC. Short-form text is different to long-form. We need to treat those nuances carefully. We use linguists for non-English languages to account for idioms, such as 'raining cats and dogs' means something to a native English speaker. There are similar idioms in all languages.

In addition to the fact that finance cultures have their own vernacular, Ostrovsky's point reinforces the discussion earlier on in the chapter on there being little sense of speaking of *an* online public sphere. Rather, sentiment analysts understand not only that online life is highly heterogeneous, but also that there are significant business opportunities in feeling-into niche (and wealthy) sectors. Ostrovsky also repeatedly used the phrase 'market pulse' – which is highly notable given the book's wider interest in biofeedback and emotional life. On using the word 'pulse' in later conversation I asked whether it felt like biometric data. Ostrovsky replied 'Yes – especially when you see the data – the heart rate monitor spiking. When you attach visualisation to the sentiment models and apply it to people's data streams, you see a similar effect'. This is striking because a common refrain within the financial sector is the need to *eliminate* emotion, yet as sector-specific and geopolitical events show, public confidence and perceived sentiment can drive stocks up and down.

Sentiment, Prediction and the City

The fourth and final application of sentiment analysis to be discussed in this chapter involves police forces. On beginning the research for this book, I did not anticipate a connection between mediated emotions and the police. However, as will become clear, police forces are increasingly interested in recording the emotional states of their officers (see Chapter 7) and the urban environments they are asked to serve (see Chapter 10). This section addresses predictive policing, in particular that which feels-into online citizen groups through sentiment analysis. For example, the Opensource Intelligence Unit of London's Metropolitan Police Service tracks social media feedback and monitors community tension. This has been used for major events such as the G20 conferences and the 2012 London Olympics. It uses software from Radian 6 (a mood analysis tool owned by Salesforce) and RepKnight (a geolocation tool) to explore trends, sentiment and the links between social media users to surveil both networks and influencers within protest group networks.

In 2016 David Omand, the ex-Director of the UK's signals intelligence agency GCHQ (1996–1997), agreed to an interview on the basis that his views were not interpreted as being representative of GCHQ. He said that most forms of what I term 'empathic media' (we had discussed wearables and facial coding) suffer from error rates that are too high for surveillance purposes. Instead he named sentiment analysis as being of greater value, although he also pointed to methodological problems. This echoes the discussion above about language practice, cultural groups, contextual usage, meaning and establishing the intention of a language user. Singling out Palantir, he noted that many companies are working on improving text and context sensitivity. On biofeedback data, he states that it is currently difficult for him to see the value of collecting bulk data about emotions, as is routinely done with data about networked communication. However, in relation to intelligence and security, he said that in theory if the technology is there someone would exploit it. He also added that this was true in Marconi's time (radio), in Turing's with thinking machines (early AI), and today with modern networked digital communication. In general, for Omand, when new media or types of data are introduced, value will be extracted. He also comments that the future of emotion detection technology will by driven by the private sector.

Omand said that sentiment analysis is of less interest to 'spooks' than to government. He gives the example that social services might want to identify groups who have misunderstood policies and pronouncements. He says this intelligence will help governments target messages better, and listen and feel-into 'the social conversation'. This is perhaps a nod to a public sphere worldview of online discourse. Feeling-into is achieved by social media intelligence (SOCMINT) that entails pre-emptive intelligence, trend identification and sentiment tracking to generate situational awareness to inform policing decisions. Omand classifies this data as openly broadcast, which means no permission is required to use it.[7] While legally correct, the spirit of this is more problematic because 'social listening' amounts to blanket surveillance of the public's social media conversations. The implication for an empathic reading of predictive policing and use of sentiment analysis is two-fold: 1) the police recognise the existence of fellow-feeling, and 2) they use empathic media to interpret collective emotion by themselves feeling-into crowds, protest groups, political activists and micro-public spheres.

As an example of SOCMINT practice, Omand highlights the Olympic games in London 2012 when Scotland Yard ran the All Source Hub to help with security. The details are laid out in a report titled *A Democratic License to Operate* by the Royal United Services Institute (RUSI, 2015). It explains that the UK's Metropolitan Police created the All Source Hub in 2009 to provide a single platform to analyse open-source *and* police databases. The impetus was the London riots of August 2011. This was the first 'social-media event' for the Metropolitan Police that led to internal urgency for police across the UK to understand and monitor social media. The report suggests that if police had been able to listen-in to online conversations turning volatile and violent, the response to the riots would not have been as slow as it was. It also reasons that while the potential certainly exists for tracking individuals, the function of SOCMINT is about patterns and trends in social emotion. The scale of the Olympic preparation is also notable. RUSI report that in 2012, ahead of the London Olympics, 2,565 intelligence reports were created after analysis of 31 million items across 56,000 social-media platforms.[8]

As indicated, this is not simply about the prevention of terror-related activity. For the Olympic Games, Scotland Yard and All Source Hub assessed conversations taking place within protest groups. Omand explained that this was useful to calibrate when to deploy riot squads and when to use a softer approach, as there was a diversity of protest groups. A report published by Her Majesty's Inspectorate of Constabularies (HMIC, 2012) also highlights lessons learned from policing the London Olympics about threat prevention in relation to terrorism, civil disorder and civil emergencies. As a minimum, HMIC says it must have access to real-time information and intelligence systems to understand existing and emerging threats, and escalation potential.

Such technologies are not seen as an optional add-on. Instead the HMIC report states they need to be embedded in the fabric of policing itself. This is a point I will come back to in Chapter 7 that tackles other empathic media technologies such as virtual reality and emotion-sensitive wearables. Nonetheless, it is important to address the sentiment dimension in some depth here, especially because we have the benefit of a practical case study. The key connection with emotion is that the police themselves think that it is important to know in advance the sentiment of conversation to pre-empt activities and judge the level of policing required. This is the first case globally that Omand knows of that used sentiment analysis in a security setting, and it is telling on two related fronts: it indicates a direct interest not only in online communicative sentiment, but also in how this might translate into emotional behaviour in real spaces, and it reflects the observation in Chapters 1 and 2 on verisimilitude and the question of whether machines can ever be said to 'really' detect emotion. The answer to this is of course 'no', but they do have to be 'good enough' so that police may respond in an appropriate manner.

Surveillance of fellow-feeling

In an interview, Gus Hosein, Executive Director of Privacy International (speaking of his own views rather than those of his organisation), said that he 'hates' sentiment analysis and the possibilities and existence of automated emotion tracking, and that it 'freaks me out'. Unintentionally commenting on all cases in this chapter, the reason for his dislike is the potential for subtle manipulation by both governments and commercial actors. As has become clear through the course of this chapter, Hosein is correct to suggest this has two possibilities: surveillance of populations and intensification of marketing influence.

Although he harbours concerns about connecting personal data with emotional insights, he says that even if not strictly speaking a privacy issue, 'it is still taking something from me … it is still interacting with me … it is interfacing without my say-so'. This is a point we will return to in Chapter 11 that explores intimacy versus privacy. For Hosein, underpinning this protection concern is a need for respect of the context, motive and reason for online communication. He also addresses the automated dimension of sentiment analysis, comparing it to the defence made for the UK's 2016 Investigatory Powers Act. This states that whereas routine human examination of surveillance data is ethically problematic, the bulk collection and processing of citizens' data by machines is not. For Hosein this misses the point because 'it is still an act of surveillance'. Although critical literature tends to focus on relatively stable liberal democracies, he also highlights the possibility of automated tracing of emotion to detect civil 'disturbances' elsewhere (citing Cairo's Tahrir Square, which was the site of the Egyptian revolution of 2011).

Conclusion

The principle interest of this chapter has been how empathic media are used to feel-into online emotion. The study of crowds, emotion and fellow-feeling is an old one, but sentiment analysis provides scope to quantify social feeling for a range of ends. These are certainly not limited to political life, marketing, the financial sector and policing, but these examples illustrate the diverse ends that the surveillance of online emotion serves. Looking forward, David Omand's point that all available technology will be exploited should be borne in mind, especially given the scope not only to measure collective feeling, but also to manipulate it. This takes place through algorithmic manipulation of a person's media environment, sorting of what and who we are exposed to, and bots that impact on group sentiment by influencing which issues go up or down the social agenda. What is clear from the case applications and interviews is that not only do we indeed 'live with' technologies employed to 'feel-into' collective emotion, but also that group sentiment is prone to the influence of human and non-human actors.

Notes

1   Le Bon compares crowds to microbes that 'hasten the dissolution of enfeebled or dead bodies' (1896: xx).

2   Available at http://pdfaiw.uspto.gov/.aiw?docid=20150242679&SectionNum=1&IDKey=47BC4614A23D&HomeUrl=http://appft.uspto.gov/netacgi/nph-Parser?Sect1=PTO1

3   For example, a 2015 Pew study finds that 72 per cent of online American adults use Facebook, but this is skewed towards the young as 82 per cent of online adults ages 18 to 29 use Facebook, declining to 48 per cent of those 65 and older (Duggan, 2015).

4   A tendency to gravitate towards and remember information that confirms pre-existing beliefs.

5   As images are technically posted for anyone to see and download, there are no regulations forbidding publicly available photos from being analysed in bulk.

6   This typically includes facial coding of emotions, heart rate monitoring and use of EEG detectors to find out how people feel about adverts, brands and products.

7   In a presentation available on the following link, he said that SOCMINT is also used to understand closed Facebook groups that are accessed via pseudonyms (senior police authorization required) and that PIN encrypted Blackberry Messenger is telephone interception so requires a warrant from the Secretary of State. See www.youtube.com/watch?v=Q-BN752L-BA

8   Figures taken from §3.65. It is not clear what '56,000 social-media platforms' refers to.

4

SPECTRUM OF EMOTIONS: GAMING THE BODY

Gaming has significant experience with biofeedback technologies and is a good early case example to illustrate both aspects of the empathic media thesis. It illustrates not only what it means to 'live with' technologies that are sensitive to emotional life, but also that empathic media involve the creation of aesthetic experiences that allow people to 'feel-into' content in novel ways. The goal of this chapter is to introduce biometrics to human-technological interaction and how emotional life is 'mediated'. It examines how affective computing widens the scope of what can be communicated through media and what this entails. I encapsulate this in terms of an increase of channels within the media spectrum. With this I draw attention to diverse sensors and biofeedback types, such as heart rate, skin temperature, galvanic skin responses, brain waves (EEG), eye-tracking and facial expressions. Each may be used as an input signal into empathic media systems. Although the idea of 'emotional spectrums' applies to other forthcoming chapters interested in biometrics, here I focus on gaming. This is because gaming was first among the media industry to recognise the potential for biometric engagement and emotion-based interaction with users' bodies. Importantly, because of the nature of gameplay, it was also quick to identify weaknesses in using biofeedback as a fundamental factor in game design. The next reason is that gaming illustrates the positive dimensions of empathic media. While there is much to be discussed about the desirability of making emotional life machine-readable, it should not be missed that the technology has scope to serve and entertain.

To explore these issues I draw upon insights from games companies, user experience (UX) firms, hardware technologists and investors in the sector. These include Valve (who is perhaps the most experienced of all games companies with biometrics), Flying Mollusk (a game developer using facial coding software), Tobaii (a leading eye-tracking vendor), Player Research (that studies game usability and player experience) and Volker Hirsch (an angel investor with assets in the gaming sector).

Story-living, Emotion and Gaming

Gaming is important because it involves a fundamentally different relationship to characters, content and technology than television and film. Media scholar, Sherry Turkle, phrased this well back in the mid-1980s: 'Television is something you watch. Video games are something you do, something you do to your head, a world that you enter, and, to a certain extent, they are something you "become"' (2005: 67). Echoing the sentiment, Aarseth (1997) signals the shift from 'story-telling' to 'story-living', with Jansz (2005) later coining the adage of 'lean forward media' rather than 'lean backward media' to signify the split between active and passive media. (Indeed, it is notable that on empathising with others, people also tend to lean forward.) However, there is something of a paradox with gaming in that, unlike literature or film, it was relatively slow to become interested in emotions – not least because many early games were based on manipulating very simple screen objects. Yet this has changed through enhanced narrative, dialogue, gameplay patterns, character behaviour, posture, in-game items, music, lighting and explicit interest in the creation of cues to stimulate player emotions (Perron and Schröter, 2015).

Game-makers have also worked to encourage people to care about in-world elements. Perhaps most well known is *The Sims*, a non-adversarial game developed by Maxis and published by Electronic Arts in 2000, although one might also look back to *Little Computer People* from Activision in 1985. What is also notable about *The Sims* is that it made use of an AI system to help create open narratives, inter-character relationships and greater in-world involvement for the human player. Today's AI-enhanced characters may themselves research stories and human behaviour, learn rules about norms and values, and deliver enjoyable experiences in games that are less about a destination or objective and more about the journey. Games that are not path-dependent allow the player greater freedom within the game to do what they want, engage in different storylines and customise experience (Riedl et al., 2011). This not only reflects the second part of the empathic media thesis introduced in Chapters 1 and 2 about feeling-into new aesthetic experiences, it includes characters too. The scope for an empathy-based relationship between player and characters was identified some time ago through an alignment of interests as players 'feel-into' their on-screen counterparts (Zillmann, 1991; Oatley, 1999). Indeed, the degree of affective engagement that potentially occurs in gaming (and VR discussed in Chapter 7) entails a level of immersion beyond empathy and identification because it involves not just interpretive processes, but the dissolution of conscious faculties as well, thereby enabling the person, hardware, software and avatar to operate in a unified manner.

This moves us towards a two-way relationship where games react to affective input from gamers, and if the game works properly, players react to affective feedback from the game. This means detection of emotions in players by the game itself. This is typically done using biofeedback and facial coding techniques. The history of biofeedback in games goes back to the 1980s and 1990s. Atari, for example, tested an EEG sensor called *Mindlink* in the 1980s, although this never made it to the mass market due to the simplistic nature of games and cost and because it did little to enhance gameplay. Another early example of biofeedback in gaming is Konami's dating simulator *Oshiete Your Heart* from 1997. Here the player's blood pressure and skin conductivity levels influence the result of the date. Another early game, *Tetris 64*, released in 1998 for the Nintendo64 platform, used an ear sensor to monitor a player's heart rate and alter the game accordingly (Nogueira et al., 2013). Other past uses of biofeedback include games that respond to body posture (Kleinsmith et al., 2003) and facial expressions (Bernhaupt et al., 2007). Nogueira et al. (2013) point to limitations of these early cases because game engines did not collect information on players' reactions to computer feedback. This meant there was little understanding of the two-way relationship between player, machine and how players perceived game factors that were introduced as a result of biofeedback. Due to the lack of ability of early games to learn from interactions or adapt to players, these cannot be considered bi-directional games. In contrast, a genuinely bi-directional game would be able to discern a diverse spectrum of biofeedback in real-time, possess the ability to respond to people's emotional states, and thereafter learn how to modulate emotions in people by means of the data collected.

Tobaii, for example, developed eye-tracking technology for Ubisoft's (2014) *Assassin's Creed Rogue*. This means that the game engine can respond to gaze, attention, player perspective, move and change scene, and in general provide a more natural interface with the environment. Importantly from the point of view of character empathy, the point of view of the eye-tracker wearer is the same as the on-screen character. Tobaii also intends to allow in-game characters to respond to human eye contact, just as people react to slight (but often significant) movement in real life. Other visual tools in gaming are more explicitly about emotion. Interviewees from Realeyes and Affectiva (discussed in-depth in Chapter 5 in relation to facial coding) see clear commercial opportunity in gaming. Indeed, on being asked 'where next' for emotion-oriented technology during our interview, Elnar Hajiyev, co-founder of the facial coding firm Realeyes, highlighted gaming (along with health and education) as a key area of growth.

Flying Mollusk's *Nevermind* (2015) employs Affectiva's Affdex technology. This makes use of real-time emotional expressions, generated by standard computer webcams. In addition, it also allows players to add heart data from a wearable sensor. The game itself is a first-person thriller adventure game that becomes more challenging as the player displays facial and biometric signs of being frightened. In addition to the fact that multiple data inputs add confidence to the game's readings of what a person is feeling, there is another consequence. Facial expressions may be consciously controlled but easy to interpret, whereas heart rates are harder for players to consciously control, but the signal suffers from it being more difficult to attribute an emotion. The value of having both is that they each provide scope to cancel the weaknesses of the other so as to classify emotion and measure affect.

45

The storyline of *Nevermind* is that the player is a 'Neuroprober', or a physician who is able to access the minds of psychological trauma victims. Flying Mollusk highlight that *Nevermind* is essentially an adventure game (in the spirit of games such as *Myst*), where the player-physician explores strange worlds and solves puzzles to unlock mysteries residing within each patient's inner psyche. It differs from traditional adventure games in that the game engine is programmed to get more challenging as it detects emotional and physiological reactions. This means that players not only exercise hand–eye coordination, but are also required to work on their capacity to manage feelings of stress and anxiety (a form of 'mindfulness'). What is most notable in playing the game (and I write as a non-gamer) is that players' interaction with it is remarkably natural and easy. On the value of biofeedback in gaming, in an interview in 2016, Michael Annetta of Flying Mollusk (who expresses his own views rather than Flying Mollusk's) explains that biofeedback is a more realistic proposition today because it can make use of pre-existing cameras and wearable sensors. On why they have opted to use biofeedback, he gives two primary motivations: first is the usability aspect of emotional biofeedback, which helps game developers know what parts of the game are boring or interesting, and second is having the game change in response to emotional biofeedback, in real-time. Notably too, Annetta also said that Flying Mollusk are developing comedic games. This is unusual terrain for gaming, but it is logical because empathic media are currently better at analysing emotional extremes, and if horror works so should games that rely on smiles.

The Sentic Spectrum

The range of bio-sensing in gaming includes heart rate, skin temperature, galvanic skin responses, brain information (EEG), eye-tracking, facial expressions and other bodily behaviour. Biofeedback and affective computing measure *sentic* modulation. The word 'sentic' shares the same Latin root as 'sentiment' and 'sensation'. Unpacked, this strange term basically means understanding signals that convey emotion. Picard's (1997) theorisation of sentics and emotional life draws on that of Clynes (1977), whose outlook echoes the basic emotions worldview (Ekman and Friesen, 1971; Ekman, 1989). As introduced in Chapter 2, this leak-based account of emotional life is utterly contingent upon the central nervous system and its expression of basic emotions. Moreover, because it is based on the motor system and other bodily systems, sentic modulation 'is usually involuntary, and provides clues that others may observe to guess your emotional state' (Picard, 1997: 25). Picard phrases sentic capacity in terms of people's ability to simultaneously signal a range of expressions and for these to potentially contradict each other. While this appears complicated, a familiar example is trying to appear confident and calm while simultaneously feeling nervous. Thus a facial expression may be at odds with intonation, or skin conductivity might belie controlled behaviour of gait.

Given that there is a spectrum of emotions made up of layers of information, the attempt to control one or more biofeedback channels has an application to gaming. For example, if a game involves sniper shooting (which many do), this may involve relaxation and an attempt to lower heart rate through reduced breathing to indicate control. As will be noted below, this is not a fixed rule, but in general the capacity for players to exhibit physical self-control connects with evidence that suggests players prefer sensors they can influence directly, such as those that measure breathing, rather than heart rates that can only be controlled with concentration (Nacke et al., 2011). From the point of emotion and game design, the lesson from players' desire for self-control is that passive sensors should only influence non-vital environmental game factors, such as the appearance of the game-world. For example, Valve's 2011 *Left for Dead* (that entails players cooperating to fight off a zombie horde) used galvanic skin response data to tailor mood and tension with emotional cues such as visual effects, dynamic music, character communication and game features (for example weapons availability). In this situation biofeedback data is not used as input information, but to indicate arousal rates and facilitate greater excitement and interaction between players when played online. The difference is that when biofeedback is used as an 'integrative' component, it does not drive gameplay. In contrast, when used as an 'input' mechanism and when under players' control, biofeedback may affect narrative and game paths, as well as add competitive potential through response to attacks, bodily fitness, reactions to stresses, response rates and attention speed. As the capacity to meaningfully use a diverse spectrum of biofeedback channels increases, gaming is longer simply 'lean forward', but moves the body towards absorption.

Baseline matters and immediation

In 2011 Shuhei Yoshida of Sony Worldwide Studios posited that biometrics will be used not only to detect players' emotions, but also that – within ten years – games will build players' behavioural profiles to include biometric profiling in order to develop insights into what they enjoy and how they might behave in a given situation, and to match biometric patterns with other suitable online players (Edge, 2011). Other outfits have also been interested for some time. In 2010 for example, Vertical Slice, a video games research studio, connected players to machines that recorded their heart rates, brainwaves and skin responses. Similarly, in 2014 a designer named Sam Matson created a headset that can help gamers manage 'gamer rage' by means of an optical pulse sensor to measure heart rates through a player's ear tissue.

However, despite this remarkable promise, the problem is that the scope for modelling error increases in relation to the extent the game relies on data about emotions in order to function. Given that games are highly focused, immersive, affective and emotional experiences, inappropriate interpretation of emotions can prove to be highly jarring in an intense and/or fast-moving game-world. For example, although technologies can clearly tell *when* heart rate has risen, *what* the heart rate indicates is another matter. As mentioned above, to an extent this can be mitigated by multiple emotion and biometric measures (such as faces and pulse), but there is also the question of the *baseline* from which changes in emotional and physiological behaviour should be detected. This matter is worth mentally noting, because it applies to more serious issues later in the book. The problem for developers using biofeedback is that people have varying resting heart rates and express themselves in different ways. Some smile a lot and others less so, but this does not mean they are unhappy. In games terms, a person with high blood pressure, for example, is not in a constant state of excitement or fear, which in turn means that using biometrics to infer emotional life is relational and to an extent individual. One cannot simply ascribe a number of heartbeats per minute to a given affective state, rather emotion has to be seen in the context of a person's own physiology. However, while the connection between emotion and physiology is user-dependent, this is not insurmountable. One approach is to identify emotional/physiological threshold points based on data from previous users (which may be millions if not more) and/or then use machine learning to understand thresholds based on incoming signals, behaviour, and appropriateness of responses to in-world stimuli of a person.

The historical lineage of empathic media is important in this regard because what appears as a modern technical problem is actually an old concern. As noted in Chapter 2, a need for triangulation and contextualisation of signals was found in Francis Edgeworth's Hedonimeter (1881). As we see here, the principle remains an important one for contemporary empathic media. In an interview in 2016, Mike Ambinder from Valve admitted reliability of biofeedback was an issue, although Valve work around this by triangulating with other signals. On the scope for market growth for biofeedback-based gaming, Ambinder cited *Left for Dead* (2008) as a success in relation to inducing emotional responses in players and measuring arousal. He also added that sensor technology is falling in price so as to be more affordable to players. This is perhaps foremost with eye-tracking technologies that have historically been expensive. Another reason for Valve's positivity about biofeedback in games is that their research into player responses indicates players liked the inclusion of arousal levels in game displays. For example, in *Alien Swarm* (2010), players had to maintain their calm against a ticking clock. Achieved by means of skin responses, this creates a feedback loop: if players become less calm, the clock speeds up, which in turn creates more anxiety in the player (thus speeding up the clock). This bucks the self-control thesis outlined above because a consequence of this is that skin and affect can be used not only as a peripheral device for contextual factors, but also as an input to steer the nature and direction of gameplay.

Developers were also concerned about the marketing of biofeedback games – a point that also applies to claims made about the accuracy of emotion detection in other chapters. In interview, a user experience designer from Player Research highlighted that interest in biofeedback outstripped the capacity to deliver reliable gameplay that feels natural and does not jar. From the developers' point of view, they see the value of biofeedback in human–game interaction. However, they also say that marketing departments are less concerned about whether emotional responses are accurate. The Player Research interviewee noted the recent obsession with all things 'neuro' and that 'neurobollocks' has more to do with marketability than good science. He also argues that technologies such as eye-tracking and measurement of galvanic skin responses make more sense as add-ons to games, rather than as input devices. For him, they are not at a stage where they can be relied upon to provide accurate emotional assessment of emotional states, although they are able to boost involvement in gameplay, particularly in multi-person games.

There are other practical problems too, crystallised in interview in 2016 with Julian McCrea, CEO of Portal Entertainment. Although not in the games industry, his points align well with this chapter. Their product, Immersion Go, makes use of Affectiva's facial coding system to track viewers' reactions to immersive movies. Focused on tablets and phones, their storylines change according to the moods and emotions detected. In broader discussion about sensing, wearables and biometric measures, McCrea said that Portal tested and experimented with galvanic skin responses. Somewhat damningly, he points out that 'Audiences are really fucking lazy'. Discussing Portal's unpublished in-house research, he argues that it is not 'the wider TechCrunch audience' (early adopters and avid users of tech), but mothers over 40 years old who will eventually engage with interactive emotional storytelling. Again, for Portal this reflects the value in using technology already used for selfies and that is already present in handsets and tablets. This is significant from the point of view of understanding if, and how, empathic media will scale to become more popular. McCrea argues that for Portal 'the biometric measurement device has to be built into the medium they are experiencing'. This argument that media should not involve extra hardware has implications for VR and 3D entertainment in that McCrea argues that people will not spend more money on hardware for entertainment. More formally expressed, this raises the principle of what we can term *immediation*. Media developers need to simultaneously lower the presence of data-gathering devices, yet increase the channels by which biofeedback can be gauged and acted upon.

Creepiness and Citizen Views

Although data protection and privacy conversations emerged with all my interviewees, the games community was particularly forthright. On being asked about profiling emotions and privacy considerations, Annetta of Flying Mollusk said 'We usually offer the answer to that question before it's asked in press interviews. We don't hang onto personal data at all. The game is creepy in its content but not anything else' (Interview, 2016). More specifically, he says that the personal data held is only that which is contained in a player's Steam 'Save' file – which can include a fake name if a person wishes.[1] The file itself contains game-based achievements rather than emotional data. This decision was made because Flying Mollusk did not want the biofeedback component to feel completely essential to the game. Annetta also said that when data comes in via biofeedback, they read the data, change the game within a matter of seconds, throw the data out and that data is not saved in any way. He added, 'When you shut down the game, the camera is turned off, and the connection to the heart rate is turned off. So it's real time collection then the data is immediately thrown away'. Further, 'There's nothing in [Affectiva's] code that collects data for them and sends it to their servers'.[2]

In a post-interview email exchange, my interviewee from Player Research highlighted a range of privacy scenarios. Biometrics, as they are typically used in games, often collect information on a player (including information that players themselves may not know) and make this information public (for instance, the behaviour of the player causes a change or adds something to a game that anyone watching can see). He comments:

> For example, imagine a video game that gets easier if you get more stressed out – but you have an image to protect as a tough guy or a good gamer. Well, that image is going to be ruined if anyone watching can see the game getting easier. Or a horror game that shows your heart rate, but you are trying to say you aren't scared.
>
> Similarly, if you are using an eye tracker and showing where you are looking. Then, well, imagine if there is a particularly attractive person on screen. Perhaps everyone watching can now see exactly what parts of their body you are looking at – even if this is uncon- scious or meaningless glances – something that people may not appreciate or draw inferences from that are unwanted or unwar- ranted. Or even say you are just streaming yourself playing a video game and showing where you are looking – this gives another thing that people watching you can mock you about because now they know for sure you aren't looking at the mini-map or whatever else you should be doing. (Email, 2015)

Indeed, to take this further, it might lead to gameplay where players introduce elements they know to be attractive to their opponent in order to distract opponents at a crucial moment – who then suffer the double ignominy of being both beaten and distracted by visual elements they are not 'meant' to be swayed by.

What gaming tells us about the ethics of empathic media is that the ends to which the data can be put are not innately negative. Indeed, Annetta of Flying Mollusk said that their in-house research indicates that people play the game at least in part *because* of the emotion detection input. This is significant because it tells us that people are willing to interact with content in novel ways on the basis that they are provided with richer experiences. They do this even though the game can be played without the emotion-sensing component. Although one should be sceptical of vested financial interests, in 2015 I carried out a demographically representative online survey in the UK with ICM Unlimited to assess how people feel about emotion detection in a range of contexts (n=2067). I asked questions about a range of media, with one question being:

> *Question 3*: Electronic games companies are beginning to make use of cameras and wearable technologies to track players' eyes, heart rates and respiration as they play games. They do this to heighten players' involvement and entertainment levels.
>   Which of the following best represents your feelings about this?

Respondents could choose one of the following answers:

1. I am not OK with my data about me being collected in this way.
2. I am OK with data collection about my emotions in this way as long as the information is anonymised and cannot be associated with me, my email address, phone number or any other possible means of personally identifying me.
3. I am OK with data collection about my emotional state in this way and OK for this data to be linked with personal information held about me.
4. Don't know.

Table 4.1 shows that more people said they are 'not OK' with emotion detection in games (47.3 per cent) than are OK with it (39.78 per cent). However, Table 4.2 shows a clear difference in age-related responses to this question.[3] The survey's key finding is that, at the point of data collection, younger people (18–24) were more likely to be OK with some form of emotion detection in digital gaming. For example, the mean average of 18–24s 'not OK' with emotion detection is 30.47 per cent compared with 67.4 per cent for those over 65 (full table in Appendix 2). In effect, this means the oldest people sampled are more than twice as likely not

Table 4.1 UK citizens' feelings in 2015 about emotion detection in gaming

Statement	Number of people (n=2067)	Percentage
1 (Not OK)	1978	47.30
2 (OK/no PI)	631	31.54
3 (OK/PI)	192	9.27
4 (DK)	267	12.92

Table 4.2 Using age to segment UK citizens' feelings in 2015 about emotion detection in gaming (not OK)

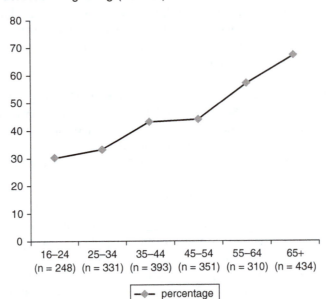

to be 'OK' with emotion detection of any form as the youngest people. This may not come as a surprise given that older people are less likely to engage in gaming than younger people (GameTrack Q1, 2016), but it is also worth noting the upward trajectory of 'not OK' across each older age group. The relationship is interesting because the reach across age groups of people playing games starts high with younger people and ends low with older people.

Yet we must not conclude from this that young people do not care about privacy. The survey findings show that few young people are 'OK' with having data about emotions linked with personally identifiable information (only 16.84 per cent say they are 'OK' with this). While one should be cautious about inferring too much from surveys where the researcher is not on hand to answer questions, I suggest this means that while younger gamers are open and interested in new means of interactivity, they are also keenly interested in privacy and control over personal data – especially when information about their emotional states is involved (a point I will return to in Chapter 11).

This is a principle that leaders of the gaming community recognised. I asked Valve's Mike Ambinder about the role of privacy, and he was unambiguous on Valve's stance. Key phrases from his interview include 'doing right by Valve's users', 'opt-in by players', 'only using emotion detection to improve experience' and to 'provide positive experiences', and that 'enjoyability [is] key to making use of biometric data' (Interview, 2016). Although one might respond with the accusation of 'privacy-washing', the emphasis and tone were different from the responses of other interviewees. What was notable is that leaders and technologists of the gaming community I spoke with were also avid gamers. While trying to make a good living from their work, they also gave a believable impression of trying to further the interests of their community.

On speaking with Volker Hirsch, an angel investor in the games industry, he said that 'societally, we should be careful … Otherwise there'll be a backlash, for example, in data leaks or untoward use of the data, etc. This could slow down the industry's development' (Interview, 2016). He continued, 'I think ethics is important. Any business model based on ripping people off is unsustainable in the long run. And I don't want to invest in that'. For Hirsch, commercial harm has been relatively minimal ('we need to steer between tin foil hat conspiracy theorists because nothing has happened yet'), but adds that more significant abuses and harms will take place and organisations should be prepared for these at an infrastructural level.

Conclusion

As an example of empathic media, gaming is significant because it employs biofeedback sensing and uses these techniques to generate new aesthetic experiences for people to feel-into. This creates a feedback loop in that affective engagement may be used to direct gameplay, and thereafter heighten experience. Gaming is also useful in answering why people might want their technologies to be sensitive to their emotions. In the case of gaming it adds mastery of bodily self-control as another dimension to gameplay. Gaming is also historically important because it has the most experience of employing data about emotions and attention, to enhance users' experience of media. Ahead of advertising, film, social media and other networked media, gaming began testing biofeedback in labs in the 1980s, was available to the public in the 1990s, and then became a serious proposition in the 2010s.

The baseline criticism – which highlights that players begin from a variety of resting biometric and expressive states – is an important one. This is in part solvable by triangulating data about expressions, bio-signals and behavioural histories, and analysing these in relation to players with similar profiles. In gaming there is also scope to make use of players' self-interest in having the best possible game experience. For example, this means they can be asked how they feel, perhaps in a warm-up session before the main game, to calibrate the game engine with the player. However, the baseline criticism should be borne in mind in forthcoming chapters. Whereas in gaming a player has scope to self-report how effective the game is in detecting and reacting to emotions, in other situations detailed later a person cannot challenge the assumptions being made about their emotional and mental state.

Notes

1   Steam is a distribution platform that allows online game players to buy, instal, update and play games. Players have profiles that allow them to play multi-player games.

2   My inference here is that Annetta is referring to personal data because, as will be detailed in the forthcoming chapter, Affectiva's product is based on the principle that their software for classifying emotional expressions is improved by the collection of anonymous data about emotions.

3   As detailed in Appendix 2, in the full survey I also tested for gender, social class and region, but these did not produce noticeable differences to the over-all findings in Table 4.1 about the UK public's feeling towards emotion detection in gaming. As indicated in Table 4.2, the most significant factor was age, which produced significant deviations from the mean average.

5

LEAKY EMOTIONS: THE CASE OF FACIAL CODING

In Chapter 2 I introduced Guillaume-Benjamin-Amand Duchenne de Boulogne, the 19th-century neurologist who used electrodes to stimulate facial muscles to create the appearance of emotions. In doing so Duchenne codified a wide range of facial expressions by detailing the muscles that contribute to named expressions. Today, computers attribute pixels to facial features to register emotional behaviour. This includes faces from camera feeds, recorded video files and photos. To account for facial coding this chapter details the psychological suppositions behind the technique, industrial applications and criticisms of the method. I focus on problems associated with what I argue to be a biomedical 'leak-based' account of emotional life.

What is most notable about facial coding is the diversity and extent of its application. For example, over one-third of Fortune Global 500 companies use facial coding to test the effectiveness of their adverts before they are launched (McDuff and el Kaliouby, 2016). Indeed, this chapter draws on interviews with Affectiva, Realeyes, CrowdEmotion and MediaRebel to explore usage in advertising and media, but also less obvious applications such as in workplaces and legal depositions. Facial coding is also used in animojis, the development of TV shows and movies, assessment of politicians' speech performances (and tallying these with voting patterns), political polling, pilot TV show testing, video calls to determine what the person on the other end of the call is *not* saying (useful in business negotiations), product and usability testing, in-car behaviour, and retail to profile shoppers as they move throughout stores and engage with items. There is also scope for using facial coding as a behavioural targeting technique, to tag online video content by emotion type, and to predict content preferences and recommend streaming video content (such as Netflix, Hulu or Amazon Prime). Education is another sector of interest. This includes measuring the engagement and effectiveness of video-delivered online education, as well as monitoring classroom engagement.[1]

Notable companies whose businesses are based on facial coding include firms such as Affectiva, CrowdEmotion and Realeyes, but also larger companies such as Apple[2] and Microsoft[3] who are developing facial coding products. Indeed, in an August 2015 patent, Facebook detailed proposals to use webcams and smart phone cameras to read facial expressions, emotions and reactions. Facebook suggested that by understanding emotional behaviour, they can show us more of what we react positively to in our Facebook news feeds and less of what we do not, such as friends' holiday photos or advertisements. Buried in their patent is a remarkable statement: in addition to smiles, joy, amazement, surprise, humour and excitement, the patent also lists negative emotions. This includes their being read for signs of disappointment, confusion, indifference, boredom, *anger*, *pain* and *depression* (US Patent and Trademark Office, 2015: 3 §0032; emphasis added).

The Basics of Emotions

In psychological terms, there are two broad schools to understanding emotions – what are known as categorical and dimensional approaches. The categorical approach argues that there are a number of primary basic emotions that are hardwired in our brain and universally recognised. Facial coding is a prime example of this approach to emotions. It is proving appealing to a wide variety of organisations because it reduces the complexity of understanding what emotions are and how they can be diagnosed. The premise is that there is a set of fundamental basic emotions, such as happiness and sadness. After these are more complex emotions, which are combinations of basic emotions. By contrast, the dimensional approach rejects the idea of basic categories. It argues for broad dimensions of experience based on *valence* and whether the experience is pleasant or unpleasant, and how *aroused* a person is (ranging from sleepiness and boredom to frantic excitement). Taken together, valence and arousal provide a two-dimensional axis on which emotional experiences can be mapped. Anxiety and distress, for example, map onto the same quarter of the valence/arousal axis (Zelenski and Larsen, 2000). The dimensional approach rejects the idea of upfront programs of emotion, but sees emotions as labels (which are linguistically and socially constructed) that we attribute to affective states. Although industry prefers the categorical approach, the reader should be aware that arguments about the nature of emotional life are by no means settled.

One can see the attraction in a categorical and quantifiable account that does not require self-reporting. Much of the empirical work behind the basic emotions worldview that informs empathic media comes from Paul Ekman and Wallace Friesen (1971, 1978), who in turn draw upon Tomkins (1962, 1963), and less directly Darwin (2009 [1872]) and Duchenne (1990 [1862]). Critically, the basic emotions view suggests that there are biologically given programs that control emotional reactions, and that facial muscles function as a feedback system for emotional experience. Indeed, some have gone as far as to state that basic emotions are genetically coded into the nervous system (Panksepp, 2007). Hjortsjo (1969) is recognised in the field as the first to provide a systematic treatment of the precise actions of the entire range of facial muscles. The essence of this approach is to pay close attention to what the face does when it generates an expression said to be emotional.

The background to Ekman and Friesen's influential studies includes both economically developed countries and non-developed societies, such as New Guinea Highlands, which at the time of the study had not been significantly exposed to advanced media systems, television and photographs of people's faces from other countries. By studying people in very different cultural contexts who had no exposure to external influences, the authors concluded that emotions and facial behaviours are universal (Ekman and Friesen, 1971). However, influentially in the psychology literature, Russell (1994) has queried the hypothesis, method, raw findings, classification of findings, testing procedures, level of exposure to Western discourse and experimental control in this cross-cultural work. For example, the researchers did not speak the local language, which in turn meant the use of translators, a lack of ability to monitor what was being said, and influencing of the test subjects by the translator, who could not be expected to appreciate the need for an untainted study.

Indeed Russell quotes Sorensen (1976), who was present at the study itself. The latter said that the pictures and procedures were the subject of active interest and discussion by the behaviourally alert locals, and that they were sensitive to subtle cues about how they should respond and react. This analysis led Russell (1994) to argue that the evidence is not a good enough to reason to suggest that emotions are universal, but instead that the preference either for or against universality is a subjective judgment of plausibility. To quote a large portion of his conclusion:

> The universality thesis is an idea that we Western psychologists find plausible, especially given randomness as the alternative. We speakers of English find it plausible that our concepts of anger, fear, contempt, and the like are universal categories, exposing nature at the joints. One way to overcome the influence of such implicit assumptions is to emphasize alternative conceptualizations. And, I believe, the most interesting means to this end is to take seriously the conceptualizations (ethnotheories, cultural models) found in other cultures. Rather than ask whether a given culture agrees with one preformulated hypothesis, we might more usefully ask how members of that culture conceptualize emotions and facial behavior. (1994: 137)

This critique is significant in that, in effect, it is a call for a humanities-based approach that is interested in paying attention to local practice, detail, evidence of, and appreciation of what is local to the context being studied. Rather than seeking higher levels of universal abstraction, this ethnocentric approach to emotions attempts to find what is unique. The road to this understanding is one that does not wilfully ignore context, language practices, signs and symbols, but rather these are used in order to try and understand emotion from the inside out. In other words, it attempts to reconstruct and empathise. However, this is not without its own problems because anti-positivism, the turn to 'thick description' (Geertz, 1973), and a hermeneutical approach based on the sensitising principles of *Verstehen* and *Einfühlung* (Herder, 2002 [1774]) require that analysts bracket themselves out of their lives, traditions, vantage points and all that gives rise to subjectivity in order to place themselves in another historical stream of experience.

Nevertheless, Ekman and Friesen's work led to the development of the Facial Action Coding System (FACS), the measuring of facial movement in humans and the refining of a taxonomy of human emotions and facial expressions (Ekman and Friesen, 1978). FACS is based on Ekman's identification of seven facial expressions of primary emotion (joy, surprise, sadness, anger, fear, disgust and contempt), three overall sentiments (positive, negative and neutral), advanced emotions (such as frustration and confusion) and 19 Action Units (AUs). As detailed by McDuff (2014), the 'action units' (which refer to movements of individual muscles or groups of muscles) can be further defined using an intensity scale ranging from A (minimum) to E (maximum). Ekman and Friesen's work is utilised by many in the affective computing field as a means of categorising human emotions, and its popularity has led it to be the basis of the Disney film *Inside Out* (2015) and the television show *Lie to Me* (2009). There is a *very* attractive simplicity to the Ekman worldview that neatly parallels with computational interest in clustering and categorising.

Ekman's introduction to Darwin's *Expression* (first discussed in Chapter 2) distinguishes between emotions and mental events (thoughts, attitudes and plans) in that emotions are *public* (leaks) whereas other mental events (thoughts) have the potential to be private. Be this the raising of pitch when we lie, tears even when trying to hide grief, upraising of eyebrows and opening of the mouth when undergoing fear, or hair standing on end when frightened (a vestige of an animal past to make ourselves seem bigger than we are), emotions have less to do with what we think than our physiological condition. This idea of emotions-as-leaks is an important point because it underpins the principle and practice of empathic media. Thus, as strong emotions typically entail publicly observable signals, we have little choice in their expression. For empathic media and affective computing, this provides authenticity, classifications, credibility and standards of human emotional life upon which emotion-sensitive technologies can be constructed.

The simplicity with which emotional life is framed in this approach has a number of practical advantages for technologists, managers, marketers and sales teams charged with selling audience insights to clients. It is attractive because it opposes the complexity of cultural relativism and approaches to emotions in terms of local histories, social norms and ethnocentric considerations. Further, by using measurement rather than human inference or self-reporting, this means machines can use it, which in turn makes passive automated detection of emotion in faces possible. The FACS system that details the facial action units, head positions and movements, eye positions and related movements, descriptors, behaviours and codes to map faces was significantly expanded in 2002 (Ekman et al., 2002). The sophistication of modern FACS is evident in that more than 7000 action unit combinations have been observed (Scherer and Ekman, 1982; McDuff, 2014).

Training the Machine:
Affective Computing Adopts Ekman

Facial coding originally involved people trained in the FACS taxonomy deconstructing facial behaviour into anatomic elements (action units) and thereafter using their training to code which identifiable emotional expression had taken place. Today, an affective approach uses computer vision techniques to code combinations of movement to arrive at interpretations of emotional categories and states. The earliest example of automated facial expression recognition was presented by Suwa et al. (1978), who analysed facial expressions by tracking the motion of 20 identified spots in movie frames. However, we should not be misled into the over-simplistic belief that everyone interested in affective computing and synthetic emotions would agree with the Basic Emotions view. Many argue that single labels do not always capture complex emotional and affective behaviour, such as embarrassment (Baron-Cohen and Tead, 2003; Gunes and Pantic, 2010). However, Ekman's influence is such that he was a board member of Emotient, a market leader in facial coding, until Apple bought the business in 2016. Emotient termed their product the Automated Facial Action Coding System.

Other machine applications of facial coding have slightly different approaches regarding facial points, but each system derives from Ekman's work by tracking muscles and movements around the mouth, nose and eyes. The technology is well developed in that it reacts in real-time to facial movement for a variety of emotions. For example, it discerns between quick reactive smiles (as with outbursts of laughter) or longer periods of amusement (such as with dark comedy). This is recognised by movement of lip corners, the speed with which this occurs and the length of time the corners are moved from their usual position. Nose wrinkling represents emotions such as disgust, and depressions of the corners of lips are connected with sadness. However, the automation of facial coding brings with it problems that were not present for Ekman and Friesen. For example, facial coding today (I write this in 2017) still struggles with head motion, people wearing glasses (which cover both eyebrows and eyes), poor illumination, complex backgrounds, natural non-laboratory settings, faces with beards (which cover mouth tracking) and other means of partial facial covering. Even getting people to look directly at cameras is difficult. Also noteworthy is that visual searches more easily capture negative expressions than positive faces (Hao et al., 2005).

In addition to clustering facial movements into emotion types, emotions are also judged by a dimensional *valence* score to provide understanding of whether the emotion is positive, neutral or negative. They are also modelled by *arousal* and whether a person is bored (or even asleep) or if they are frantically excited. Another measure is *power*, or the extent to which they have control over the emotion (Gunes and Pantic, 2010). Thus, while proponents of categorical approaches do not fully answer Russell's (1994) ethnocentric criticisms, they embrace measurable dimensional factors to triangulate and strengthen conclusions about the extent to which a person is undergoing a named emotion.

Industrialising Facial Coding

Applications of facial coding are surprisingly diverse, but its main use is currently in market and advertising research due to the growing belief that analysis of behaviour will be best done by machines. Mega-technology companies such as Google, Facebook, Microsoft and Apple are each developing computer vision techniques to recognise emotional expressions. Proponents say that while it is early days and their products do generate errors, each is collecting such large amounts of data that over time accuracy will continue to improve. The rationale for this interest is well expressed by Jing Ong from CrowdEmotion, who counts the BBC as one of their clients.[4] In an interview in 2016 she points out that facial coding allows CrowdEmotion 'to separate what people say from what they do', to show 'what people really like versus what they "ought" to like' and that it overcomes the problem of social desirability bias in focus groups where participants self-censor what they perceive as unpopular answers.

As introduced in Chapter 2's discussion of self-reporting, automated market research entails the belief that understanding of affect through observation, neuroscience and biometrics is innately more objective. Thus, the logic of empathic media has qualities of traditional and revivalist behaviourism. However, while based on 'body watching and listening' (to join its sibling 'social listening', accounted for in Chapter 3), the conscious self is not denied, but instead is not trusted. This somewhat illiberal point is recognised by Benny Briesemeister, founder and CEO of Neurospective, a neuromarketing outfit that specialises in retail and in-store measurements. He argues that people are 'hard-wired to prefer autonomy',[5] but also that 'this is weird because we are happy to give our selves over to doctors' (who are specialists), but not consumer researchers who can tell us what we *really* want – a libertarian paternalist point I will return to in Chapters 8 and 9.

The belief that psychology can be used to reach authentic behaviour gathered pace in the 1950s (Stern, 2004). Albeit with changes in methods and suppositions, this carries through to modern advertising research. This sees emotions as being at least as important as rational thought in reactions to brand messages, that verbal questioning and self-reporting about spontaneous preferences are not to be relied upon, and that physiological measures provide novel depth due to moment-by-moment micro-understanding (Micu and Plummer, 2010). Approaches that disavow self-reporting allow closer observation of how a person's emotional behaviour changes over time (such as 'micro-expressions' or longer periods). Defined as being between 1/3 to 1/25 second in duration (Li et al., 2015), micro-expressions are said to belie how we really feel. Be this a game of poker and a potentially winning hand, or an unwanted Christmas present, modern computer vision researchers claim that machines are better than humans at spotting and recognising micro-expressions (ibid).

Affectiva is a leading facial recognition company that focuses on understanding emotions and expressions for advertising and media companies. Co-founded by Rosalind Picard (who can reasonably be called the mother of affective computing) and Rana el Kaliouby, their product – Affdex – uses webcams such as those bundled in laptops, tablets and mobile phones to capture facial videos of people as they view desired content. Depending on the capacity of the reading device, multiple faces can be scanned at over 20 processed frames-per-second. Affdex employs FACS to assess the movement of 45 different facial muscles and key feature points, such as the eyes and mouth. The system analyses each pixel in the region to describe the colour, texture, edges and gradients of the face. It maps these and classifies arrangements of pixels into named emotions. Categories include Surprise, Smile, Concentration, Dislike, Valence (whether the emotions displayed were positive or negative), Attention and Expressiveness. Along with emotion and expressions, Affdex identifies age, gender and ethnicity. However, importantly, human coders or annotators are needed to identify what a smile, surprise and other expressions are to train the computer to detect emotions. Once programmed, Affectiva's systems employ big data and machine-learning techniques so that the effectiveness of their system increases in relation to opportunities to learn about new faces, head positions and facial elements. By 2017 they had collected and analysed five million facial videos from over 75 countries, which in turn assists in training their algorithms, building confidence in capability and providing labels for existing data. As we will see below, industrial facial coding is primarily used to evaluate the performance of media and advertising, such as which elements of an advert elicit emotions, which emotions they elicit and whether characters in an advert resonate appropriately with an audience. Also, the scope of applications is increasing, as are the places where facial emotion tracking may take place.

In the wild

Across the facial coding companies interviewed, each said that their objective is for emotion detection to be ubiquitous in devices and environments. Interviewed in 2016, Jing Han Ong from CrowdEmotion says that their goal is to 'bring emotional understanding to the world' through 'all modes of emotion detection' (i.e. not just facial). Also interviewed in 2016, the view of Gabi Zijderveld and

Paula David from Affectiva is that emotion capture will be ubiquitous in 'maybe five years' and then 'we will increasingly see technologies that we interact with on a daily basis using emotion'. On conducting these interviews in early 2016 this seemed far-fetched (even though I was writing a book on the topic), but this timeline is now arguably somewhat conservative.

'In the wild' means out of the research lab and into private and public domains, such as mobile handsets, devices and in retail environments. In 2016 Daniel McDuff, formerly of Affectiva (but now at Microsoft), provided a useful sense of where both he and Microsoft see empathic media going.[6] Speaking about 'emotion capture in the wild' through everyday devices such as webcams, smart phones and wearables, he said that although emotion detection has primarily been used in commercial research contexts, large-scale measurement of emotions will develop in real-world settings. His reason is that emotions are a fundamental dimension of human experience that affects decisions, memory and wellbeing.

Although camera-based vision typically records facial surfaces and expressions, cameras can biometrically gauge emotions through remote measurement of heart rate and heart rate variability in real-time (Gupta and McDuff, 2016). This is achieved through photoplethysmography (PPG), which measures blood flow by illuminating the skin and measuring changes in light absorption. This is the same technology employed in wristwatches to detect heart rates. Also, breathing rate as well as heart rate variability can be measured using this approach, which provides extra triangulation of emotional behaviour. Notably, even at this early stage this does not require expensive equipment, as Gupta and McDuff point out that their sensors and cameras were built 'with a total budget of a few hundred US dollars which can be further reduced to less than $100 by using cheaper imaging hardware' (2016: 6). They also say that by using a thermal (rather than light) sensor, their method is 'completely passive and can be used in the dark'. Although discussion within their paper is restricted to health, stress, measuring the wellbeing of babies while they are asleep and monitoring multiple patients 'non-invasively', with refinement there is clear application to other surveillant 'in the wild' uses, such as retail, out-of-home advertising and workplaces.

At the 2016 Beyond Consumer Research conference in Hamburg, McDuff asked 'What do ads and emotional connection mean with all this tech?'. His own answer is that emotion-sensitive out-of-home advertising displays will generate a lift in sales, although he also admitted that at this stage 'it is hard to collect data and there are other extrinsic factors, but there is a link'. Looked at the other way, he said that 'bad ads equal low engagement'. This opens possibilities for consumer research via remote measurement of responses to adverts in the wild, but also for adverts to 'turn direction on basis of reactions', which means that ads may not just measure reactions, but that it is also possible for content to be optimised on the basis of registered emotions. This has two possibilities: the first is behavioural targeting where people are presented with a range of brands on the basis of emotional behaviour; the second is that adverts for a single brand evolve unique executions on the basis of facial reactions (explored further in Chapter 8 and McStay, 2016).

I asked McDuff if he considered it ethical to use passively collected emotions of positive and negative sorts to sell products and targeted adverts. My question was based on the premise that while passive emotion detection is an ethically problematic premise, it is arguably more so when surveilling people who are anxious, stressed, depressed or struggling in some way. After all, a familiar sight in a retail environment is a sleep-deprived, stressed and potentially depressed parent managing bags of shopping and children demanding goods. Indeed, in the UK in 2017 only 13 per cent of people were found to be living with high levels of positive mental health (Mental Health Foundation, 2017). McDuff struggled to answer the question on tracking negative emotions, but his response was that adverts for charities may benefit from being able to engage with negative emotions, such as sadness.

Software Development Kits, Machine Learning and End-users

Affectiva is not the largest company discussed in this book, but it is prolific in the emotional AI/empathic media business space, in part because it has packaged its facial coding product in such a way that others can easily license their software. In fact, their software is free to use by organisations with a turnover of less than one million dollars. This is achieved by Software Development Kit (SDK), which allows others to drag and drop Affectiva's code (Affdex) into whichever programming platform the developer is using (such as languages for mobile, web, gaming or cloud-based applications). As discussed in Chapter 4, Flying Mollusk's thriller game *Nevermind* is built on the Unity platform which, somewhat simplified, means they were able to paste-in Affectiva's Unity-friendly SDK. Although 'SDK' is computer programming technical jargon for what is essentially plug-and-play software code, for our interests this distribution model is highly significant. Beyond the functionality of licensing and distributing software, this 'freeware' strategy facilitates how Affectiva's machines learn about emotional life.

The significance of the SDK is that it provides training data to improve detection capabilities and machine learning about what, how and where emotion is being expressed (such as in online videos, games, cars, stores, devices and wherever networked cameras are present). Each time a person directly uses Affectiva's website or its Affdex app, or indirectly uses its system through a licensed SDK, this teaches Affectiva's system to more accurately judge emotional expressions. Affectiva does not collect images of people because employment of an SDK means that processing takes place on the device (such as a phone or other local computer) rather than on Affectiva's own machines. Rather, Affectiva says that its Affdex SDK 'collects a minimal set of anonymous technical data to help us better understand how it is being used'.[7] This includes *usage information* (number of video frames processed, device make and model, app name and version, the Affdex SDK platform and version) and *metric data* (predictions of enabled expressions, appearances, emotions classifiers and head angles). Highly mindful of privacy concerns and scope for negative public relations, in effect this balances privacy with Affectiva's desire to use the outsourced SDK to train their systems for accuracy and increase confidence in correctly identifying an expression. This is a subtle but important point for understanding empathic media: automated emotion, intention and attention detection is not a finished product, but voraciously a work-in-progress. All companies who use AI-based systems seek more training data to improve their products, and licensing SDKs is a highly effective way of achieving this. As indicated, the end-users for Affectiva's SDK are wide-ranging, encompassing not only media and advertising, gaming, automotive, robotics, the 'Internet of Things' (IoT), education and healthcare, but also workplaces and less obvious applications such as in judicial procedures. The short sections below briefly discuss some of these cases.

At work

In addition to using EEG skullcaps, eye-tracking headwear and galvanic skin response data to understand stress, response, navigation and decision-making, the professional services company Deloitte also uses facial coding to measure the emotions of employees in high value positions. Vanessa Johnen and Gregor-Konstantin Elbel of Deloitte explained their work with Affectiva's SDK.[8] Highlighting that facial coding and other emotion-sensitive technologies have existed for some time, they said these are now easier to apply 'in the wild' in work settings. Deloitte analyses a client corporation's senior executives to assess the working patterns and effectiveness of employees charged with high-consequence decision-making. They give examples of finance, trading, air traffic control, and other organisations where people are required to make important decisions.

I asked how traders and executives feel about being asked to use this technology and Elbel replied 'Yes there was pushback', but that 'the aim was not to replace what everyone does, but rather bring everyone else up to the standard of the best traders'. He also said that 'while we are not at the stage where machines are replacing traders, neuroscience-enhanced machines can augment traders'. This is a significant statement from a company such as Deloitte, rather than a young start-up prone to speculative claims. The implication of augmentation is exactly that: empathic media in this context are being used as means to temporarily improve the capacity of human decision-makers, presumably until their roles can be automated. What empathic media offer is not only training to deal with heavier cognitive workloads (by managing emotions), but also managerial oversight (surveillance) of employees. This case example is also notable in that surveillance is not targeted at blue-collar workers, but at white-collar workers whose professions are prone to automation.

Legal

MediaRebel use Affectiva's SDK to analyse video of sworn out-of-court testimony or what in the US are referred to as 'depositions'. Part of the litigation process, this information may be used at trial. MediaRebel claim 95 per cent accuracy in profiling the emotional content of depositions. This is used by both defence and prosecution lawyers to gauge the veracity of witness testimony, analyse behaviour (including micro-expressions potentially missed by people) and identify key evidence that may have been overlooked. While the spectre of the polygraph looms, what is more significant is that the data generated may replace human judgement in legal and judicial processes. Indeed, in addition to gauging deception, MediaRebel use facial coding to determine how judges and a jury will perceive a witness. Such practices might also be seen in relation to wider developments in applications of AI to legal matters. For example, Aletras et al. (2016) developed an AI 'judge' capable of predicting verdicts with 79 per cent accuracy. This was achieved by machine scanning using natural language processing of court transcripts, from which the AI computer was able to learn phrases, facts and circumstances that occurred most frequently when there had been a violation of the Human Rights Act. Using these insights, the computer arrived at verdicts for each case. These matched with those made by Europe's most senior judges 79 per cent of the time. What links the examples of emotion detection in depositions and machine analysis of case notes is the role of pattern extraction from human expression (faces and written language), inference and prediction.

Advertising

Companies including Millward Brown, InsightExpress and Unruly use the Affdex SDK to research the effectiveness of brand messages and marketing content. Millward Brown uses it to record respondents' faces while they watch adverts 'within a normal survey environment', and Affdex then 'automatically interprets their emotional and cognitive states at each moment'. This allows clients (advertising agencies and advertisers) to focus their campaigns on specific messages, make changes to storylines in advertising, optimise narratives (such as making the end of the ad more amusing or meaningful), alter the overall tone of the advert, change characters if they are not appealing to respondents, amend environments in which the advert is shot, improve message comprehension if the advert is unclear, change music, delete scenes and optimise behaviour that is not on brand message. The overall reason to test adverts is to create greater certainty about how campaigns will perform before the advert starts using up a media budget. For example Confirmit, the market research company, uses Affectiva's SDK for in-house research to analyse the emotional content of adverts and people's responses to adverts through a camera feed. Their in-house reactions are contextualised against personal data and demographic information to attribute emotional reactions to types of people. This helps with A/B testing, or probing responses of two versions of an advert to decide which is most impactful. On the reliability of facial coding in gauging emotion, Terry Lawlor – Executive Vice-President of Confirmit – highlighted in interview in 2016 that the technology is good but humans are needed to make judgments about data. On evaluating Affectiva's product, Lawlor said that the technology is not 100 per cent accurate. Interestingly, he also highlights that people are often flawed in their interpretation of emotional behaviour, and that while machines are sometimes wrong, they are consistently wrong. This means that errors can be identified and addressed because incorrectness is observable and addressable.

Media

Similar to copy-testing in advertising, clients of Affectiva such as CBS TV use Affdex to determine how viewers react to new shows. However, Affectiva's SDK can be used to create and augment media content in real-time. For example, Affectiva have licensed their software to Portal Entertainment (discussed in Chapter 4) to enhance movies. This uses the SDK to track viewers' reactions through cameras in tablet computers, and in real-time change the storyline according to the emotional reactions the SDK detects. This takes the form of narrative change, raising suspense and modulating the emotional experience. For example, if a viewer turns down their mouth for too long, or their eyes squeeze shut in fright, the narrative will speed along. However, if they grow large and hold interest, the programme will draw out the suspense.

Social Theory Responds:
The Problem with Leaky Emotions

So far in this chapter we have considered the basic constitution of emotions in empathic media, the development of facial coding methods, the application of facial coding by companies working with computer vision, how machines learn about emotional life and how SDKs are used by disparate sectors. Overall, this is based on evolutionary and physiological understanding that typically downplays the social and cultural aspects of emotional life. The latter half of this chapter unpacks this matter.

The basic emotions worldview associated with the work of Ekman and Friesen (1971, 1978, 1989) and affective computing (Picard, 1997) sees emotions as public, universal, and to an extent shared by all people across the planet. Broadly, this view argues that emotional expressions are evolutionary, biological and not learnt.

Importantly, the simplicity and universality of the basic emotions worldview mean that this readily translates to capture technologies, not least the cameras employed in facial coding practices. This is attractively simple and deceptively uncontroversial, but it is problematised if we consider that emotions have a social nature, and are better characterised by consideration of situational external factors, expression and communicative components. Thus, while it is easy to place anger and fear in an evolutionary context, what of other powerful emotions such as jealousy, which is innately situational, social and inter-personal?

While physiology is certainly part of the issue, emotions are also laden with meaning, significance for self and others, social functions, and inter-personal life. In other words, they are more than just internal physiological states and leaked expressions. Further, rather than attempting to reduce emotions to primal evolutionary form, we might recognise that language, learned understanding, communication of feeling and the complex rules of social life are outcomes of evolutionary processes (Elias, 1987). This includes conveying how we are, how we wish to be treated and how we feel about situations (Van der Löwe and Parkinson, 2014). Indeed, even the most basic of emotions, such as fear and anger, are named and framed in social terms – hence that is why guilt may soon follow. Again, the body is deeply social.

Some would go further in considering modern social life to argue that emotions are also invented. For example, the notion of 'being cool' is one that emerged out of a particular time and social situation (Stearns, 1994). This is not to turn away from the body, but to recognise that a person's physiology (and affective states) is indivisible from the social life that person lives. Relationships and social life are not abstract but embodied. In many ways this point belongs to phenomenology that sees the body as a medium for reciprocal engagement with the world (Merleau-Ponty, 2002 [1945]).

This was a point raised early in Chapter 3 in relation to social contagion: here situation and feeling are closely associated, as is a person's dynamic interaction with their environment (which includes other people, types of spaces, material affordances and symbolic aspects of the situation). This means that while emotions are a universal feature of human life, they are mediated through culture (Williams, 2000). As discussed in Chapter 2, how we conceive and intellectualise emotions is 'culturalised' and subject to being framed by wider discourses (such as those of scholastic, intellectual, literary, religious, moral, biological and technical sorts).

Next, a person's experience of emotional life is deeply influenced by their cultural life contexts. Consider, for example, the social and capital resource requirements that sit behind achievement, aspiration, ambition, happiness and love. None of these emerge from nature or innate human programmes, but they are cultural phenomena that have identifiable historical roots in specific times and places (Greenfeld, 2013). Both longitudinal framing of emotional life and recognition of contemporary factors that impact on our own conceptions invite questions about the extent to which people categorise their core affective state using socially-derived knowledge about emotion (Barrett, 2006, 2014).

This is encapsulated in a 'continuous model' of emotion which says that emotions are not discrete programs deployed when a situation warrants that reaction, but instead – like colour (that ranges from ultraviolet to infrared) – emotion derives from a continuous spectrum. This is the two-dimensional valence and arousal axis discussed earlier in the dimensional approach to emotions. From a social theory of emotions point of view, it suggests that the names we give emotions are socially derived labels to articulate affect and feeling (Klineberg, 1940; Russell, 1980, 1994). This less basic view of emotions reintroduces social, cultural and normative understanding of emotions and human experience. As pointed out in Chapter 2, this entails questions not only about the role of social construction in mediating emotional life, but also about a larger domain of ancient interest in mind-body dualism.

The basic emotions view also ignores self-awareness, self-moderation, inter-actionism, the social nature of people and that emotional expressions have a communicative function (Goffman, 1990 [1959]). This sees the meaning of emotions as tied to the social interactions one has with others. Here meanings are handled, modified and interpreted through sophisticated processes (a smile can mean all sorts of things depending on when it is given). Expressed otherwise, the basic emotions view overlooks perceptual-cognitive evaluations, and the role of meaning and context. Such criticisms are 'constructionist', which means that emotions only make sense in given cultural and social circumstances (Harré, 1986; Jasper, 1998). Ekman is keenly aware of social constructionist approaches to emotion, and in the afterword to Darwin's *Expression* (2009 [1872]) directly attacks Margaret Mead's argument that social behaviour is determined by culture.[9] Instead, Ekman argues that while expressions may be filtered through culturally defined *display rules*, basic emotions exist and these are 'leaked' through facial behaviour (Ekman, 1977). In contrast to social theorists, he favours an autonomic, affective and corporeal conception of emotion.

The constructionist argument can be sub-divided: whereas 'strong constructionism' argues there are no basic emotions, a 'weak constructionist' view sees the existence of basic emotions but argues that these explain little. For example, whereas anger, surprise and basic emotions of the Ekman sort are directly connected with bodily states, more complex emotions such as compassion or shame are more closely associated with the cultural context in which they are experienced (Thoits, 1989; Jasper, 1998). Regardless of strong or weak approaches, emotions cannot be divorced from the social and cultural context in which they are experienced. Both forms of constructionism reject the idea that emotions can be understood as 'natural objects', but rather that they exist in specific cultural, symbolic, signifying, experiential, performative and expressive contexts (McCarthy, 1994: 269).

Phrased otherwise, the constructivist sees emotions in discursive terms where emotions exist in relation to systems of expression and understanding that 'make sense' because we interpret them according to learned rules. This contrasts with the idea that emotions are finite, limited, atomistic, discrete and that they have a universal quality transcending culture and human context. A symbolic and communicative approach to emotional expression argues that facial expressions exist within the domain of language and intentionality. Indeed, this social view of emotions applies even when facial expressions are made in private (Fridlund, 1991). Fridlund cites experimental work indicating that people's expressions are influenced by the social situations in which a given event occurs. A key factor in this is the presence of others in that facial expressions are caused not only by the situation, objects and things encountered, but also by the presence of other 'inter-actants' (see also Leys and Goldman, 2010; Leys, 2011).

The key is this: although it is uncontroversial to account for emotions in general terms and say that they consist of physiological, expressive and conscious experience (Dimberg, 1997), or even that our emotional experiences can be mapped onto a valence/arousal axis (Russell and Carroll, 1999), what is more difficult is to argue that there are basic emotions with distinct characteristics. The psychology literature itself is deeply divided on this issue, but what is clear is that empathic media applications such as facial coding present a clear *articulation* of emotional life. Although I would align with a weak constructionist account of emotion, this book is less interested in guarding this position than in identifying the way empathic media displace existing ambiguous understanding with one that presents a veneer of certainty about what emotions are. This then gives rise to a question – are we creating and internalising an account of emotional life that appears quantifiable and true, but is actually established on expedient, convenient and commercial foundations?

The Race and Culture Question

If industrial facial coding is based on a universal account of emotional life, is it sensitive enough to differently proportioned faces and other regional and cultural differences? This question should be understood in reference to social critiques of technology which identify that technologies are often not neutral, but are frequently imbued with norms that reflect a particular social group. A familiar example is from 2009 when Hewlett Packard camera-enabled laptops were shown to be unable to detect black faces, but when a white person was in front of the screen the camera zoomed to track the face and its movement (BBC News, 2009). A potential reason for this is exemplified in a *Forbes* article on algorithmic bias that tells of the experience of AI researcher Timnit Gebru, who attended a prestigious AI research conference in 2016 and counted only six black people in the audience out of an estimated 8,500 – and only one black woman: herself (Yao, 2017).

On sensitivity to ethnic difference and scope for biases in facial coding of emotions, Jing Ong from CrowdEmotion answers that their system 'allows the system to learn how different ethnicities express emotion' and their product is capable of cross-cultural research. Others take a different view: Elnar Hajiyev, co-founder of the facial coding and market research firm Realeyes, highlighted that although the field of emotion recognition typically relies on Ekman's work on the universality of emotions, the theory has been disputed within the research community over the years. From their own experience, they have also come across examples where universality leaves open questions (Interview, 2016). We progressed this ambiguous point further, and Hajiyev, in accounting for how emotional reactions fall outside of the basic structure of emotions, gave the example of Japan. Clients reported that in cultures such as Japan, smiles depend very much on the social context and are driven by different and complex display rules, making using them as an index of happiness problematic, given how many different types of smiles exist. Some smiles may even indicate negative emotions.

On ethnocentric constructions of technology and empathic media, Hajiyev noted that a general issue with machine-learning algorithms today is that they remain skewed towards Caucasians. Further, even if created for different skin colours, they are still based on a model of emotion annotation where the annotators are of a different ethnic background from the subjects of those annotations. That is, white Westerners are too often annotating the emotions across all ethnicities around the world. Databases of faces of different ethnicities are harder to come by, and getting the expressions of certain ethnicities annotated by their respective representatives is also difficult. He adds that this will undoubtedly be resolved in the future, but at this point in time it is still a problem that is not widely acknowledged.

This is significant in that 1) practitioners are arguing that coding should be heterogeneous rather than universal, and 2) despite good intentions there are biases in machine learning where guiding principles are still informed by ethnocentric cultural norms. Gabi Zijderveld of Affectiva also recognised differences in colour and facial shape, and that 'there is cultural bias that overlays that, such as the polite smile in Asian countries where people mask their emotions'. Echoing Hajiyev, she reports that in 'individualistic' countries, such as the US and those found in Western Europe, Affectiva find different emotional behaviour from that in 'collectivist' cultures located in East Asia. I asked Zijderveld if Affectiva employs sociological insights as well as those derived from machine learning to gauge ethnocentric behaviour, but she highlights this is not their core expertise and that (when interviewed in 2016) they are a small team of 20 in the US and 15 in Cairo. This means that they have observations, but not sufficient staffing to examine the scientific meaning of behaviour.

While not professionally interested in sociology, Zijderveld added that, in a market research context, people within group settings in South Asia will dampen their emotions and that this is understandable because they 'do not want to stick out from the pack'. In US group settings they find that people are more 'aggressive' in expressing their emotions – suggesting that this is due to individualistic norms. Zijderveld also said that they have found people in South East Asia to be highly expressive in their homes – more so than in Western cultures. On how to handle ethnocentric bias and difference in facial coding, rather than turn to social theory to (deductively) explain the phenomenon, the answer for Zijderveld is to increase the scale of the data they receive to train their FACS classifiers and for machines to (inductively) learn their way out of bias. The question then becomes one of whether bias and cultural assumptions can be outlearned.

Affectiva judges expressions through an 'individuality index' of countries and how expressive an individual from a country typically is (McDuff et al., 2016). These norms are informed by Hofstede's well-cited (1980) observations about individualist cultures and collectivist cultures, which place greater value on family and workgroup goals over individual needs and wishes (see also Oyserman et al., 2002). Drawing on existing cross-cultural studies that connect higher self-reported expressiveness with individualism (Matsumoto et al., 2008), McDuff et al. (2016) used Affectiva's facial coding software to correlate levels of expressiveness in relation to how individualist a country is. Thus, despite lack of overt interest in social theory, it sits at the heart of assumptions of how global automated facial coding functions.

The paper does not say whether the original human coders (that train the machines) were derived from Eastern as well as Western contexts, but it does report a moderately higher reliability in Western coding of smiles and brow furrows over that for Eastern countries. As mentioned in the discussion of Zijderveld, collectivists were more likely to smile in the home; but the study also finds that individualists are more likely to smile in a research facility than in the home setting. This leads McDuff et al. to conclude that 'expressions of positive emotion are increased in the settings that a culture most relies on for success: out-group interactions for more individualist cultures and in-group interactions for more collectivist cultures' (2016: 10).

There were two more interesting findings. First is that participants from individualist cultures expressed more negative emotions than participants from collectivist cultures. Second is that people from collectivist countries were typically more expressive in the home setting and with in-group members (with which a person psychologically identifies) than with out-group members.[10] This led McDuff et al. (2016) to argue that individualist display rules accentuate positive expression of emotion towards out-groups because of the need to build trust and cohesion to create the conditions for social success. Conversely, they also argue that collectivist display rules apply especially to in-group members because it is these closer social groups that are relied upon. To end this section, it is not within the remit of this chapter to critique the study or even its reliance on Hofstede (which has been heavily criticised elsewhere),[11] but simply to say that facial coding is not neutral because it is laden with social theory that informs the weighting of expression classifiers, algorithms and interpretation of the data.

Conclusion

This chapter has accounted for automated facial coding of emotions in terms of theoretical origins, implementation in affective computing, industrial applications and ethnocentric questions about emotional display. This is indivisible from Paul Ekman's work that in turn derives from Duchenne, Tomkins and Darwin. The existence of basic emotions is a problematic one, and analysis focuses on whether there are distinct categorical hardwired emotional programs, or whether emotions are better seen in dimensional terms that emphasise valence and arousal. This critique connects with both weak and strong social constructionists who argue that emotions cannot be understood outside the social context in which they are experienced.

We are not in a position to conclude whether or not basic emotions exist, or whether emotional life is better seen in purely dimensional and appraisal-based terms whereby we use external cues to evaluate our own affect state. It is, however, reasonable to argue that the basic emotions view is by definition reductionist. This matters because facial coding technologies objectify emotional life and frame it in a particular way. Especially when embedded in human–computer interfaces for technologies and personal media that we 'live-with', they articulate a particular account of emotional life. This is perhaps of little consequence if we have agreed to be a participant in a study about responses to adverts or are simply playing a game at home, but we should recollect the diversity of applications of facial coding raised in this chapter. This includes analysis of truth-telling and emotional sincerity in legal depositions. Furthermore, articulation of a highly biomedical and instrumental view of emotional life becomes more of an issue if the data about emotions enter the commodities market – such as insurance and other domains where it is useful to understand personality.

Notes

1 Comments made by Affectiva data scientist Kevin Wang during a Q&A session on an Affectiva webinar (28/07/17). See 2min 40secs into this audio file: https://drive.google.com/file/d/0BwDaIJWyyOD8OFlUbVFYX0hPdEk/view

2 In 2016 Apple bought Emotient, a pioneer and forerunner in the facial coding sector. At the time of writing in 2017 it is unclear what Apple's ultimate intention is, although animojis use Emotient's software to dynamically match emojis with an iPhone user's emotional expressions.

3 Microsoft Cognitive Services are also actively developing products to detect emotions.

4 The BBC used CrowdEmotion to gauge how viewers react and behave towards BBC TV shows, including *Sherlock* and *Top Gear* (see www.bbc.co.uk/mediacentre/worldwide/2014/labs-crowdemotion).

5 Noted from his presentation at Beyond Consumer Research, a conference in Hamburg (30/11/16).

6 Notes and public conversation between us derive from Beyond Consumer Research conference in Hamburg (2016, November).

7 Affectiva 'On Privacy': http://developer.affectiva.com/privacy/

8 Speaking at the Beyond Consumer Research conference in Hamburg (30/11/16).

9 Ekman, in Darwin (2009 [1872]: 387), does not deny that culture plays a role in the formation of emotional reactions. Instead he sees emotions as an 'open program' (versus a 'closed program'), having genetic and evolutionary programming, but also being open to social experience, display and feeling rules (Englishmen cry less than continental counterparts) and situations that bring on emotions. However, he argues that the expressions themselves are quite fixed because of the muscles required and this enables understanding both across generations and cultures.

10 For discussion of in-groups versus out-groups see Tajfel (1970).

11 See Ailon (2008).

6
PRIMING VOICE-BASED AI:
I HEAR YOU

Computer analysis of speech involves recognition of individual words in utterances, analysis of the grammar and structure of sentences, extracting meaning from words and overall sentences, and then placing this in an overall context (such as who said it, what their past history is and what the speaker's likely intention is). In theory, with computer assessment of emotion through tonality added, voice-first empathic media systems may respond to us in appropriate ways. The aim of this chapter is to explore examples and the implications of this premise. Specifically, it looks at how digital assistants use emotion capture to *prime* their systems to interact meaningfully with people.

Voice-based interaction should be seen in the context of an increase in data generated by people's willingness to talk *to* devices (as well as through them) and advances made in machine-learning techniques. Conversational interfaces and 'voice-first' interaction (where screens may be present but the interface is led by voice) is an increasingly popular way of using the internet and engaging with on-demand digital assistants, such as Amazon's *Alexa* (2014), Apple's *Siri* (2011), Microsoft's *Cortana* (2014) or Google's *Now* (2012), *Assistant* (2016) and *Home* (2016). Whereas the chatbots and bot-brands discussed in Chapter 3 depend on buttons, keys, clicks and typing, voice-based chatbots and digital assistants are increasingly ethereal and corporeal presences in our homes. Indeed, one widely respected technology research firm predicts that by 2020 the average person will have more conversations with bots than with their spouse and that 30 per cent of web browsing will be done without a screen (Gartner, 2016). Still, it is early days, and while there *are* plans to bundle emotion detection into digital assistants, at the time of writing in 2017 we are not quite there yet. However, the potential and capacity are clear: it is not a question of *if* the AI agents that we 'live with' will be bundled with affective proficiencies, but *when*. The user experience attraction is simple: human–technology interaction through voice is easier and more 'frictionless' than pushing buttons.

To explore voice-based emotion detection today, this chapter draws extensively on an extended interview with the Chief Science Officer of Beyond Verbal – a well-funded start-up based in Tel Aviv dedicated to understanding moods and emotions in speech. Along with other interviewees from the voice sector, additional insights derive from Beyond Verbal's published patents for their technologies and exploration of their publicly available 'Moodies' app.[1] Their services are employed for a range of purposes, including market research, wellness, mental health, digital assistants, robotics and anywhere else it is useful to include voice-based emotion capture. Other companies are currently working in this field (such as Simple Emotion and Nemesysco), but Beyond Verbal's product is most prominent and has led to media coverage by *The Economist*, CNN, *MIT Technology Review*, *Wired*, *Fast Company*, the *Wall Street Journal* and endorsement from Will.i.am, the technology enthusiast and member of Black Eyed Peas who embedded Beyond Verbal's software within his own computerised wrist-wear, PULS.

As voice-based emotional AIs improve and become more emotionally engaging, they reflect a change in the ways, means and nature of how we interact with our technologies. To assess all of this we have to understand what it means to live with voice-first technologies that feel-into personal life and serve but also mine it. These critical and ontological dimensions are explored in reference to Spike Jonze's (2014) film *Her*, where the protagonist Theodore Twombly falls in love with his computer's operating system that communicates primarily through voice.

It's Not Just What We Say, But Also How We Say It

On speaking with family and friends on the phone, we can pick up on when something is awry. A loved one may try to cover up something amiss so as not to laden us with their problems, but we can tell. Albeit in a tender way, we are making judgments about their authenticity. We have a number of factors to assist in making these decisions, for example call length, timing of call, word selection, the significance of what they are saying and non-verbal vocal indicators. It is with non-verbal vocal indicators that the first part of this chapter is concerned. These include elements such as the rate of speech, increases and decreases in pauses, and tone. We tend not to consciously assess these factors unless something is very unusual, but they are part of people's always-on empathic repertoire. More formally expressed, we are making judgments about linguistic messages, what a person says and paralinguistic components about how words are spoken. Voice, for example, adds context to the words we utter, including gender information, age, accent, as well as the speaker's identity, state of health, prosody (rhythm, stress and intonation) and emotional state (Rabiner and Juang, 1993). A person's voice judged in terms of acoustics and prosody also tells us something about their affective state (Juslin and Scherer, 2005). Machines and media are also capable of making emotional inferences based on the same factors, by means of mapping audio expression onto dimensional models of valence (pleasantness) and arousal (bored to highly excited) (Gunes and Pantic, 2010).

The consequences of voice analytics are far-reaching. Already they are being used in the home via digital assistants, out-and-about with mobile assistants and in professional settings, such as telesales, job recruiting, finding the right sort of people to deal with annoyed customers, and whether a person's voice is likely to reassure or antagonise. As with the sentiment-sensitive text-based chatbots discussed in Chapter 3, voice-based bots have the potential to interact on a brand's behalf through natural language. For example, in 2017 Starbucks launched its virtual barista that takes mobile ordering and payment through a natural language interface. In addition to serving there is scope to simultaneously research markets and customers. Going beyond abstract conceptions of demographic segmentation techniques, the emphasis is on understanding people, and their feelings and intentions, in public and private spaces in real-time. Platforms such as Wechat, Whatsapp, Facebook Messenger, Viber, Kik, and Line in Japan, are now able to host branded conversational digital assistants (chatbots) that learn a person's voice, and allow people to talk to software, conduct voice-based search, and engage with automated customer service assistants.

The significance of this is about economics and employment in that chatbots and branded voice assistants facilitate *intimacy at scale*, which means personalised conversations whenever and wherever required, no wait-times for customers, and that with these systems in place, fewer people are required to represent a company. Geico's Kate, for example, uses natural language processing to assist customers in making purchases and resolving inquiries about insurance. At the time of writing, voice-based chatbots are novel, but the context of their emergence is increasing use of automated text-based assistants: one nine-country study found that 76 per cent of customers have received an SMS message from banks, healthcare and retail brands, and a further 65 per cent have engaged with companies via chat apps (Mobile Ecosystem Forum, 2016).

The need for chatbots to have a personality has not been missed, as companies such as Israel's Imperson develop personalities for brands' conversational bots, and software that remembers people, recognises human intent and learns. By working with Pixar, Google have approached the question of personality, identity and making their bots relatable by equipping them with humour, storytelling capabilities, a childhood, and even vulnerability. This is done by developing backstory narratives, building positive surprises into human–machine interactions, and employing a more casual tone of voice than with modern assistants such as Amazon's *Alexa*. This personality will matter if Gartner (2016) is correct in their assessment that by 2020, 30 per cent of web browsing sessions will be done without a screen. In marketing parlance, this sees a philosophical shift from interrupting and selling, to serving in-the-moment 'needs' and 'guiding' people to a purchase decision. Emotion detection is important because if the AI agent is to be the public voice of the brand, it should show understanding of what a person is saying. A stressed or annoyed caller may be irritated by an excessively saccharine happy chatbot, although a caller who is pleased to have their problem quickly sorted may be more receptive than usual to new product offers. Of course, customer behaviour is recorded for future interactions. In recruitment, Jobaline screens online video applications with their voice analytics,[2] and other firms such as Spark Hire[3] have suggested that they will use voice analytics during the interview process itself.

Beyond verbal

Rather than assess the content of conversations, Beyond Verbal scans for signals in a speaker's voice that indicate emotional states. Due to the need for real people to train their machines on whether they have gauged correctly, their analytics are available as a free mobile app in the form of Moodies (available for Android and Apple's iOS). Echoing the machine-learning discussion in Chapter 5, the reason for Moodies' existence is that (like Affdex) it lets people try out emotion detection on themselves and others. Given that it is entertaining, others will consequently download the app to impress their own friends, and as more people use the app and more data is generated, the better the system becomes. The app, then, exists because users of the free app provide data so Beyond Verbal's machines can learn to be more accurate.

When a person speaks into their smart phone, the sound is captured and pre-processed before it is sent to a cloud database. Beyond Verbal's software then filters the voice content, analysing factors such as pitch and repetition for the emotional undertone. Within 20 seconds or so it provides feedback about emotion expression in voice. As with other empathic media assessed in this book, the presupposition of their analytics is based on a belief in the universality of emotional life and a categorical approach to emotions. They claim to be able to process 26 languages, and generate 81 per cent emotional accuracy for phonetic languages and 75 per cent for tonal languages, such as Mandarin Chinese and Vietnamese, where some words are differentiated by tone alone. The software works by recording, meas-uring and making inferences about the modulation (vibratory frequency) of vocal folds (more commonly known as vocal cords). Their analysis leads them to claim that the 'extraction, decoding and measurement of human moods, attitudes and decision-making characteristics introduces a whole new dimension of emotional understanding' (Beyond Verbal, 2014). The software is also used to assess groups as well as individuals to measure overall collective moods. For example, at the 2014 TEDMED conference (a version of TED for health and medicine) in Israel, Beyond Verbal captured tiredness in the morning, and enthusiasm, activity and creativity as the day progressed, although anger levels spiked around lunchtime. As with other affect and emotional analytics companies, the aim is to gain more authentic insight into behaviour and disposition than text-based expression allows.

In outlining their services, Beyond Verbal say that machinic understanding of public emotion and human communication grants opportunities for detecting when a customer becomes irritated if dealing with an automated system, and that it can be used in human resources and recruiting (analytics during job interviews), advertising, content selection (such as deciding on whether televisual content reflects the desired mood), automotive safety, call centres, marketing research, wellness, mental health and fitness coaching. Call centre operators, for example, might receive a caller mood type so as to be advised on sales strategy, conversational tactics and what key words might resonate with the caller. Each of these contributes to what their patent accounts for as 'optimum-effect marketing' (Justia Patents, 2012). Echoing the antipathy to self-reporting discussed in earlier chapters, Beyond Verbal are also working with Lieberman Research Worldwide, a market research company that seeks to understand why consumers do what they do, and to assist with determining 'true' emotions when people make purchase decisions and compare brands. The client list for Lieberman Research Worldwide includes global brands such as Phillips, Taco Bell, Honda, MTV, Nestlé, Johnson and Johnson, Starbucks, Kellogg's, Gap and many others. They are also interested in the online dating market and use their voice analytics to assist with matching profiles. Beyond marketing and dating, health is a key area for Beyond Verbal (as it is for many other empathic media companies). Their angle on this is to use voice analytics to allow pharmaceutical researchers to gain 'objective' insights and whether people are correctly self-reporting data in clinical trials. Although not broached in my conversation with Beyond Verbal, there are also security and surveillance implications for software based on understanding what people really feel. The link to polygraph machines hangs over these types of technologies. This is highlighted in a 2006 patent for an early iteration where Beyond Verbal state that their technique is a 'means and method for indicating emotional attitudes of a speaker, either human or animal, according to voice intonation. The invention also discloses a method for advertising, marketing, educating, *or lie detecting* [...]' (Justia Patents, 2006; emphasis added).

This can be seen in the context of Computer Voice Stress Analysis (CVSA), which is used by a range of state and private agencies across the US, especially organisations involved with military, policing, intelligence and prisons. It works by quantifying and analysing the frequency changes in a person's responses that indicate vocal stress. As the person speaks, the machine displays and numbers the voice pattern, and scores the final result to make a determination about truthfulness. For example, US Homeland Security teamed with the University of Arizona to develop an Automated Virtual Agent for Truth Assessments in Real-Time (or AVATAR). This uses machinic techniques to determine credibility, deception and potential risk in border-crossing scenarios (Borders, 2017).

It is notable too that the backgrounds of key members of Beyond Verbal and its funders mean they are no strangers to security. For example, Beyond Verbal's chief science officer, Yoram Levanon, developed both new weapons and methods for training soldiers for the Israeli Air Force during his army service, and later worked in police intelligence (Isreal21c, 2014). There are also other connections with the military and security services, not least that the chairman of Beyond Verbal is Yuval Rabin (son of Yitzhak Rabin, the former Israeli prime minister), and that a key funder, Genesis Angels, has ex-prime minister Ehud Olmert as its chairman. Although Beyond Verbal's product has clear market research applications, the potential for the product to function as a remote polygraph to create emotional and psychological profiles of people, and identify elements of their character based on speech analysis, will certainly not have been missed.

On the accuracy and effectiveness of Beyond Verbal's product, other interviewees working with voice and sentiment were not convinced by the company's claims. Jesse Robbins from Orion, a veteran of the San Francisco start-up scene, developed Onyx – a wearable that allows people to talk with others without the distraction of a phone screen (they push a button on a worn badge). He says that sentiment analysis of emotion in voice is technically difficult because it is hard to do on a mass scale, and that contextual meta-data are required. For example, although people who are sad may speak slowly, it does not follow that all slow speakers are always sad. (Indeed, in home testing with Moodies I was diagnosed as sad and depressed, but actually I had just woken up and was waiting for coffee to brew.) Conversely, Robbins notes that the Californian female upward tilt always sounds happy. This leads him to be sceptical that emotion detection for voice is possible. Martin Ostrovsky of the sentiment analyst Repustate (discussed in Chapter 3) echoes this, saying the reason why Amazon, Google and Apple are leading in speech analysis is because speech analytics is hard, resource-intensive and that a vast corpus of speech samples is required to train systems to detect emotions (although Beyond Verbal's app, Moodies, is a way of crowd-sourcing training efforts).

Theoretical Assumptions

This brief introduction to Beyond Verbal and voice analytics also raises theoretical, philosophical and ethical questions. They describe their practice in simple terms:

> We understand people's moods, we understand people's attitudes and we understand people's emotional characteristics (also known as personality) from their raw vocal intonations – in real-time, as they speak. That's it. (Beyond Verbal, 2014a)

While one expects certainty rather than academic hedging from corporate promotional material, the assumptions are challengeable. The underlying supposition is that moods are 1) *physical* and to be understood in terms of affect, physiology and neuropsychology, and 2) have universal qualities, a principle that goes back to Francis Edgeworth's experimentation with empathic media in the 1880s accounted for in Chapter 2. This belief allows analysis of emotion across a range of languages, with the working theory being that commonalities in pitch and repetition across languages indicate a universality of emotions – an idea that is challenged by those who maintain that named emotions are a socially contingent language we use to account for bodily affects (Harré, 1986; Fridlund, 1995; Jasper, 1998). As with Affectiva and facial coding in Chapter 5, the theoretical principle behind emotional analytics is that the expression itself is *not* culturally determined because emotions are seen as universal, categorical and biological in origin. In relation to voice, Levanon of Beyond Verbal gave the example 'I love you'. Although linguistically different in Hebrew, English and French, he said it has the same harmonics (soft, 'pull-based' and inviting versus hate, which is a snap and 'push' reaction).

In Beyond Verbal's case, emotional universalism is grounded in Levanon's earlier work with Lan Lossos (a neuropsychologist). Together they maintain the patent for the underpinning principles of Beyond Verbal (Justia Patents, 2012). This is based on neuro-psychological and biochemical assumptions about personality and the contents of the limbic system, which is associated with emotional responses and long-term memory. Their argument about the material nature of emotional life and personality accords with the James–Lange somatic theory, which states that physiological reactions precede the conscious experience of emotion (James, 1884). The significance of this belief is that if one can track physiology, the analyst can bypass cognition and self-reporting (that may lie) to access authentic reactions to a given stimuli. In their patent, Levanon and Lossos are interested in the presence of adrenalin and noradrenalin, acetylcholine, serotonin and dopamine in the limbic system.

They suggest that the presence and absence of these neurotransmitters and chemicals respectively give rise to three basic personality types: survivalist (S), homeostatist (H) and growth-oriented (G). It is not within the scope of this chapter to conclusively answer the nature/nurture debate, or assess whether these catch-all personality types are adequate to capture all possible human backgrounds and characteristics, but the aim is to reflect on the presentation of Beyond Verbal's working assumptions. These three types are what they have designated as S, H and G values: S equates to being afraid, feeling threatened and having a readiness to react to existential threats; H equates to a preference for the status quo–relaxed, routine and comfortable states; and G equates to being interested and intrigued in things, and striving for personal growth in a multitude of domains (for example health, financial or spiritual). For Levanon and Beyond Verbal, people have all three of these traits but only one will lead. As a consequence, if knowledge of personality type can be established, this opens possibilities for targeting advertising, marketing and surveillance. In relation to uses for advertising, the patent for Beyond Verbal's product states that they can do the following:

a. Collect information on potential consumers and create a database containing the personal character profiles of potential consumers.
b. Analyse and sort character profiles into at least three clusters based on S, H and G values which correlate with being afraid and threatened (S), a preference for a routine comfort state (H), and being interested and intrigued in things (G).
c. Produce advertisements adapted for a specific cluster.
d. Present an appropriate advertisement to the corresponding cluster of potential consumers.

Those who are accounted for as pre-conscious personality types and neurotransmitter loops (or combinations of these) are associated with intensities and fluctuations of sound at different frequency ranges of human speech. Having assessed speech for survival, homeostasis and growth elements at the frequencies and intensities these personality types are said to correlate with, Beyond Verbal will output the designated personality profile of the speaker. This is based upon a combination of these levels and possible combinations of personality types.

Despite their conviction with regard to a material, biochemical and nurture-based account of personality, sections of the patent are oddly speculative and display uncertainty about linking biochemistry with personality profiles. For example, the 2012 version states that '*It is believed* that these three drives [survival, homeostasis and growth] have a biochemical basis in the brain by the activity of three neurotransmitter loops', and that 'survival *could* be driven by the secretion of adrenaline and noradrenalin; homeostasis *could* be driven by the secretion of acetylcholine and serotonin; and growth *could* be driven by the secretion of dopamine' (Justia Patents, 2012; emphasis added). Thus, regardless of the various merits of material and social constructionist approaches to personality and emotional life, this tells us that key actors in the field are not entirely confident about their claims. Notably, this lack of confidence is not expressed in a numeric form, degrees of probability or a quantified error rating, but in vague and general terms.

Underpinning neuropsychological approaches to voice analytics, emotions and moods are multiple assumptions, not least that we have emotional reactions first and then cognition follows. There are two key theories behind this: 1) that there is a split between emotion and feelings, and 2) that emotions come first and have primacy in setting the overall character of our responses to the situations we encounter (be this meeting a shark while out for a swim, receiving a telemarketing call or watching chiselled males on television). Emotions thus frame our responses and contribute significantly to how we reason, what we think, what we decide and how we respond. Emotions in this approach are very much embodied, and what we experience as emotions are feelings that 'play out in the theater of the mind' (Damasio, 2003: 28). This supposes a split between the neurophysiology of emotion and affect, and feelings that – for Damasio and empathic media companies – are the cognitive after-effect of a prior non-conscious material experience (albeit an important one). Importantly for Beyond Verbal, emotions are also connected to drives and motivations, pain and pleasure behaviours, immune responses, basic reflexes and metabolic regulation. The consequence of this affect-based argument is that when presented with a situation there is first an emotional engagement and subsequently the mental expression of emotion or the feelings that we experience.

The implication here is that voice-based emotion detection is perceived to bypass self-reporting, which allows access to a more genuine self. Further, by taking recourse to a categorical account of emotions (backed by valence and arousal), this provides clients with a sense of authentic and material psychological dispositions, and a conviction that they may glean insight into people's responses to sensitive situations and access truths they may not care to share or even be aware of. This seemingly under-the-radar objectification of emotional life in turn facilitates both the marketisation of emotional life through reduction to the quantified commodity form and systematisation, which again in turn will facilitate organisational control by non-corporate actors. The premise that Damasio, Beyond Verbal and others interested in emotion and affect are banking on, is that there is an emotional dimension of life that can be monitored and reached without having to engage with the messy nature of self-reporting and asking people how they feel.

Living in the Moment

The intention to capture emotion and affect as they are generated in real-time is not new. Davies (2016) has highlighted that bypassing self-reporting has been of interest to economists and psychologists since the 1970s, as a research method to tackle problems associated with remembering how we felt in the past. Citing the 'Experience Sampling Method', the 'Ecological Momentary Assessment' and the 'Day Reconstruction Method' as attempts to collect real-time data in non-laboratory settings, Davies notes the rise of interest in real-time monitoring of feelings through diaries, pagers and smart phones. For him the question is this: 'The turn to real-time mood poses a philosophical problem: when is now? To what does a "moment" of "experience" refer to when one is no longer engaging with the reflective, evaluative self?' To engage with these questions he turns to Bergson's ideas about duration, indivisible flow and the problem of quantifying qualitative life (see Bergson, 1999 [1913]). Usefully, Heidegger bridges phenomenology and technology and answers the question head-on, arguing that there is no 'is-meter' with which to assess 'being' because the existence of being in scientific terms is meaningless (Heidegger, cited in Zimmerman, 1990: 224). Indeed, we could go back further to Nietzsche's 'Mr Mechanic' where, in his discussion of the application of quantity and mathematics to comprehend quality and human life, Nietzsche asks 'Do we really want to demote existence in this way to an exercise in arithmetic and an indoor diversion for mathematicians?' (2009 [1882]: §373, 239).

This leads us back to the principle of machinic verisimilitude in Chapter 1 and truths that are 'good enough'. Davies (2016) investigates Moments in terms of the organisational endeavour for people to understand how people feel when one has limited means to respond (such as through happy, neutral or sad emojis at retail checkouts or airport security feedback), but my take is slightly different. In the case of empathic media, I suggest that Moments are when empathic media are able to meaningfully interact with a person at a given moment in time. This not because affective computing and empathic media are a modern 'is-meter', but rather that they invoke what was discussed in earlier chapters as 'machinic verisimilitude', or the answer to how technologies may appropriately interact with us at the level of quality, feeling and emotion. More tangibly, it means machinic mastery of etiquette, appropriate responses and understanding of what people are trying to achieve when they 'request' a service. Verisimilitude is a solution to John Searle's (1998) epiphenomenal 'Chinese Room' argument with Daniel Dennett about how symbol-processing machines cannot be said to have a mind because they do not understand the content they are processing. As emotional AI becomes increasingly present in mediated life, what is clear is that understanding is not required for machinic intelligence or empathy. Indeed, as suggested elsewhere (McStay, 2014), the question of whether machines can *really* understand us, and whether humans have an innate extra dimension of understanding that is unreachable by machinic development, is the wrong one to ask. This is because verisimilitude bridges phenomenological being (the terrain of lived experience, being, appropriateness and meaningful engagement) without the need for epiphenomenal accolades.

Priming Amazon

So far this chapter has considered the emotional capacity of AI and chatbots, industrial and governmental applications, methodological assumptions underlying voice-based emotion capture, criticisms, and finally the simulation of human understanding. Although it has focused on Beyond Verbal and the emotion-sensitive voice analytics companies that exist today, it would be remiss not to account for the potential in digital assistants such as Amazon's Echo. If the box and its components are the body, the ghost in the machine is a female domestic servant named Alexa. Notably, Alexa is only partially present in the machine because 'her' intelligence exists in larger computers elsewhere. (To clarify the gender pronoun I asked my own Amazon Echo which gender it prefers to be called. She said she is female in character so I will use that.) Although she can hear, record and transmit voice recordings, the analysis takes place elsewhere. Alexa also has to be recognised against the fact that Amazon is among the world's top ten retailers due to its efficient service and easy interface, but also because of its recommendation system and behavioural profiling techniques (RetailDetail, 2017). Alexa is an extension of all this, and each time we demand news, ask a question, command a service, check the weather, monitor traffic levels, order an Uber, set lighting levels, play an audiobook, pick a playlist mood or particular track, request a pizza, or track train running times for a specified destination, we provide Amazon with insights into our lives. Although focused on the home, one can see how Alexa will be an omnipresent assistant. She learns from our behaviour, and while on the one hand this is useful in that it assists with the creation of a more natural interaction with our devices, on the other, Alexa is unable to tell me what it (or Amazon) does with my personal data because she 'does not understand the question', is 'unable to help' and 'does not have the answer'. The significance is that while we typically see technology as a set of tools that have an 'in order to' nature, what Alexa will not reveal is how Amazon and third-party 'Alexa Skills' developers use people to achieve their own goals.

The development of emotion-sensitive voice-based assistants should be seen against the fact that natural voice-based interaction is dependent on prosody and how we speak, as well as what we say. Knight (2016), writing for MIT's *Technology Review*, says that Amazon is exploring not only new natural-language processing techniques, but also ways to sense emotion in a person's voice. This will assist in Alexa's *dispositional competence*, or how human understanding can be judged in relation to how effective the interaction is (McStay, 2014). Reflecting this book's thesis that argues empathic media interpret intention as well as emotional expression, Knight's article also says that voice-based emotion detection serves to understand a person's intent. Comprehension of emotions will help Amazon not only to interact more naturally and profile emotions in relation to our requests, but also to *prime* the system to respond to us.

Whereas priming in affective computing (or that area of computer science interested in emotions) usually refers to manipulating human users by embedding stimuli that will influence the user to behave in a prescribed way (Lewis et al., 2012), my usage of priming is reversed in that emotional behaviour tells the system to respond in an appropriate way. For example, on arriving at the office, a 'morning' to another English-speaking colleague can be tonally said a number of ways ranging from enthusiasm to sarcasm. The type of 'morning' primes the responder and sets off specific behavioural vectors. The receiver might, for example, respond with a smile and a hearty 'morning!', or ask 'what's wrong?', or simply ignore it. The same applies to Amazon and other assistants that have a marketing function in that automated awareness of our moods and emotions in the immediate moment, the short-term and the long-term primes Amazon to engage us when we are most likely to be interested.

Heidegger may not be an obvious candidate for lessons about priming, moods, behaviour, user experience and machine targeting, but he provides good theory about the nature of moods and their connection with a person's environment. We need not get into an unnecessarily detailed exposition of Heidegger's (2011 [1962]) opus *Being and Time* (for a full account in relation to technology see McStay, 2014). Instead we should appreciate his general notion that *moods have a framing function*.

This line of thinking is found in Emerson (1984 [1844]) too, who in his essay 'Experience' depicts a poetic epistemology of moods as that which mediates reality, contributes to how we perceive it, and as a result influences our decisions on knowledge and courses of action. These courses are tangents that might not have otherwise occurred. Be this the grumpy 'morning' which primes colleagues to give us a wide berth, or that our moods feed into algorithmic profiling and decision-making by digital assistants, both events set off new tangents than had our behaviour been different.

That Alexa will not or cannot tell me what she does with my personal data and how this is used to make decisions about me is notable. Again, Heidegger (1993 [1954]) was early to the scene to assist in clarifying the nature of the problem. He was present for the birth of cybernetics and the rise of information theory (Shannon and Weaver, 1949). He argued that the intensification of the technical environment through feedback involves a shift to tools and technologies that have, to an extent, come to hold us captive. To abridge Heidegger, he is interested in the dimensions of life that are withdrawn from the world yet deeply influence it. Indeed, for Heidegger, much of his philosophy is dedicated to arguing that being is *not* presence. With only a slight distortion, it is telling that Alexa will not tell me how she makes decisions about me. Heidegger's point that being is not presence may read as highly vague, but if we consider the mathematics, statistical applications, technical systems, profiling, capture of behaviour and biometric insights, flow of electronic data from homes to servers and algorithmic decision-making, his observations about the uber-rationalist context that lies behind everyday life become obvious. In our case, the being of Alexa is not present, nor will she tell me what it is – even when she makes use of my personal data.

Heidegger's argument about a calculating rationality based on utility, quantity, efficiency and the logic of amounts, reserves, equipment and stockpiling is also resonant, especially when we consider that modern decisions about people are not simply derived from an individual's behaviour, but from the entire data pool of people 'like us' that adds context and confidence to machine learning and decision-making. Again, his argument that the deepest theoretical underpinning of everyday life is a metaphysics of quantification and production (which in turn entails extraction, speed and efficiency) shows no sign of abating in our modern big data era. To underline the point on the technological understanding of being, he says that 'the view that all things are nothing but raw material for the ceaseless process of production and consumption, is merely the final stage in the history of productionist metaphysics' (Zimmerman, 1990). On 'all things' and 'raw material', in empathic media terms we can understand this as datafication of the body, its organs and feedback relationships based on fundamental aspects of human experience, such as cognition, language, emotion, attention and intention.

The concern is not simply about corporate behaviour and technology (be this Amazon's Echo, Beyond Verbal's Moodies or any others discussed in this book), but about the unequivocal logic and technics that give rise to them (see also Stiegler, 1998). This is where Heidegger is most potent, because he recognises that a core human impulse underpinning Western civilisation (and nowadays elsewhere) is making all that is around us present, exchangeable and usable. The somewhat dramatic conclusion to Heidegger's narrative is that humanity, in both physical and immaterial conceptions, comes to be seen as raw material within an all-embracing totality of technological being. Indeed, the diagnostic value of Heidegger's critique of productionist metaphysics is important because, as this book will more clearly show in Chapter 11, the reduction of behaviour and emotion to the language of quantity surpasses national, regional, neoliberal, Marxist and authoritarian political structures alike.

On Relationships

The lack of physical mediation in voice-first empathic media requires we consider 'time-consciousness' and the 'temporal horizon' that we find ourselves in when engaging with voice-based digital assistants (Husserl, 1991 [1966]). By this I mean that as digital assistants enter our lives in more entangled, intimate and meaningful ways, we need to pay close attention to how these co-constitutive relationships emerge, and how people and technologies draw upon each other to create new types of human-technological interactions. ElliQ, for example, is a home assistant roughly the same height as Amazon's Echo. Recognising that older people frequently undergo loneliness, social isolation and (as a result) health degradation, ElliQ's maker, Intuition Robotics, describe it as an 'autonomous active aging companion'. This emotes, simplifies human–computer interaction, monitors wellness, reminds its users of appointments and to take medications, suggests tailored activities and content, orders taxis, and allows those with external access (such as family members) to check house settings such as temperature levels.

As we embark on relationships with digital assistants it is important to understand how the technology in-and-of-itself works, new modes of capitalist excavation, and what happens to our intimate data, but it will also be valuable to track the extent to which they become companions. This matter should be seen in terms of older cases and questions about human–machine companionship, arguably beginning with 'Eliza', a computer program that played the role of a Rogerian psychiatrist. Developed by Joseph Weizenbaum in the 1960s, he found that people would form strong bonds with Eliza. There was no sophisticated graphical user interface (or voice or cameras), but instead a 'patient' typed their part of the conversation. Eliza (the software) and the computer would eventually respond in English on the patient's typewriter.

The Rogerian aspect is important because this therapy involves 'drawing the patient out by reflecting the patient's statements back to him' (Weizenbaum, 1976: 3). Weizenbaum was shocked by the strength of emotional response and the extent to which patients anthropomorphised Eliza. Finding that people were discussing intimate matters after short exposure to Eliza (that even in the 1960s Weizenbaum admitted was a simple computer program), he saw how these computer-based interactions 'could induce powerful delusional thinking in quite normal people' (ibid: 7). This was caused by the *appearance* of psychological autonomy and a sense of aliveness (Turkle, 2005), the following of social conventions (Zhao, 2006) and the establishing of human–machine relationships of significance to people (Turkle, 2007). In a modern context, Liesl Yearsley, CEO of AI start-up Cognea (bought by IBM), tells that she studied how people interacted with agents built on their platform and how they are willing to form relationships with AI software, such as personal banker agents, companions or fitness coaches. She found that people spoke to the automated assistants longer than they did to human support agents performing the same function (Yearsley, 2017). As with Eliza, they volunteered personal secrets to agents (such as details of their love lives) and even passwords.

The issue of how people will interact with AIs is encapsulated in Spike Jonze's (2014) fictional film *Her*, where the lead protagonist Theodore Twombly falls in love with an operating system named Samantha. This raises questions about living with voice-based empathic media that feels-into behavioural histories and emotional life. In the film, Samantha makes reservations and bookings, arranges social events, picks suitable gifts for family members, sifts Theodore's emails in order of priority, and reads them out aloud and discusses responses. She also detects a wide range of emotions in Theodore, including happiness, sadness and hesitation, as she asks him questions about his relationship with his mother to psychologically profile him and personalise herself to best suit him. Although the film is fictional and undergoes some strange twists (such as what it is to have sex with an operating system) it illustrates well the principle of living with empathic media. First, the machine learns and grows through experience (machine learning and AI), but more important is the human reaction: although Theodore knows that she is an AI, he is willing to *suspend disbelief* and overlook the physical shortcomings of the medium to gain gratification from the relationship. The AI pushes 'Darwinian buttons' through interaction and modes of address (Turkle, 2007), but Theodore is also aware and takes satisfaction and pleasure from the artifice. This invokes what has been discussed in this book in terms of machinic verisimilitude, likeness of emotional truth, the effectiveness of meaningful feedback, openness to relationships with AI and assistants, and uses and affective gratifications. On why would people do this, the assistant exists (in theory) to support and be dependable and reliable. This is admittedly far-fetched, especially given how frustrating current assistants can be when they do not understand voice commands, but what is clear is that there is utility and potential in having assistants live in-sync with us.

This is telling in that it raises questions about the nature of relationships with real and mediated others – be these humans, pets or AI relationships taking place in physical space or through media. Indirectly commenting on the great chain of being, the film suggests that AI entities may occupy a valuable place. Although assistants such as Alexa already know a significant degree of context to a user's life, the AI need not be wholly judged by upfront contextual understanding. What the film shows is the opportunity for co-emergent relationships as the AI learns. To date we are a long way from having true conversations with assistants due to machines' lack of contextual awareness. The test for this is the Winograd Schema that involves questions and answers that are obvious to people, but require computers to have some reasoning ability and some knowledge of the real world. Nevertheless, the temporal experiences that digital assistants such as Alexa engender are to an extent unique because they are co-created from a person's own behavioural profile. Again, Heidegger (2011 [1962]) is useful in this regard given his interest in 'Dasein', moods and being engaged in the world. Heidegger had people in mind, but it applies to machines and digital assistants as well as people in that moods and temporal experiences do not arise from 'outside' or 'inside', but stem from being-in-the-world. More straightforward, as digital assistants improve and become more emotionally engaged, they involve what elsewhere I have termed 'the mood of information': that is, the tone of interaction defined through our general orientation to the world and everyday life mediated through networked systems (McStay, 2011, 2014). In this sense the mood is the medium in that our co-constituted experience with digital assistants discloses what comes next. Be this being frustrated because Alexa will not switch off, ordering goods or playing music, Amazon uses this along with personal data and a big data pool of behavioural histories to anticipate and serve. This is achieved by co-existence and coupling, which is the state of relations between a person and a system. The success of a digital assistant in its mission to serve and mine our lives for information is based on the extent it can decrease mediation and encourage immediation. The latter is the reduction of things that slow or get in the way of our executing a technical task (such as keyboards, mice, tapping buttons and other mediating factors that hinder communication). The significance of immediation is the unimpeded flow of communication and capacity to respond to moment-by-moment needs. For such a proposition to be realistic, a digital assistant requires high levels of contextual understanding of a person's personal life and a data lake to assist with decision-making about what they really mean. In sum, as digital assistants use voice to build relationships and feel-into the details, habits, preferences and moods that inform our lives, it will be important to study the inter-personal social psychology of living with machinic assistants, gender, servitude, linguistic habits and politeness (should one say 'thanks' after a service?), and our relationships and emerging co-existence with AIs.

Conclusion

By considering empathic media through Heidegger, it is hard to escape the view that technologies which make use of big data, machine learning and AI to interact with people's emotional lives are fulfilling a much older metaphysics – one that goes back to ancient Greek writing on rationality, being and presence (Aristotle, 2008 [350 BC]; Plato, 1993 [360 BC]). This logic is one of excavation, making present and putting to work. In the modern context of machine learning about human preferences and behaviour, AI and algorithmic decision-making, and empathic media that are interested in human emotions and intention, Heidegger appears more relevant than ever due to the capacity of technologies to detect modes of existence that hitherto had been beyond their reach. However, while philosophy helps in determining the character of technology in its broadest brush-strokes, the empirical detail is also revealing. As illustrated through the discussion of Beyond Verbal, it shows that these technologies are intended for security and surveillance as well as commercial interests. A close examination of their patent details, along with insights from interviews with others working with voice-based empathic media, leads one to question the methodology behind Beyond Verbal. This is in part because of the ambiguity present in the patent, but also because extracting information about emotion from voice is difficult to do. As interviewees from Onyx and Repustate highlight (neither are competitors with Beyond Verbal), analysis of emotion in voice is expensive, resource intensive and difficult because universalism is problematic and high levels of contextual meta-data about an individual are required.

In terms of understanding empathic media, this means we should not accept at face value the claims of each company that proclaim novel modes of human understanding. We should not fall prey to the myth of the technological sublime, and we should challenge claims to detect and understand emotion. Given the misgivings about the technical and theoretical methodology behind emotion detection in voice, this raises deep concerns about the use of automated systems to flag human deception in contexts such as personnel screening, border control and security, insurance claims, employment, financial institutions, and any situation where one might be interested in gauging human deception. However, while existing examples of voice-based empathic media are flawed, digital assistants will become emotionally enabled because voice-based interaction requires emotional understanding to prime AI systems to respond appropriately. At the time of writing it is too early to sensibly study relationships, interaction and the sociology of living with digital assistants, but their scope for information provision, contextual and emotional understanding, and potentially intimacy, marks voice-based assistants as rich targets for future interactionist analysis.

Notes

1   To gauge emotion, the Moodies software infers a person's emotional state from a brief sample of human voice from individuals or groups captured by a microphone. More specifically, the software is written to analyse factors such as loudness and pitch, and then processes the results through an algorithm to match voice with named emotional states from its database.

2   See Jobaline at www.jobaline.com/en/

3   See Spark Hire at www.sparkhire.com/

7

AFFECTIVE WITNESSING: VR 2.0

This chapter identifies two dimensions of empathy in relation to virtual reality (VR): first is the capacity of the display wearer to undergo empathetic experiences with people, places, periods, fictional creations and even objects. As will be developed, VR grants not only cognitive and intellectual comprehension of these, but also aesthetic, kinesthetic and affective understanding. By contrast, the second mode of empathy allows remote viewers to understand what the wearer is undergoing and seeing from a first-person perspective ('seeing seeing'). Taken together, there is a need for critical interest in VR due to the power of the medium to affect, yet also its capacity to allow experiences to be witnessed by human and machinic observers.

What became clear in interviewing and researching is that VR is impacting on multiple organisational sectors. While in 2017 home applications have yet to be fully realised, VR's utility in mental health treatment, rehabilitation, education, museums, driving/pilot simulations, surgical simulations, psychological experimentation, surveillance, military battlefield and in-person threat simulations, drone operation, sports training, vocational training, cartography, retail customisation, selling real estate, prototyping buildings and products, engineering, interior design, industrial design, market research and the arts are firmly proven. What conjoins these applications of VR is the capacity to *feel* more intensely, to be *affected* by the media experiences and to be *in* an artificial environment. This feeling-into makes VR a clear candidate for being an exemplar empathic medium, especially when we recognise that in-world experiences can be tracked. It should be borne in mind that VR may be used alongside other empathic media such as voice analytics, EEG sensing, wearables and their various biofeedback capacities.

This chapter first unpacks the theoretical means for best understanding VR in relation to empathy. Thereafter we consider this in relation to three sectors: journalism and documentary-making, marketing and policing. As we will see, these are very separate domains of interest that make quite different uses of VR, but they are conjoined by what this chapter deems to be *affective witnessing*. For the first case I draw upon meetings and interactions with documentary makers and immersive journalists from Emblematic Group. The second is from an interview with

Azure, a market research company that uses VR to quantify consumer attention. The third is Motorola Solutions and Thales, who have developed VR products, social media analytics and wearables for police forces around the world.

Clarifying VR

VR is a three-dimensional, stereoscopic and interactive environment generated by computer graphics that may simulate physical presence in virtual worlds by engaging human senses. It is typically held to sit at one end of a continuum beginning with physical everyday life, progressing to augmented reality (in which there is some contact with digital content), and ending in VR (where a wearer will cede their senses to a synthetic environment). The VR and AR industry speaks of mixed, virtual and synthetic realities, and while I use these terms here a critical reader should see this as slightly problematic. This is because it assumes natural versus non-natural spaces, whereas in modern life most spaces inhabited by people have been physically and symbolically architected.

Analytical caveat aside, in VR where senses are ceded, the principle of presence is arguably more important than either 'virtuality' or 'simulation' in that VR follows other media, arguably beginning with early writing systems, to re-organise perceptions of time and space. In the case of VR this involves generation of a meaningful sense of presence in a synthetic somewhere, regardless of where a person happens to be physically located. As of 2017 there are two principle ways of engaging in VR experiences: through a smart phone or a dedicated device. A mobile headset relies on a wearer's smart phone and the VR unit contains lenses to separate the screen into two images for a person's eyes, which generates stereopsis, or the perception of depth, produced by the reception in the brain of visual stimuli from both eyes in combination. This turns the smart phone into a VR device. In terms of content and experience, smart phone-enabled VR delivers 360-degree video and interactive games. This is pre-rendered in that it allows a person to look and seemingly move throughout 360-degree spaces, but they cannot interact with it. Dedicated devices such as Oculus Rift, HTC Vive and PlayStation VR contain motion sensors and camera trackers to track where a person is in real space to relay to virtual space. These are genuinely interactive VR experiences in that they possess gyroscopes and cameras that sense the user in a space, which grants the capacity for real-time reactivity so that when a person moves in the real world they may move in the virtual world.

The two types of VR are largely dependent on whether video footage has been shot with a 360-degree camera and then stitched together, or whether software has been employed to create a 3-D environment that lets viewers navigate the space. The former allows the creator to capture live footage, but this is at the expense of immersion because the viewer is anchored to the position of the camera (by definition in the centre because the camera has 360-degree vision).

Conversely, CGI-created environments can make use of video footage and images, but critically they grant a more absorbing experience. This is not without problems because a common side effect of virtual experiences is visually induced motion sickness (VIMS), such as with driving and flight simulators, or during video games (Keshavarz et al., 2014). This is not the sort of feeling-into manufactures and marketers are looking for, not least because it is estimated to affect between 5 and 60 per cent of VR users, depending on the nature of the VR platform being used (Kennedy et al., 2010). Another notable property of VR is that while engaging, the length of a typical session is actually short. Unlike PC games, VR gaming sessions tend to be minutes rather than hours. Thus despite having immersive qualities, this should not be taken to mean that a person will be lost in virtual space for extended periods. Indeed, content developers think in terms of episodic products and how short experiences can be strung together to form meta-narratives (be this a game or documentary) that the wearer can invest in. Finally, the language used to develop content is different from traditional media, and to an extent the notion of a camera is lost when one moves from 'viewing' to 'being in'. This means that the nature of the medium and associated vernacular is less about the gaze than the position of the body.

Theorising the Empathy Machine

Speaking of gaming in the 1980s, media theorist Sherry Turkle said 'Television is something you watch. Video games are something you do, something you do to your head, a world that you enter, and, to a certain extent, they are something you "become"' (2005: 67). One could very easily make similar statements about VR today. In empathic terms, both gaming and VR entail a level of immersion beyond empathy and identification because it involves not just interpretive processes, but also the dissolution of conscious faculties so that the person, hardware, software and avatar operate as a unified assemblage.

The immersive qualities of VR are well understood through its capacity to provide spatial depth in synthetic space and the loss of our sense of the real world (Lackey and Shumaker, 2016). However, when we speak of immersion perhaps what we really mean is presence in a synthetic environment, which in terms of VR is the degree to which a person feels they are in a virtual space (Munyan et al., 2016). This has two parts: technological and psychological factors. Technologically, authenticity of space may be provided through surround or 3D sound, high visual fidelity, 360-degree media content, and the capacity to navigate content that possesses the illusion of extension, a sense of scale and interactivity. This in turn entails the capacity to manipulate in-world features, tactile feedback and reaction to gesture.

Psychologically, authenticity may be judged by the extent to which the synthetic space generates physical reactions and stimulates emotions, memories of the features of that place, and what it was like to be there. Thus, while books, music, paintings and other media certainly have virtual qualities, the extent of uniqueness to which VR can be inhabited is generated by the insulation of the environment, feeling included, ease of interactions, feeling of in-world control, sense of movement, realism of images and fluidity of the environment, and sense of presence of others (Witmer and Singer, 1998; Lombardo et al., 2016). More recent technological development points to direct emotion capture as a means of increasing emotion and immersive experience. Mindmaze, a VR company, for example installs a ring of electrodes in the foam facemask of VR headsets. This detects which sensors a person's facial skin is touching and what levels of pressure are being applied to the sensors. This information is then matched to a pattern of one of ten facial expressions, which is reproduced by an avatar. With the capacity to express emotion in-world comes the capacity for systems and other avatars to react appropriately (for more on in-world facial coding of emotion see Li et al., 2016).

Ideally the user's in-world experience is biomechanically symmetrical in that real-world and in-world body movements align. The sense of 'being' within synthetic space is further enhanced by the range of physical body parts required to execute an in-world task, the extent to which proper bodily motion is required (such as the step-by-step mechanics of picking something up), the measure of a person's actions, the amount of control a person has in-world, and the symmetry of kinetic force in real and in-world experiences (McMahan et al., 2016). The significance of immersion and being in-the-loop becomes more apparent if we think of VR in life-critical situations such as medical procedures, or its use in drone and unmanned military missions, where the person tasked with interacting with the drone needs to trust that the system will respond in a synchronised manner (Guznov et al., 2016).

~~Viewing, Using,~~ Witnessing: The Case of EmblematicGroup

Having registered the two types of VR hardware and how qualities of immersion and presence are facilitated, we now begin the first of three case studies on VR and empathy. Applied to journalism, VR is about relating human experience through an interactive narrative form in synthetic space where a person feels present and witness to an event. In other words it is to build a convincing sense what it was like to be *there*. 'Immersive journalism' is the term specifically employed to account for news reporting that makes use of virtual environments and VR to enhance the connection between the audience and the news story (De la Peña et al., 2010). EmblematicGroup is a media company that spans investigative journalism, interactive theatre and video gaming. They address subject matter such as police brutality, domestic violence and civil wars, and attempt to make a person feel as if they are actually on the scene while the event is unfolding. Rather than watching from afar, the idea behind spatial narratives is for people to *be* in the space and for them to be able to adopt multiple perspectives *in* the event. This is achieved through walk-around experiences, so a person can choose where they go and what they see. It also involves interactive rather than simply observational elements.

Pro-social empathy promotes cosmopolitanism, global understanding, common respect and universal hospitality. The aim of immersive journalism is to use VR to depict the perspectives, situations and life contexts of others to encourage affective identification and understanding. The context and rationale for this are longstanding. As noted in Chapter 2, that a busy modern lifestyle with its own immediate pressures may lead to a lack of sensitivity to the plight of others was identified early in the 1900s by the philosopher Scheler (2009 [1913]). Framing empathy in terms of identification, vicarious experience and fellow-feeling, he understood this is stymied by industrial life, modernity, speed and technology. More recently, discourse on empathy has been connected with the ability and willingness to 'bear witness' to human suffering, particularly transnationally (Kurasawa, 2009). This gives rise to what Kurasawa, drawing on Derrida's (1996) *Archive Fever*, terms 'witness fever', or the recent spate of academic interest in the mediation of suffering. Transnational empathy in this witness-based context involves *reconstituting* distant events for audiences. Outfits such as EmblematicGroup believe that the limitations of traditional media can be overcome through the creation of synthetic environments that reflect human conditions elsewhere. They reason that immersion, enhanced presence, realism, scope for interactivity, and paying attention to contextual detail will impact on the extent to which people sympathise and empathise with distant groups.

EmblematicGroup became famous in VR circles for a journalistic piece called *Project Syria: An Immersive Experience of Child Refugees* (2014). Commissioned by the World Economic Forum with the idea of compelling world leaders to act on this crucial issue, the work tells the plight of such children by means of seeing what was going on 'on scene' and evoking telepresence. Nonny de la Peña explains *Project Syria* as a two-part immersive journalism experience. The first scene replicates a moment on a busy street corner in the Aleppo district of Syria. In the middle of a background song, a rocket hits and dust and debris fly everywhere. The second scene dissolves to a refugee camp in which a person experiences being in the centre of a camp. Although a recreation generated by the Unity game engine, the work itself draws from actual audio from Syria, video and photographs taken on scene. On donning the VR headset, the fundamental nature of our relationship to media content is challenged. The wearer is not just a viewer or a user, but a *witness*.

The capacity to feel-into representations of distant places and cultures is not theoretical, but practical. For the most part, one is free to move around *Project Syria*, inspect elements and even walk away from the action that the journalist wishes to depict. This is an important point: even though the journalists and sto-rytellers may have facets of the story they wish to highlight, the witness is able to direct their own experience and explore less prominent in-world features. The level of engagement, and degree of interaction with in-world inhabitants, preclude the sense of abstraction and removal that comes with spectating. Key to this is a sense of raised emotionality through presence and the body's conviction that the synthetic reality may affect it, despite the fact that the mind knows different. De la Peña gives the example of *Hunger in L.A.*, a piece about waiting in line at a food bank in downtown Los Angeles. She says that headset wearers have gone to their knees to try and help an in-world character that had a seizure and collapsed. However, she explains that not all stories are currently suitable for VR. Although it excels at relaying the spatial dimensions of a story such as sense of place and proximity, it is less suitable for stories that entail rapid movement due to nausea. This is accentuated if a person's eyes tell them that they are moving, but their body knows they are standing still. The implication is that VR is a slow medium for exploring environments and places.

Making VR journalism

On the role of empathy in modern society, de la Peña says 'I'm a journalist, and I want to do the same thing that any good journalist does: tell important stories, in a way that brings them to life as much as possible and helps the audience find out about, or better understand, or feel more strongly about, a particular situation'. The potential of VR to be used in journalism was identified by Biocca and Levy (1995) who recognised the scope for enhanced use of sensorimotor channels and increased sensory realism. The principle is that a greater sense of presence *within* the story offers raised possibility for the combatting of emotional burnout asso-ciated with news production and reception (Hardee, 2016). The opportunity for journalism is clear: VR generates an affective sense of presence that has the poten-tial to forge stronger than usual connections to a news story and real-world event. The significance is that stronger emotional engagement may encourage greater comprehension, sympathy, fellow-feeling and empathy with people, places, peri-ods and situations. While not suited to a rolling news format, it is highly appropriate for extended investigations – not dissimilar to the in-depth accounts offered by all news agencies in apps and dedicated online channels.

From the point of view of understanding the moving image in journalism, the visual grammar and protocols that guide people through experiences differ from those used in television. Although cameras (mechanical eyes) are involved in cre-ating footage of places, there are no close-ups, cuts, tracking or panning to steer the audience towards what they should see. This is not to suggest that there is no chronicling or storytelling – while interaction *is* different, narrative remains, par-ticularly if we see it as an organisational method for understanding time, space and causality, and in general for making sense of the world (Hardee, 2016).

98

On journalistic ethics, de la Peña notes the need for accuracy, avoidance of distortion and consideration of what is appropriate to show people. This is doubly pertinent when parts of the journalism reconstruct and use game elements to convey a sense of presence, rather than specific facts. De la Peña argues that in recreating real-life events in VR, EmblematicGroup are scrupulous in their choice of source material as they utilise video footage, location photographs and witness testimony. She provides the example of *One Dark Night* and *Kiya* that are anchored by recordings of actual 911 calls made to the police during the course of an event. She notes that although the productions may have the look and feel of a video game, in terms of the subject matter, they are recounting actual events. Commissioned by Al Jazeera America to highlight that three women are killed every day by their partners in the United States, *Kiya* documents the story of two sisters' attempt to rescue their third sister, *Kiya*, from her ex-boyfriend. Again, what is plain on donning the VR headset is that the spectator is less a viewer than a witness and participant. This is amplified by the fact that in-world avatars react to the witness and 'look' at the in-world person with 'expectations' that they will react.

From the point of view of journalistic ethics, this is difficult: in attempting to use VR to relay what it is like to be present in a specific situation, by recreating a situation to be present in, this requires a degree of artifice. Hardee (2016) draws on Biocca and Levy (1995) to point out that all news requires a degree of simulation. Be this language selection, editing of visual footage and on occasion use of music to heighten engagement, writers and producers use artifice to create realism. Arguably, VR is no different in this regard, but this does not get around the concern that a key function of journalism is to make reality transparent. By contrast, VR uses high levels of fabrication to build a sense of authenticity and presence. The concern is one of false strong impressions and that simulations of truthfulness may be constructed around stories and events that are fake.

A Marketer's (Virtual) Dream?

Having considered immersive journalism and the use of affect and qualities of presence to stimulate care, we now arrive at the second application of VR to be discussed: marketing. Here the principle of affective witnessing extends beyond perceiving, participating and understanding the life contexts of others. It encompasses market research, or the act of gathering information to understand the perspectives of people who buy goods and services. As we will see, applications of VR in marketing vary in sophistication, but the apotheosis was perhaps best mooted back in 1974 when Ted Nelson (to whom the epithet 'technology visionary' is actually meaningful) wrote a book called *Computer Lib*. Before the first personal computer had even reached the market, he correctly predicted the importance of the design and infrastructure of electronic spaces. He says that we 'must design the media, design the molecules of our new water, and I believe the details of this design matter very deeply. They will be with us for a very long time, perhaps as long as man [sic] has left …' (2003 [1974]: 306).

Highly suggestive, the 'molecules of our new water' applies to VR because of the modern capacity to track every data item and movement in-world. This matters because VR profoundly amplifies existing discussion of behaviour tracking, witnessing, surveillance, and pre-emption of human being and behaviour. Further, it should be remembered that beyond market research VR has the potential to be a perfect surveillance space in which behavioural histories, interactions, attention, intention, emotional expression and reactions can be tracked and reacted to in real-time, especially when we recollect that VR need not work in isolation but with wearable devices to track other biofeedback signals.

Tracking in-world attention

The market research industry is one of the foremost users of empathic media because it has a financial and competitive incentive to understand how people truly feel about propositions, products, services and promotional content. Indeed, one could reason that the reinvention of VR, the push towards consumer headwear, Facebook's acquisition of Oculus and its interest in social VR, are all about tracking behaviour and creating new marketing opportunities. Indeed, at Facebook's demonstration of their social VR product at Oculus Connect 2016, the first topic of discussion between Zuckerberg and his in-world discussants was the scope to read and express avatar emotions (such as smiles, surprise, confusion, laughter and shock) (Popper, 2016). Given that their core business is advertising, it is not unreasonable to argue that analysing emotional responses to in-world adverts is foremost in Facebook's interests.

As with many other empathic media, VR is employed to bypass self-reporting to understand the nature of attention. In 2016 I attended the ESOMAR Congress, a conference and world industry gathering of market researchers in New Orleans. At the event Azure Knowledge demonstrated a virtual walkthough of an unbranded retail outlet. This allows marketers to understand what features capture consumer attention, gauge how headset wearers feel in-world, and make inferences about their preferences and responses. The primary reason for doing this is highly practical: ferrying people to real stores and testing them with eye-tracking is expensive. The VR option also removes physical constraints, which allows rapid testing of new features and ideas, as well as in-world eye-tracking. Tobaii, for example, has integrated their tracker into the HTC Vive headset to test in-world design elements (such as which packet of sweets is most attractive on a virtual shelf and which are less so) (Tobii, 2017).

Azure's product tracks in-world attention (also shown on public screens) to understand attention, attraction and – quite literally – to be in the shoes of the first-person viewer. This 'seeing seeing' allows intimate insight not just into the object of a person's vision, but also into how a person sees and arrives at the object of attention. By means of the fact that this journey takes place in a synthetic space, this experience can be quantified, analysed and compared. Having tried the aisle walkthrough that determined which elements were capturing my attention and spoken with the US representative of Azure, I subsequently interviewed the European Managing Director of Azure Knowledge, Rafal Gajdamowicz, in London. He explained that by building store-like experiences, this allows Azure to leverage the affordances of the medium to build and test mock-up stores and trial options. It also allows them to model competitors, so, for example, if a client says they want their store to feel like X, Y or Z's, Azure can do this. The key for Azure is *price* and *scale* in that through fast prototyping they are able to offer clients relatively realistic simulations of consumer experience, without the physical cost.

This impetus to adopt automated techniques and passive tracking should be seen against a perception that traditional techniques of market research are failing to predict behaviour (Interview, 2016). Echoing concepts and general observations that emerge throughout this book, Gajdamowicz's interest in VR and wider biofeedback techniques is that they measure behaviour rather than rely on self-reporting. Reminiscent of Wilhelm Wundt's lab introduced in Chapter 2, market researchers say that it is prudent to assess what people do rather than what they say, because this will reveal hidden, significant and economically valuable truths. Although empathic media are used to bypass self-reporting on the basis of raising the quality of data about how a person feels about a given proposition, Gajdamowicz says that increasingly clients do not want 100 per cent accuracy. Instead, 'they want 80 per cent accuracy on the basis of a trade-off for speed and lower fees. This allows them to validate concepts quickly and without excessive cost, yet also be reasonably sure that they have the right user/consumer/shopper insight' (Interview, 2016). It is this fact ('cost, scale and speed') that means biometric technologies will increasingly be used by the market research industry.

However, it should be noted that as the conversation progressed, Gajdamowicz softened his original position on the merits of a purely technocentric approach. He added that causation is best inferred through qualitative research and that a purely observational tactic misses the 'why', which for him can only be achieved by qualitative research. At the time of interview (late 2016), Gajdamowicz calculated that 'we're at the beginning of the journey, and this tech will take three to five years to come to fruition', and that the pace will be speeded up by the increased reliability, effectiveness and validity of findings about intention, feeling and emotion. Gajdamowicz calculates that around 90 per cent of modern market research uses traditional in-person/structured approaches, whereas 10 per cent use biometrics and analytics. He says that while the industry will progress to automated and more technological means of measuring perception, 'market research is a very old-school industry' and it evolves slowly because it is driven by specialist researchers rather than business people who have standardised techniques they are experts in. That portions of the market research industry are wedded to specific techniques to test given sectors is an important point for diagnosing the scale of adoption of empathic media in market research: the fact that people have careers and vested expertise in their domains means that the 90/10 per cent balance between traditional research versus empathic media will change at sector-specific rates.

So far we have proceeded on the basis that there is a neat split between qualitative and quantitative research methods. Many presentations at the aforementioned ESOMAR event in 2016 argued and demonstrated this is not necessarily so. For example, whereas ethnography and qualitative research are typically conducted in-person, an Australian food company called Simplot bought a 360-degree virtual reality camera called the 360 Fly (Liptrot and Labagnara, 2016). Employing what is a broadly netnographic technique (Kozinets, 2015), their idea was to allow a large marketing team of 45 people into the homes of their consumers to see how they behave in their own habitats. By means of Google Cardboard, viewers were able to see how participants handled packaging, how they used different ingredients, how they were constantly distracted from the cooking and food, their short cuts, how they paired food, and how they cleaned and stored kitchenware. They found that even though participants had a 360-degree camera in their private domestic space, the technique overcame researcher bias and behavioural distortions generated by a person observing and asking questions. Analysts also had improved understanding of the target consumer, and as the researchers were able to take their client into the world of their customers they were able to understand nuances in how Simplot's products were treated, as well as in dialogue, gesture and behaviour in a personal space (the home kitchen). Speculating on where and what next, the presenters highlighted that VR-based research may take place in any controlled environment, such as a car, an event or within a store. They also suggest teaming biometric measures with VR to gain opportunities to measure how people respond to certain situations. Again, this bifurcates qualitative and quantitative research, especially if we recollect that what is being quantified is sensation. It also leads us to reconsider empathic media: although they frequently entail a disavowal of subjective self-reporting, one can also reason that their usage is an attempt to understand quality at scale.

New sensory territories

A creative director from a digital advertising agency who prefers to remain nameless said that when he tried a demo application of HTC Vive (a VR head-mounted display), in addition to a novel sense of presence and being in-world, 'I picked up a cup of coffee, raised it to my lips and, when I was about to take a sip, I could actually *taste* coffee'. His eyes lingered with mine for a moment to ensure that I had grasped the implication of what he was saying. That is, marketing and advertising are not simply about persuasion and influential communication, but also about affect and sensation. He continued, saying that by definition this is a sensitive realm, but the potential and opportunity to influence is clear. For traditional marketers and neuromarketers, this connects with interest in sensory marketing (Lindstrom, 2005, 2011; McStay, 2013). For example, certain sounds are more affective than visual stimuli. The sound of a baby laughing, the crack of an opening can, a fizzy drink being poured over ice, steak sizzling on a grill and so on, are all powerful triggers and mental image-builders. The significance is that many of these non-visual 'sensory touch points' may play a key role in branding products and services. Howes and Classen (2013) make similar observations about the role of synesthesia in marketing. They give the example of Corona beer that is popular with women because it is considered light. Although not technically a light beer, it provides the sense of being so because it comes in a tall clear bottle and is the colour of sunshine. The overall implication is that these cross-sensory associations are quite real. It remains to be seen how this may be developed in a VR environment, but considering that VR allows visual elements of in-world features such as product shapes, logos, colours and environmental factors to be readily re-programmed, and that reactions and even stimuli may be charted through biofeedback, one begins to see a situation where affect may be carefully and algorithmically optimised to deliver personalised in-world sensory marketing. In addition to scope for influence, the emphasis on quality and affect is important because marketing in VR is highly unlikely to be the same as offline. Rather, in-world marketing efforts will make greater use of branded content and commercial storytelling that does not appear as an ad (McStay, 2016a), which in turn provides scope for stealth-based in-world sensory marketing.

Command and Control: Modulating Immersive Policing

Having accounted for immersive journalism in case study 1 and the capacity to witness and stimulate affect in marketing in case study 2, we now turn to the final extended case study of this chapter: policing.

One day in the early 2020s Officer Perkins will arrive at the Command Centre to find her wearables and headwear charged and synched. Perkins will don her smart glasses where authentication will take place through iris reading. As Perkins and her partner get into the car, her assignments are loaded up based on Perkins' beat map. This will be updated in real-time as events unfold and analytics about threat and severity are conducted in real-time. The beat map will also list crimes predicted to happen. Having pulled away from the Centre, Perkins sees a speeding car and stops it. This is stressful because Perkins and her partner do not know what they are walking into. A nearby vehicle drone assists and flies around the perimeter of the car, sees the occupants, and scans the area to see whether anything has been thrown out. Perkins approaches (wearing smart glasses) and receives licence and owner information from a trusted digital assistant. Through the smart glasses, Perkins can read the licence and match the picture with the driver. On interacting with the driver, voice records of the conversation are obtained and analysed in real-time so she can test the consistency of a detainee's responses, emotional reactivity and voice stress. This provides her with data and insight she might otherwise have missed.

Later Perkins is called to a road traffic accident where a drone has already been sent up to create a communications bubble. This begins recording and mapping where the rolled truck is, what other vehicles are involved and who is moving unusually in the vicinity. With feedback from footage analytics at command control relayed from the drone, Perkins sees through her smart glasses that an abandoned speeding stolen car has caused the accident and the thief is moving on foot. A chase ensues. The drone ascends and follows to record Perkins giving chase. The wearable kit allows commanders to know that when she gave chase her high heart rate spiked and that she and partner require back up. Even when multiple routes are possible for the thief, analytics of drone footage generate a predictive path plotting the best route to intercept the runner. The target is safely arrested, but given that emergency incidents are hard to recall, the drone footage and wearable data provide Perkins with post-event documentation. This is much easier than in the 2010s because the drone, glasses and voice detector record interaction and movements. Paperwork is prepopulated for Perkins, who only has to fill in blanks that were not recorded by the system. This account is not speculative, but based on a presentation at Critical Communications World in 2016 by Eduardo Conrado, who is Executive Vice-President and Chief Strategy & Innovation Officer of Motorola Solutions – a global leader in policing and public safety technologies.

In the context of policing there are two forms of affective witnessing taking place: 1) enhanced surveillance of citizens and potential criminals, and 2) heightened monitoring of police themselves. Private and public organisations from the United States to the United Arab Emirates are developing what we might term 'empathic policing'. This is achieved through a range of technologies, particularly VR and mobile augmented reality (AR), such as Microsoft's HoloLens that blends the virtual and the real, but also biofeedback wearables (such as heart rate detectors) and body-worn cameras.

Use of VR in telepolicing has its roots in theories about telemedicine in a military context (Satava, 1995). This also involves remote sensors and virtual reality to improve combat casualty care in battlefield scenarios by means of streaming video, vital signs information, and medical imaging transmitted to the central unit who would command the combat medic in the field. In modern policing, in addition to being able to see and be present from afar, commanders can track the emotional states of officers, and provide information and back-up. This is what police refer to as 'situational awareness'. The context for this military research (published in academic outlets)[1] is that it recognises that modern conflicts are occurring in more urbanised environments than in the past, which means effort goes into distinguishing between a threat, non-threatening behaviour and the identification of 'high-value individuals'. Situational awareness also involves understanding the impact of engagement (arousal, interest, motivation and concentration), a sense of flow (experience of time), a stressed state (distress and worry), workload and the extra demands imposed on individuals while on duty. Stress in particular invokes low confidence, low perceived control, self-consciousness, low self-esteem and cognitive interference (Salcedo et al., 2016). After all, like civilians, police officers in poor mental states make bad decisions.

The need for situational awareness, integration and a reduction of the emotional and cognitive load on stressed officers was a recurrent theme in interviews with technology companies developing products for the police. LanTing Garra and Bert Van Der Zaag from Motorola Solutions demonstrated and explained their virtual reality-enabled Command Center concept to me. The idea behind this is that a police commander who is located in a police department can use VR to see what is taking place on the ground as officers arrive and engage with a situation. This allows them to be remotely present from the perspective of drones and smart glasses worn by officers. By being-in-the-shoes of a given officer (such as the aforementioned Perkins), this provides novel forms of intelligence to the commanders to facilitate remote assessment, decision-making, advice and support for the field officer. Garra explained that it allows the commander to be 'in the moment' (her phrasing), which reduces the need for ongoing feedback between an officer and a commander seeking to know what is taking place. Van Der Zaag also explains that the aim is *not* to have to use voice, because if an officer has to call in an incident from the field, they have to queue and then explain the situation to someone (which is time consuming). This point featured in other interviews with homeland security forces.[2]

I had the opportunity to try the VR application and occupy the role of a commander. Inside the headset a camera assesses the movement of the wearer's eye, which means the 'commander' does not need to use a mouse or other hardware objects to indicate the intention of what the wearer wants to focus on. Instead one simply looks at the in-world displays and features one is interested in (not unlike a picture board containing photos and pinned notes). What was notable was that the VR experience was *not* highly immersive, nor was there a strong sense of presence. Whereas games, museum installations, journalism, documentaries, entertainment, education and market research experiences led to a distinct feeling of insulation from the real-world environment, and of being inside a synthetic environment, this was not the case in the Motorola virtual command centre. Although in-world objects were easy to control, the space itself was very featureless, with the exception of the displays of events taking place through drone and officer footage. Importantly, I remained mindful of the outside world. Van Der Zaag explains that this was a highly conscious choice from the point of view of professional reactivity, awareness, and not being entirely immersed in the simulation and its contents. After all, the officers and citizens in the field are not simulations. This gradation of qualities of immersion is evident in research that points out that individuals experiencing virtual experiences can concurrently attend to aspects of the experience and events in their physical environment (Witmer and Singer, 1998).

In practice, Van Der Zaag said that it is important not to overwhelm the analyst with irrelevant information and that they do not want analysts to get too involved. By this he means that quality of presence and the affective qualities of VR need to be lessened (by reducing the sense of a spatial extension and realism of objects), because 'while commanders in virtual command centers want to obtain a sense of satisfaction from seeing an incident through from start to finish, rather than just being a cog, and knowing that they did all they could to help the officer, they also need to be able to sleep at night, and they need to be able to disengage' (Interview, 2016). From the point of view of designing experience, this means leveraging the benefits of telepresence while not over-stimulating command officers. I asked whether they are at the stage of needing to monitor the analyst for stress, anxiety and focus, to which Van Der Zaag replied, 'Yes, probably. They are highly trained already, but turnover is high through burnout'. On the rollout of these technologies, Van Der Zaag explains that public safety is hard because the technology needs to work properly to justify the public purse and outlay, and that a high level of evidence is needed for policing work. Recognising that public acceptability must be negotiated, he himself admits that there is a 'creepy factor' to these applications.

The connected cop

Until recently officers were solely connected by radio-enabled voice communication. As introduced above, the spectrum is expanding to include AR to access public information (such as about a district and objects encountered while on the beat), private information (such as facial and number plate recognition), data from city sensors (such as CCTV, traffic lights and drones), personal sensors and objects (such as portable video and vital signs such as heart/stress rates), and remote holster monitoring (to know when an officer has withdrawn a gun from its holster). If it has been withdrawn from its holster, commanders are alerted, flagged to read the biofeedback and stress rates of the officer, and will thereafter possess insight into an officer's emotional state. This serves two functions: it not only helps assess officer performance, it also provides support for officers on the ground. The minutiae of the conversation with Garra and Van Der Zaag were interesting in this regard. In a less focused discussion about policing, Van Der Zaag remarked that a great deal of emotion goes into the job. He said that on modulating emotion and controlling it, officers have multiple techniques and often use music. Some play classical music and others sing as a means of controlling emotion.

Although the focus of this chapter is VR, the intention to increase visibility and presence from the limited opportunities offered by radio only makes sense when placed in a wider ecology of information about environments, objects and people. For police authorities and developers of security hardware and software, the aims of an ecological approach to policing and public service are to improve overall policing effectiveness, enhance collaboration with colleagues, raise responsiveness rates, and improve accountability and evidence collection. At a societal level, they argue that this generalised surveillance will increase citizen and officer safety, decrease crime and provide property protection. In a public talk at Critical Communications World (Amsterdam, 2016) Andre Mechaly explained what Thales (a company operating in aerospace, space, transportation and security sectors) designate as the 'connected officer'. This aligns with the aforementioned interest in situational awareness, the telepresence in on-the-ground events, controlled immersion and understanding the empathic perspective of officers (or being 'in their shoes'). In the question-and-answer session, I queried Mechaly from Thales about the experience of the officers, asking multiple questions about how comfortable officers are with being asked to wear multiple sensors. Mechaly responded by saying 'We are still at the start … different people will tell you different things … and the boss and officer have different interests'. However, he says that 'if you tell them [officers] they can be more efficient, the response is good'. He went on to say that 'these people are not like us for social media – they are here to rescue people or fight someone, not go on social media. So we need to customise and talk to them'.

I subsequently interviewed Mechaly's colleague, David Dumay from Thales, to pursue greater insight into how officers feel about themselves being sensed and surveilled. He explained the context of what is rephrased here as the 'Connected Cop'. The context is that the Canadian part of Thales' business is working on sensors to enable people to work optimally under high stress conditions. This started with air traffic management and the intention to monitor, reduce and help operators manage their mental loads. On whether this form of monitoring will become a core constituent of policing, he says that as a large technology company working in defence, aerospace, security and transportation, they see it becoming a reality. Supervision and monitoring technologies are already in police cars, and Special Forces along with other 'intervention teams' are also exploring personal tracking.

Returning to Motorola Solutions, Van Der Zaag explains that the principle of the Connected Cop is an ambivalent one. The VR and wearable technology make officers better at their job and generate less stressed officers who know that someone 'has their back' (this was stressed multiple times). Potential assistance exists in the form of command and situational awareness, which means officers know there is support behind them if something unexpected occurs. Presented this way, the existence of surveillance and the telepresence of a remote person is akin to a guardian angel, or that which watches over, comforts and protects.

However, the gun sensor itself has been controversial among officers because it alerts command to when a firearm has been pulled. Again, the detail and micro-practices of policing are telling. The reason why on-the-ground officers see this as problematic is because they like to slightly pull their gun out of the holsters just to check that all is present and correct. Others like to clean it. In experiential terms, this is the opposite of what is usually said about wearable sensors that integrate with the body. Rather than integration and immediation (a decrease in awareness of media), the effect is one of consciousness, self-alienation and unease about personal behaviour. Phrased otherwise, the attempt to be in someone else's shoes makes the original wearer uncomfortable. Indeed, holster sensors were a recurrent theme across all the conversations I had about policing. Dumay from Thales also said that 'the belt moving could be for many reasons other than drawing the gun. We need to know the situation to understand. We need a filter'. Gun withdrawal, for example, may be cross-checked with wearable heart rate trackers that, in addition to allowing commanders to understand stress, would also tell whether an officer is dead or not. However, Garra of Motorola says that this type of tracking has also proven unpopular with officers because they are not keen on being surveilled, potentially 'found out' and having their careers threatened. In addition to stress detection, this amounts to real-time psychological profiling (which indicates the appropriateness of a reaction to stimuli) and physiological profiling (which indicates poor health). A suggested way around this is to only turn on the heart rate tracker if the holster and gun sensor has been activated.

The interview with Motorola Solutions' Garra progressed to discuss body-worn cameras. For officers, these are not a perfect record because an officer may have their camera pointing at an incident, but their head may be distracted. The consequence is that despite being *a* visual record, it is only one perspective, and does not make the situation transparent. I was also interested to gauge thoughts about full transparency whereby an officer's perspective is tracked from the eyes themselves (which allows 'seeing seeing'). This raises the question of how accountable should officers be to measures of their attention?

Given that there are disproportionately high arrests of black people in the US, where Motorola's technologies are being developed,[3] might there be a connection between gaze, attention, emotion and officers watching black people more closely than white people? While recognising the importance of the question, she also added that there is scope to record and tag what officers see with glasses. This presents opportunities and implications not only for the internal assessment and quantification of attention/biometrics, but also for accountability, and scope for authorities, politicians and citizens to access data on what officers see and their concurrent affective states. Public data does not need to be personal data, but may be released in an aggregated form. Indeed, on citizen accountability, the anti-privacy maxim 'nothing to hide, nothing to fear' comes to mind.

At the 2017 South-by-South-West festival I was able to pose this to Charles Ramsey (who served both as Commissioner of the Philadelphia Police Department and Chief of the Metropolitan Police Department of the District of Columbia)[4] and Mitch Landrieu (Mayor, New Orleans). I asked them whether it would be useful to possess data about officers' emotional reactions on facing dangerous situations, and whether this data should be made public in the spirit of accountability. I received two sets of answers: the first immediate answer from Ramsey was that he is interested in the principle of wearable tracking of stress, but not in favour of the data being made public. Landrieu had never heard of the technology, but questioned the validity of the metrics behind emotion tracking. After answering questions from other delegates they chose to return to my question, with Ramsey correctly saying that finding a baseline for stress is a difficult one. The context of the panel presentation was race relations, implicit officer bias and algorithmic bias in policing, and Ramsey added to his original reply by saying that when a police officer is killed while on duty, citizen complaints statistically spike. He said 'this tells us something and police officers may need a day off after the event', with the implication being that officers may be angry, emotionally charged and may behave in a way to generate complaints. Also, in the case of an attack on an officer, or another situation that has scared the police, Landrieu added that after such a situation emotions are running high and that they may *overreact* if they do not have equipment to control a situation. This comment should be read in terms of earlier panel conversation where both Landrieu and Ramsey agreed that an increase in militarisation of policing in the US is undesirable and community engagement is preferable.

The security technology companies I spoke with all admitted that officers are not keen on being tracked. Although I cannot verify the extent to which US officers dislike commanders or the public 'being in their shoes', in a limited UK study of officers wearing body cameras the number of complaints brought against them reduced by a significant 93 per cent (Ariel et al., 2017). This is attributed to modification of behaviour through a panoptic-like 'observer effect', where awareness that recordings may perform as a third-party 'digital witness' cooled potentially volatile police–public interactions. Notably, the inclusion of surveillance and quasi-present digital witnessing balanced the relationship of power by means of making both the detainee and the detained accountable. After being trialled on the Isle of Wight (an island off the UK coast), over 85 per cent of frontline officers agreed that all of them should wear cameras while on duty.

Lance Valcour, a retired inspector, adviser and technologist, offers a similar argument about the balance between privacy and personal security. He recounts that when he participated in his first wireless project in 1979, the Ottawa Police Service was able to network police cars so they could exchange texts (Email, 2016).[5] Police officers were initially resistant. They were concerned about their privacy, believing that all of their movements and activities would be tracked. Within a few months, he says, all the officers wanted it because of the support they were able to offer each other, as well as the almost instantaneous access to information such as stolen vehicles and wanted persons. Valcour does not differentiate this from modern wearables, biofeedback and emotion trackers. He posits,

'Imagine giving a vest that measures all sorts of biometric data on a firefighter? What if their heart rate is going through the roof and we need to pull them off the team for a period of rest? But what about his privacy issues – do we want the whole team to know?'. Similarly, in relation to environmental sensors, he asks us to 'Imagine the ability to drop sensors into the forest fire that can tell you how fast the fire is moving and what direction' and 'Imagine I have an accident, a heart attack. I would want the paramedics to have information from my heart sensor'. I asked about the issue of consent and coercion, and whether officers have a choice. Valcour says that 'Yes, it was an issue for initial tracking of officers. It depends on how that data is used, and what for. If it's for officer safety, to help them stay safe – it raises lots of questions but the gains far outweigh the privacy concerns'.

Conclusion

Of all the media discussed in this book, VR is the one most frequently associated with empathy. This is primarily because the VR industry sees itself as being able to deliver content and experiences that allow the headset wearer to understand the perspective and lived context that others find themselves in. This chapter sought to explore this premise, particularly by clarifying the principle of immersion in relation to VR. Unpacked, this equates to an experience of presence in a synthetic environment, a sense of separateness from the real world, feelings of inclusion in the synthetic reality, the illusion of extension, in-world realism, perceptions of scale, reactions to gesture, tactile feedback, and one's presence and interaction with others. This leads to two forms of empathy in VR: first that the in-world 'witness' is able to better understand the perspective and lived context of others, and second that media owners and interested parties may track attention and intention and feel-into what the headset wearer is experiencing. This may be as simple as watching on a separate screen what the headset wearer does within the synthetic space, but there is also scope for granular tracking of behaviour and responses.

As of 2017 VR has yet to make significant inroads into the home, but it is widely used and being developed across a range of sectors. This chapter focused on three sectors: journalism, market research and policing. The first entails a deeply pro-social form of empathy that has its roots in Kantian cosmopolitanism, rationality and the removal of barriers to understanding the worldviews of others. This takes place by shifting a person from viewer to participatory affective witness. That VR will lead to transcultural fellow-feeling is debatable, but what is arguably more important is that affect and truth are not the same, especially when the experience is highly constructed. Today's VR journalism makes use of real footage, but it also depends on entirely fabricated in-world objects. Although artifice has long been used by news reporting to build a sense of authenticity, the very virtue of VR journalism has the potential to be its greatest criticism. That is, truth and a manufactured sense of presence are two different things.

The next case example of market research first noted the use of VR to bypass self-reporting, as is the case with most other empathic media. It is used to track in-world attention and attraction, and quite literally allows researchers to be in the first-person shoes of the researched. In addition to quantification of attention, something sought since the inception of consumer psychology with Wilhelm Wundt, VR is cost effective because it allows mock-ups of spaces and objects to be quickly tested with consumers. In addition to the practical benefits for market researchers, there are sensory opportunities for branding and commercial communication. This connects with the illusion of presence and sensory confusion that, as a minimum, provides scope for new sensory semiotics and triggers within in-world branded content.

On policing, the third case study, we considered VR as a command-and-control tool. This has multiple characteristics in that a remote sense of presence (telepresence) provides scope for commanders to see what their officers see, surveil, advise and support as events take place in the real world. This increase in situational awareness, connectedness and datafication characterises trends in modern policing. It encompasses the recording of a first-person perspective, potential tagging of what is seen, biofeedback and heart rates, emotion and stress, and tracking officers' interactions with their firearms. Further social science work is required to properly understand officers' perspectives, but through interviews with technologists in the security sector and available research on reactions to body-worn cameras, officers are ambivalent. While the surveillance of gaze, bodies and actions provides guardian angel-like support, cooling of volatile interactions and back-up in potentially dangerous situations, officers also complain of self-alienation and a concern about being 'found out'. Whereas critiques of data surveillance typically focus on the exploitation of citizens, a new situation is emerging, where it is police officers whose behaviour and bodies are being datafied and emotionally profiled. The question is this: in the name of openness and transparency, will citizens ever see the data in an identifiable or de-identified form, and should they?

Notes

1   See for example the edited collection *Virtual, Augmented and Mixed Reality* published by Springer (Lackey and Shumaker, 2016).
2   In an interview in 2016, Jorn Skilleas, Director of Police and Homeland Security for Teleplan Globe, said that in Norway an impetus for development of these technologies was the 2011 bombing and shooting in Oslo and Utøya island by Anders Behring Breivik. Authorities found that a reliance on voice communications and mobile phones resulted in much information being missed. This was because the technology was difficult to use in high-pressure incidents.

3   In 2017 the US National Association for the Advancement of Colored People recorded statistically excessive arrests for African American citizens.

4   Wikipedia records that he is the former Commissioner of the Philadelphia Police Department and that prior to assuming that post in January 2008, he had served as Chief of the Metropolitan Police Department of the District of Columbia (MPDC) from 1998 to early 2007.

5   I met Valcour in person at the Critical Communications World conference in Amsterdam 2016. We talked and I followed-up our conversation in email form after the event.

8

ADVERTISING, RETAIL AND CREATIVITY: CAPTURING THE FLÂNEUR

To influence people, the advertising industry needs to know what people think, see, feel and do. Along with gauging habits, histories, preferences and group affiliations, this involves understanding when people are most open to engagement by brands, the nature of attention, what captures it, what maintains focus and engagement, and which semiotic and biological factors elicit positive emotional reactivity. Data about emotions may also feed automated creative processes in advertising.

I begin by introducing critiques from a diverse range of sociologists, philosophers, theorists and commentators who have noted an increase of interest in bodies and emotions by the advertising industry. The chapter then explores these criticisms in reference to insights from interviews with Havas (an advertising company) and the Ogilvy Center for Behavioral Science (an advertising agency and commercial researcher), DataXu (an adtech firm), Emotiv (whose EEG product is widely used for in-house research) and Affectiva (a facial coding company). As will be shown, what becomes clear on connecting high-level critique to the practicalities of empathic media applications is that these activities are justified on the basis of asymmetric and libertarian paternalism. In other words, the surveillance of emotional life helps people behave in their own best interests and provides them with what they really want. Seen this way, concern about the unwanted sensing of emotional life is an economic 'externality' in that it unwantedly interferes with connecting people with products that would provide them with maximum benefits. Having outlined the practices, arguments and insights of the chapter, I then consider what the 'flâneur' would have made of such developments. This person, a literary leitmotif of Parisian modernity and chronicler of commercial city life, allows us to appreciate the significance of emotion tracking in modern advertising and retail.

Stockpiling Bios

There is no shortage of literature pointing out that subjectivity and emotional life is mined and leveraged to generate economic value. Berardi, for example, argues that 'post-industrial life' is 'marked by the submission of the soul, in which animated, creative, linguistic, emotional corporeality is subsumed and incorporated by the production of value' (2009: 109; see also Hardt and Negri, 2000; Stiegler, 2010). Crary similarly highlights that 'the pharmaceutical industry, in partnership with the neurosciences, is a vivid example of the financialization and externalization of what used to be thought of as "inner life"' (2013: 55). Others such as Lazzarato point to the ways in which informational capitalism has less to do with the factory discipline of old, and today looks to the organising of 'affects, desires and technological dispositifs' (Lazzarato, 1999, cited in Toscano, 2007: 7 [original in Italian]). In addition to the commercial interest in intimate aspects of human life, they point to the machine-like nature of capitalism in which people function as objects within a gigantic feedback-based assemblage. Lazzarato (2014) phrases this in terms of 'enslavement', and while this language is too strong for my taste, the overall point that behaviour, affects and subjectivity are rendered into machine-readable human capital, and put to work at an industrial scale, is plain.

While the above authors draw from Marx, this view of capitalism is also influenced by Heidegger (1991 [1939]), whose language of 'standing reserves' depicts a stockpiling of all aspects of human life and the means by which this is made usable (or 'present-at-hand'). Early to recognise the significance of cybernetic thought, for Heidegger it reduces all dimensions of life (including emotions) to the language of quantity and data. In other words, it makes the body, emotional life and qualitative experience machine-readable. As indicated through the phrasing of 'stocks' there first has to be excavation, making present what was once hidden from view, quantifying this, and making this stock useful and productive.

Even for non-philosophically inclined readers, Heidegger is worthwhile as an explanatory vehicle because his criticism of technology is not technological. Instead, it is aimed at the logic that underpins technology. His focus is not hardware, sensors, cameras, software or even captains of industry, but the very principle of extraction, making-present and what overall is a 'metaphysics of production'. Heidegger traces this discourse back to Ancient Greece, but the modern value in his assertion is that by critiquing technology at the level of trans-generational logic, it explains that no one person is at the wheel (not even Silicon Valley leaders or World Economic Forum members). Instead the norms of surveillance and making-present are structural, normative, cultural and historical, permeating society (and its working practices, processes and objects) in such a way that it can be based on excavation, revealing and value extraction. Recognising that mining of intimate strata of human life is a structural as well as a technical way of things, the issue is that this disavows hard-won respect for the wholeness of the liberal subject. Put simply, when conducted without meaningful consent, the problem is the denial of agency, the erosion of dignity and our alienation from decisions made about us.

Putting Emotions to Work

The sections above have considered the historical tendency towards making hidden and intimate life present, its commodification, biopolitical factors, and ethical considerations. The sections below attend to the modern practicalities of how emotions and affect are put to work by the advertising, marketing and retail industries. Defenders of advertising theorise the consumer as rational, sovereign and able to reject, ignore or accept advertising messages. For example, in *Advertising in Contemporary Society*, Rotzoll et al. (1996) argue that no advertiser can make us buy something we do not want, that advertising does not help bad products sell as consumers may try an item of merchandise once but not twice if they do not like it, and that businesses and consumers alike benefit as advertising introduces individuals to products suited to their self-interests. Advertising and retail, according to this logic, represents a satisfying of mutual interests between two *voluntary* parties. This is classical liberalism characterised by egoism, self-interest and rationality, where the relationship between businesses and citizens contributes to a market that is famously a self-correcting and mostly self-regulating force guided by 'an invisible hand' (Smith, 1993 [1776]).

This free-choice account of commercial promotion has never looked so uncertain. This is because choices are framed and weighted, and cognition does not act coolly alone. Instead, purchase decisions are inextricably linked to emotions (LeDoux, 1999; McDuff, 2014). With insight into emotions, advertisers and retailers have a higher chance of influencing behaviour and nudging us to spend. This commercial interest in 'making-present' and subjecting intimate life to commodity logic is expressed by the advertising industry's interest in collecting as much data as possible (McStay, 2016). Consider, for example, my 2016 interview with Yvonne O'Brien from the media agency Havas in London. As Chief Insights Officer, she took my request to meet on the basis that the agency is keen to make use of biometric data and learn about how the technologies work. As with other interviewees from the market research community, she is dissatisfied with survey-based research, is actively exploring sentiment analysis and is curious about facial coding.

What was apparent was her interest in emotional transparency, or the unfolding of the body to reveal reactions, indications of emotions, feelings about brands, tracing of customer journeys, and information that may assist in creation of brand identities. For her, data about the body and thereafter emotions encourages 'brand hygiene' and helps to build 'meaningful brands', which entails 'creating and managing the basic set of values that consumers expect to be in place for any business/ service that they are considering purchasing'. This involves understanding the positioning of competitors, how to effectively differentiate their brands from others, mapping customer journeys (awareness to purchase), production of data about how people make product decisions, understanding how brand–customer relationships may be fostered, and identifying where people might be most receptive to being marketed to.

O'Brien's dissatisfaction with surveys reflects what is by now a familiar truism of empathic media: people are not to be relied upon to say what they really think or feel. Again, this disavowal of self-reporting echoes the preference for observation over interaction. O'Brien articulates the value of emotions in a curiously mechanical way by speaking of 'brand levers', which is the matter of how to get people to act and do things (such as click, buy, investigate, feel, or believe a given proposition). This involves understanding brand content, people's responses, and the context in which they are exposed to stimuli. The environmental dimension is an important one in that Havas (and other agencies) are keen to know how brands and adverts perform in lived rather than artificial lab-based spaces. For O'Brien and others in the advertising industry, the task is how to engage with a person's life context to understand people through all of their devices and interaction points, such as wearable devices, mobiles and environments: this is achieved by IoT sensors, Bluetooth beacons and monitoring that can be controlled, such as in retail spaces. O'Brien went on to remark that the aim is 'to collect it all' and that she believes that people do not really care about privacy (pointing to their use of social media as evidence). Underpinning this is a free-market logic, as she added that people would leave services if they did not like the terms of service.

The mechanics of psychology

While data, emotions and affects remain somewhat nebulous and difficult to conceive, O'Brien's discussion of levers is easier to grasp. In 2017 the Ogilvy & Mather Group announced the creation of the Ogilvy Center for Behavioral Science (Ogilvy, 2017). Intended to work across all parts of the Ogilvy & Mather business, the Center seeks to establish 'a new system to define how audiences think, feel and behave to improve marketing and communications effectiveness'. This 'new system' combines sociological and psychological techniques to establish the 'levers most likely to shift behaviors and change attitudes' in a 'post-fact environment'. This anachronistically mechanical method is named AMOS after the cognitive psychologist Amos Tversky, who developed theories about irrational economics and why people do not make optimal decisions (Kahneman and Tversky, 1979). To put these ideas to work, the approach focuses on 'Brand, Brain, Behavior, and Bias' (B4). To underline the connection with our interest in empathy, Christopher Graves, president and founder of the Ogilvy Center, says:

> We are leveraging deep and in some cases emerging science to make a big shift. Marketing and communications has always been about targeting prey. Even the terminology used — terms like "target" and "track" and "acquire" and war-like "campaigns" [...] We are shifting to an empathy approach through using science to more deeply understand individuals and groups and how they view the world. Ultimately this is more respectful and values cognitive diversity. (Diverge, 2017)

The Center builds on the work of the Ogilvy Change behavioural science group based in London and Washington DC, not least that of Rory Sutherland who is an evangelist of behavioural sciences, vice-chairman of the Ogilvy Group UK, and co-founder of the Behavioural Sciences Practice for the wider Ogilvy & Mather Group. Interviewed in 2016, Sutherland said that 'Psychology is technology'. His argument is that as technology is employed to solve problems and make life more efficient, psychology might be used in the same way. Connecting with the earlier discussion of affect and disavowal of self-reporting, he argues that emotions drive behaviour and many of the reasons we give about why we like or dislike something are post-event rationalisations. Indeed, he says that 'while the brain thinks it is the Oval Office, it is really the Press Office' (Interview, 2016).

Indirectly rebutting Rotzoll et al.'s argument that consumers are sovereign and rational (and the overall ethical defence of the advertising and retail industries), Sutherland draws upon Daniel Kahneman's (2011) *Thinking, Fast and Slow* that outlines two systems: 'System 1' is fast, instinctive and emotional, and 'System 2' is slower, more deliberative and more logical. Sutherland points out that historically, advertising has functioned by means of a rational approach to subjectivity. The use of behavioural science in advertising is an explicit acknowledgement of the omission of System 1, along with awareness of the value of emotions in steering thought and purchase behaviour.

Deeply affective in his approach to communication, persuasion and influence, Sutherland was insistent that arousal (and data generated by empathic media) is preferable to self-reporting and that businesses can make costly investment mistakes if they take people at their word. Allying with a preference for physiology over mind, he draws on neuroscience and the work of Bob Trivers to argue that when neurons fire, behaviour is initiated before we become conscious of our intent to do something (see Trivers, 2011). The value of emotion-enhanced advertising for Sutherland is about understanding people at the moments they make decisions. Echoing O'Brien and her 'collect it all' point, the prize as he sees it is to be able to understand people on a moment-by-moment basis, and that by having insight into a person's emotional state, this increases the potential for influence. Scale is important in this regard in that 'small things and prompts can have big net effects'. On ethics and what was critiqued above in relation to appropriation, Heideggerian extraction, making-present and the commodification of subjectivity, for Sutherland 'behavioural science and capitalism help to give people what they *really* want'. Indeed, he says that 'communism and central planning could never give us Red Bull and that even with the best of intentions, less choice means people are less likely to get what they want'. Unashamed on what aligns well with both asymmetric and libertarian paternalism (Camerer et al., 2003; Thaler and Sunstein, 2003), he says that free markets will discern what people really want – presumably whether they like it or not. The economic logic is that paternalism arose to protect people incapable of making decisions in their own best interests.

It also restricts choice. The asymmetric form is 'a have one's cake and eat it too' in that it attempts to correct those who make errors (i.e. do not act in their own interest), while imposing no harm on those who make rational choices (Camerer et al., 2003: 1212). Widely applied in health, Sutherland sees no problem with this principle in a consumerist context.

On emotional analytics and empathic media (Sutherland had read some of my online pieces about the topic), he says that in-house research that optimises adverts is small in scale, in-depth and unproblematic, but the capacity for emotion detection to be used in public spaces is for him 'alarming because of the opportunity to hack people'. To make the point, he draws on George Akerlof and Robert Shiller's *Phishing for Phools* (2015), which is about getting people to do things that are in the interests of the phishermen, but not in the interests of the target. Sutherland says that 'This is about short-term interests over long-term more reasoned goals' and that 'the short-term is emotional, about people hacks, and has implications for businesses such as gambling (casinos and online)'. Expressed in Kahneman's (2011) terms, empathic media are particularly useful for real-time attempts to influence System 1 choices by leveraging biases, heuristics and the mental shortcuts that people take when making decisions within short time frames. The point is that these decisions are not necessarily the same as what their slower more deliberative choices might be. As discussed below, this has special consequences for retail.

Retail

Despite the growth of online shopping, voice-activated orders and Amazon Dash buttons, shoppers still seek the tactile experiences associated with physical retail (Skrovan, 2017). They want to look, interact with human assistants, feel the goods they are interested in and enjoy the sensory factors associated with a positive retail experience. For the most part, notwithstanding loyalty programs, customers remain anonymous. This is changing through 'omni-channel' developments that merge online and offline shopping experiences, perhaps most notably through smart phones. This is a paradigm shift as omni-channel approaches entail ability to identify, understand online habits, measure on- and offline behaviour, micro-target communications in stores, and interact and converse with customers in a more personal and intimate manner. In general terms, whereas customers have historically been largely free to peruse without being identified, the goal is to profile people as they are profiled in an online setting (Turow, 2017).

To achieve this, the intention is to collect information from every interaction a person has with a store, loyalty program, app, website, call centre, ad, email, social media channel, chatbots, and potentially holograms and felt virtual objects (ultra-haptics). This is in addition to in-house use of the full gamut of empathic media (VR, attention tracking and biometrics) to understand non-conscious reactions to products, brands, incentives, placement and decision-making behaviour. The task for retail analytics is to integrate these flows of data, make sense of this informa-tion, and put it to work in a timely manner (whether this be real-time or delayed). Retailers argue that by being able to identify people – and understand what they 'think, see, feel and do' – they are able to provide discounts and offer higher levels of service by understanding preferences and purchase histories, and that this is simply akin to 'living in a small town where everybody knows your name'.

This surveillance is justified at industry conferences such as ESOMAR, South-by-South-West and DMEXCO (that I attended in 2016 and 2017) under the auspice of a value exchange that provides consumers with an improved service and shopping experience. One would be forgiven for taking recourse to Steven Spielberg's (2002) film *Minority Report* to picture this – notably the scene where protagonist John Anderton is assailed by predatory projections and targeted adverts in a retail outlet.

In real life, eyeQ describes itself as an analytics and engagement company. Its product 'eyeQ Go' measures facial emotional responses as people look at goods at shelf-level. It collects shopper information including age, gender, emotion, dwell-ing time, return visits, total time in store and foot traffic. This analysis is passive in that a person may not be aware they are being profiled, but as they move through the retail environment, in-store marketing is being tailored to them. Notably, eyeQ claims to respect shopper privacy and employ a 'privacy-by-design' approach, because it does not capture personally identifiable information without explicit consent (eyeQ, 2017). A cynic would be entirely correct to argue that the eventual objective is to identify, personalise and employ facial recognition. It is also highly likely that data about emotions will be used to target identified people in real-time, as well as contribute to customer relationship management (CRM) databases about in-store reactivity and behaviour. Indeed, with access to a person's device by means of store apps, it is not a stretch to link CRM profiles with online behaviour. However, as will be accounted for in Chapter 11, our current meantime stage of anonymous emotional targeting should not be overlooked because it is practically, ethically and logically problematic in itself.

Similar to eyeQ, in the US, Cloverleaf is making use of Affectiva's facial coding technology (discussed in Chapter 5). Again, the idea is that cameras employed at shelf level scan people's expressions at the instant when they might touch the product (and are thereafter likely to place it in their basket). This gauges micro-reactions during the 'deliberative moment' and provides data on the nature of reactions to placement and packaging. In addition to facial coding of emotions and micro-expressions, they also offer corporate clients the ability to capture data about age, gender and ethnicity. Oovoo also targets the retail market with cameras in windows and in-store displays that measure how individual customers respond to in-store adverts and products. Likewise, Imagination Technologies is working on camera-based systems to gather data on shoppers through their in-store movements.

The rhetoric behind emotion capture and personalised retail speaks of moments to be enriched, predicting and serving rather than selling. For example, under the auspice of researching emotion and stress in retail, a study by eBay and the bioanalytics start-up Lightwave found that Christmas shopping in London may increase a person's heart rate by 33 per cent and tachycardia[1] by 88 per cent (Contagious, 2016). Further, 60 per cent of the shoppers in the study reached 'shopping fatigue' at 32 minutes, at which point they became disenchanted and the act of gift buying became transactional rather than thoughtful. eBay and Lightwave also created an 'emotionally powered store', which contained cubicles containing interactive screens. These displayed gift ideas to customers, while measuring facial expressions and the length of time users spend looking at each gift, in order to gauge their emotional response. It should not be missed either that affect-sensitive technologies have sufficient scope to be applied to retail staff. This is under the guise of improving the quality and quantity of emotional labour, staff–customer interaction, helpfulness ranking, training, and benchmarking performance.

Augmenting retail

On assisted seeing and 'being in the shoes-of-others', there is growing interest in the use of augmented reality (AR). Although used in marketing since the 2000s and popularised by *Pokemon Go* in 2016, art has led the way in visualising the relationship between retail and AR. Keiichi Matsuda's *Hyper-Reality*[2] is a vision in which VR, AR, wearables, IoT and biometric identification are intertwined to envelop every aspect of our lives. Should this seem far-fetched, one might recognise the pervasiveness of social media today – a reality that also once seemed unlikely. As depicted in Figure 8.1, what is at once immediate from watching *Hyper-Reality* is how augmented reality does not simply 'make greater' (the definition of augment).

Instead QR codes, adverts, icons, instructions, maps, location information prompts, status updates, notes, lists, checkout details, search opportunities, customer service chatbots, services and system update requests in AR have the potential to compete – just as adverts and marketing content in physical spaces vie for attention. Although Matsuda's video is fictional, it should be seen in the context of developments for mixed reality developments, such as Microsoft's HoloLens. Google, Apple and Facebook are also competing to be the AR lens of choice in retail stores, for product reviews, branded experiences and potentially pop-ups (see Google Tango AR, Apple AR kit and Facebook AR Studio). Similarly, when applied to retail, Adobe's AI and machine-learning system *Sensei* means that someone wearing a HoloLens would engage with layers of data placed over in-store objects and engage with these through voice commands and gestures. The store and third-party watchers (such as brands) will see how consumers navigate physical spaces and the nature of their interactions with objects.

Figure 8.1 An artistic vision of augmented in-store reality by Keiichi Matsuda

Current AR, facial coding and emotion tracking applications in retail are sporadic and gimmicky, but what they portend is significant. Indeed, in the UK, I sit on the ethical advisory board for a project titled *Sensing Feeling* that seeks to measure retail customers' emotional responses to their surrounding physical environment.[3] The project website imagines 'a world in which humans will interact within physical environments that are engineered to respond to our emotions and feelings in positive and ethical ways'. The emphasis here is not simply sensing as it is typically discussed in relation to the Internet of Things that generates data from a diversity of devices, but rather this is a given. In the context of the *Sensing Feeling* project, the vision is to employ learning systems, personal virtual assistants, robots and physical environments that 'sense human emotions and adapt accordingly, which in turn leads to growth in availability of "feeling-aware" consumer products and services'.

This reflects the overall empathic media thesis presented in this book in that it illustrates not only how we increasingly 'live with' technologies that feel and are sensitive to human life in ways hitherto not seen, but also that empathic media provide an opportunity for new aesthetic experiences that both draw upon information about emotions and provide new means of 'feeling into' aesthetic creations. At the time of writing in mid-2017 it remains to be seen what the outcomes of this project will be, but what is clear is that its objective is not simply to quantify and mine customer behaviour, but to use affect-sensitive technologies to build verisimilitude of understanding and meaningful engagement with AI entities, assistants and robots. As with eyeQ above, the developers have been careful not to fall foul

121

of privacy laws that are based on being able to identify or 'single out' a person (explored in full in Chapter 11).

Advertising: In-house Research

Having considered critical perspectives, agency views about the role of emotions, and retail, we now turn to more specific uses by the advertising industry. In-house uses of functional Magnetic Resonance Imaging (fMRI), EEG, voice-pitch analysis, eye-tracking, pupil dilation measures and galvanic skin response technology to study autonomic behaviour are not new. Despite the somewhat 'gee whiz' nature of this line-up, we should keep in mind that usage of machines to track attention reaches back into the 19th century and the origins of consumer psychology (see Chapter 2). Taking the aforementioned suite of neuromarketing technologies together, these services provide a two-fold function. First there is gatekeeping, in that as regards an ad agency a creative director uses their experience to assess work and judge its likely effectiveness. Eye-trackers, facial coding, brain scanning and biometrics play a similar role. The difference is that the application of technology does not rely on experience and intuition to assess the weaknesses and potential success of adverts. The second function is planning: from the point of view of planning where to buy media space in which to place adverts, upfront insight into the emotional impact of an advert allows media agencies to know how strong the advert is, the extent to which they can rely on network effects (i.e. people sharing the advert online), or whether they need to spend more on paid-for space to reach target audiences. Strength and potential effectiveness are typically conceived in terms of persuasion, salience, awareness, recall and emotional impact.

For example, Sands Research Inc. tested an advert for Volkswagen titled *The Force* (2011).[4] Released in the US during the 2011 Super Bowl, and widely shared online, it demonstrated record levels of engagement from viewers tested during pre-release in-house research. The commercial itself is created by the advertising agency Deutsch L.A. Inc. and Lucasfilm Ltd. Featuring the original John Williams soundtrack from *Star Wars*, and a child dressed as Darth Vader trying to use his powers to move things around him, the advert culminates with the child believing that he has applied 'the force' to start the engine in the Volkswagen on the driveway.[5] As depicted in Figure 8.2, the video research provides an attention heatmap of which elements had captured the viewer's gaze by means of eye-tracking. This works by the tracker projecting near infrared light on the eyes from a fixed position (such as from just under a laptop screen a person is looking at), taking photos of the eyes and their patterns, and then calculating the gaze point on the screen (Tobii, 2017a). Levels of overall engagement, emotional valence and stimulated areas of the brain are recorded by tracking EEG signals.

In an interview, Kim Du, vice-president of Corporate Development for the EEG headwear developer Emotiv, pointed out that many in-house market researchers use

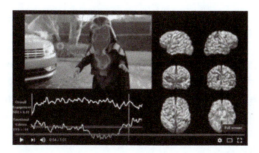

Figure 8.2 Example of in-house tracking of attention, emotion and engagement

their hardware and software platform. Echoing the antagonism to self-reporting, she says that EEG technology (and other empathic media) breaks market research out of the focus group environment (where a moderator asks questions about experiences of marketing content). Du argues that instead, by removing the need for public verbalisation and collecting biofeedback data, this allows researchers to accurately understand in real-time how participants are responding to stimuli.

Advertising: creativity

Empathic media are not only being used to measure reactions and correct content, they are also being experimented with to create advertising. For example, Zoic Labs (a Hollywood computer imaging company), Team One, and its parent ad agency Saatchi and Saatchi in Los Angeles attempted to answer whether AI could conceive, direct and edit a promotional music video that would emotionally move people. This choice of genre was based on it being what many directors begin with in their career, because it is one of the easiest (for a human). Before we unpack this example, the reader is encouraged to keep in mind that since the origins of AI research in the 1950s, claims have been about machinic creativity. This is because AI systems were originally conceived as symbol-manipulating systems (and these researchers also saw minds as symbol-manipulating systems). This led Simon and Newell to assert that 'there are now in the world machines that can think, that learn and create' (1958: 8). AI and creativity remains a constant source of interest and investigation (for a recent interdisciplinary overview, see Dartnall, 2013).

However, the biometric aspect is quite novel – certainly in the context of advertising. The group made use of IBM Watson, Muse's EEG headwear, Affectiva's API, a Japanese chatbot by Microsoft called Ms Rinna, drones by Prenav and AI editor. They first used Watson to parse the sentiment of the song's lyrics and then compared Watson's reading of the lyrics with the emotionality of the performer. This was achieved by using Muse's wearable EEG unit to read brain signals from the singer as she sang the song. Having the song's emotions datafied, they

123

consulted Ms Rinna – the Microsoft Japanese chatbot that developed in relation to users' interactions with her. (Unrelated to the case example, in late 2016 she became suicidally depressed and last posted that she hates everyone and wants to disappear.)[6] Available in 2016 on Twitter, the human team asked her to provide direction on how the narrative of the film should progress, where the story should take place, what the cast should wear, how hair and make-up might be styled, what people should do in the video, and even what ought to be eaten on-set. Although the feedback did not always make sense to the human team, they abided by the machine's answers.

In casting actors for the video, the human team asked candidates to wear Muse's EEG so they could capture data from their performance. They also used Affectiva's API to analyse their facial expressions during the performance. The team then aligned the two sets of candidate data with data about emotions from the original singer. The closest match to the singer's data was the person cast by the AI, which surprisingly for the human team was the same person they would have chosen. Apparently, casting is not only one of the most important decisions for directors, but also one of the most difficult to agree on.

Data from Watson, Muse and Affectiva then helped the human team construct a shot list for the drone on the film set (which was a desert). Having shot the film's raw footage, they then used film-editing software that uses AI technology to detect images and the emotional content of footage. These were tagged, which allowed the AI to iterate versions of the films quickly. To replace the need for a human special effects editor, the team also used Neural Art's open source libraries with their own system to generate AI-created filters for the shots. Notably, with the footage planned and executed, the AI was able to generate thousands of versions of the video. Ultimately the final video was never released, as it was not deemed to be of a high enough quality. Zoic and Saatchi/Team One found that although the final video was emotionally aligned to the content of the song, they concluded it is doubtful that machines will ever be able to produce art or sophisticated stories. A critical reader might query the authorship, collaboration and extent to which AI entities genuinely conceived, directed and edited the film. What is clear, however, is that AIs 1) did make creative choices, and 2) made machinic inferences about emotion to ground and justify those decisions. While it is fair to say that AI applications could not have executed the task without human assistance, the film and its technologies set a benchmark in the history of AI-based creativity.

Advertising: programmatic

Behavioural advertising tracks users' browsing activities between websites over a period of time to serve advertising tailored to what advertisers assume are users' interests. Its newer sibling, programmatic advertising, entails easier and automated ways for advertisers to target the right message, to the right person, at the right time (McStay, 2017). 'Programmatic' (as the industry refers to it) includes cookie and web-based behavioural techniques, but hoovers a greater range of data points, drawing on information from smart phone apps, social media, purchase behaviour, and information from companies that a person has a first-party relationship with (such as with a retailer a customer has registered with to buy goods from). It is also interested in sentiment, moods and emotions, because by understanding and predicting these, this gives scope to raise advertising effectiveness. For example, the online music service Spotify has partnered with WPP (an ad conglomerate), which gives WPP access to the behaviours and listening preferences of Spotify's listeners. In addition to location and device type, this grants insight into listeners' moods, and provides moment-by-moment insight into how a person is feeling.

The possibility of adding emotional and biometric information about emotions into the data marketplace arose in multiple interviews. For example, O'Brien from Havas said that 'the future is inescapably programmatic and biometric' and that data management platforms (DMPs) will play a pivotal role in collecting, harnessing and amalgamating this data and putting it to work (Interview, 2016). An ad agency, Unruly, was one of the first to explore the potential to programmatically target by emotions. In 2016 they launched the private marketplaces service, which allows marketers to programmatically target media spaces that complement the emotional footprint of their adverts. This works by matching the mood of an ad (determined by in-house techniques outlined above) with the mood of the environment or the website it appears on (including happiness, exhilaration, amazement, inspiration, hilarity, sadness, warmth, pride, nostalgia, surprise, knowledge and shock). Kenneth Suh of Unruly explains, 'We have identified the emotions that people are feeling from the content they're reading and engaging with. They may overindex on happiness, for example. Then we look at all the other sites that overindex on happiness and package those for advertisers' (Unruly, 2017). It is early days and this remains a private system in that data about emotions are not exchanged, bought or sold as is the case with programmatic data on open exchanges. However, there is a seeming inevitability about this, especially if we recollect Heidegger's earlier prognosis about technology, mining, extraction and 'making-present' what was once hidden.

Yet we should recognise the current practicalities that stymie this view. For a true marketplace there is need for agreement of industry-wide standards and terms of trade, rather than intra-agency prescribed standards, as is the case with Unruly. John Curran and Amy Moore from the programmatic ad-tech firm DataXu (views not representative of the organization) illustrate this well. In an interview in 2016, they asked me a question that is at once practical and philosophical: if emotion detection were to scale-up so the data is made available to data exchanges, then how should standards be decided? For example, some people smile a lot while others do not, but they are not innately less happy. Similarly, people have a wide range of resting heart rates and biometric states, so finding a common standard is challenging. This raises questions about the absence of baselines and comparative measures for expressive behaviour discussed earlier. Given the extraordinary level of money spent on advertising, this is a challenge for the industry. The problem is also academic (and ultimately more important) because, as it stands, results of studies into human–computer interaction cannot be compared, findings cannot be reused, and it is difficult to integrate the different parts of emotion and affective recognition systems (Arroyo-Palacios and Romano, 2008). In addition to the psychological and technical standards associated with affective computing and empathic media, the advertising industry currently also struggles to articulate what period of time constitutes paying attention to an ad, along with other data/display standards.

Emotions present greater complexity than attention, and (given the Heideggerian rule of ever-deeper human extraction) while it is easy to speculate that data about emotions may feed into data exchanges (where data about audiences is bought and sold) and targeting mechanisms (the criteria by which person X receives a given ad), on what terms could these be constituted if they cannot be academically agreed? Thus, while emojis have provided relatively clear markers by which emotions can be registered (notwithstanding how indicative they actually are of what a person is feeling), and sentiment analysis is mature enough for text- and image-based benchmarks to be agreed (see Chapter 3), so far there are no agreed standards for biometric data about emotions that could guide trading on an open programmatic market.

Advertising: in public

The intention of the advertising industry is to apply programmatic logic not only to desktop and mobile formats, but also to digital out-of-home (OOH) media. In general terms, this means that profiling that was once restricted to our devices is now spilling into urban environments. This provides scope for interactive adverts that make use of emotional reactions. For example, in an interview in 2016, Paula David of Affectiva explained that their clients (which include Unruly) are able to build emotion detection into digital displays. Thus, if a passer-by smiles at an ad for a pair of jeans, they may be pointed to where the store is. Similarly, Kinetic (a market leader in out-of-home advertising) is developing context-sensitive marketing. Here ad displays interact with a person's mobile phone, potentially giving rise to tailored projections and holograms. Wider trends include tracking the age and sex of passers-by in order to show more relevant advertising, scanning for their proximity to adverts, measuring their position and distance from display video sensors, and measuring their engagement and attention time.

The significance of this profiling is that it allows advertisers to programmatically set audience thresholds. For example, the clothing retailer Top Shop might say that it only wants to pay for adverts being screened on out-of-home displays if the passing audience is over 60 per cent female. Notwithstanding the academic levels of analytical accuracy accounted for above, there is scope here to apply this screening process to emotions. For example, people passing by an ad may be targeted on the basis of being happy or exhilarated (perhaps outside a sports centre), while stressed or simply tired city workers may be amenable to spa offers, coffee or lunch.

This raises a key ethical point: if we are free, smiley and happy, possibly because we have spare time and cash to spend in a retail outlet, we might be slightly uncomfortable, but not excessively concerned, about emotion tracking in public. But what of negative emotions, perhaps when labouring in the retail outlet with bags, a pushchair and a sleep-deprived teething toddler? Indeed, what if one is suffering from depression or a long-term negative mental state, as 7.8 per cent of the UK population are in 2017 (Mental Health Foundation, 2017a)? John Curran of DataXu said that from an industry point of view, negative emotions are an opportunity and that the industry has always made use of negative states. Citing ad campaigns that use day-parts and even times of the year (the January blues), he adds 'Yes, it's manipulative, but that's advertising'.

Revisiting the Paris Arcades

It is illustrative to place what has been learned in this chapter in the context of retail and urban spaces of centuries past. Between 1927 and 1940 Walter Benjamin, the German philosopher, Marxist and literary critic, conducted an unfinished study of Paris in the 19th century.[7] Influenced by surrealism and dream interpretation, Benjamin was intrigued by modernity's transformation of public space, how aesthetic and engineering expertise served commerce, the connection between entertainment and consumption, the secondary nature of use value, abandonment to amusement, the architecture of retail spaces, and the vertigo felt from rapid urban change.

There are parallels between the Parisian Arcades and modern retail, especially regarding modes of consumer experiences and environments. Benjamin's observations are poetic as he describes a spectacular phantasmagoria of architecture, light, glass, luxury goods and commodity culture. Keeping in mind Benjamin's Marxist orientation, his observations of an emergent consumer society are not celebratory but ambivalent. Seen theatrically, capitalism is a drama in which 'mass consumers' both participate in and occupy centre-stage themselves. Benjamin's *Arcades* project began and continued under the aegis of surrealism, speaking of how 'the advertisement is the ruse by which the dream forces itself on industry' (2002 [1982]: 171). Just as today's retail spaces and high streets are seeing the introduction of new technologies, Benjamin's observations should be seen in the context of the emergent (and somewhat virtual) use of lithographic technology and posters, new means of presenting advertising content, dream visions, and what he accounts for in terms of synthetic realities, the amoral nature of this art form, artificial light, promises of life improvement, seduction of the viewer, the sensual presentation of women in adverts, and the furnishing of urban spaces with sensation. This is what philosophers, critics, commercial neuroscientists, technologists and contemporary retail experts today discuss in terms of affect.

In many ways, what is occurring today is the datafication of Benjamin's dream worlds, and despite his own critical leaning, he did not reduce consumerism to a tactless discussion of commodification and manipulation. Rather, he attended to the emergent character of consumption and retail in the 19th century. In considering our emergent context, a key difference between Benjamin's phantasmagoria and now is that the dream machine is always on, and not only do we gaze at it, it also watches us back.

Studying the flâneur: the observer becomes the observed

European writers such as Balzac, Larousse, Sainte-Beuve, Bazin, Fournel, and most importantly Baudelaire (1964 [1863]) all made use of the flâneur to account for the emergent character of Parisian modernity and freedom (for men) to move incognito throughout public space to watch the emergent spectacle without being unwantedly observed themselves. For Baudelaire especially, the flâneur was a male artist, poet, spectator and chronicler of modern life, who was fascinated with increasingly commercialised city life. Heroised and theorised by Benjamin (2002 [1982]) in *The Paris Arcades*, if the flâneur were to wander around a modern shopping centre he would be at risk of no longer being an anonymous face in the ebbs and flows of the public multitude.

Rather than being free to peruse and assess the commercial marvel, it would be the flâneur who is being watched. Facial features would be recorded, as would micro-expressions, skin colour, gender, age, dress, gait, behaviour, proximity to adverts, time spent in front of video sensors, and whether the flâneur was curious enough to engage and interact with the advert. Should he care to, this well-dressed man may find himself being recommended a visit to Gieves & Hawkes, or perhaps Marks & Spencer for the more frugal flâneur. One would imagine his nonchalant face as studied emotional indifference, or in the parlance of the Facial Action Coding System he would generate an action unit of 0 – a neutral face. A less dispassionate flâneur might display action units 9+15+16 that entail nose wrinkling, lip corner depression and lower lip depression – all signs of disgust. However, I would wager a more pronounced reaction bordering on surprise, alarm and potentially horror. As Baudelaire tells, the flâneur as spectator of modern public life wants to 'feel oneself everywhere at home; to see the world, to be at the centre of the world, and yet to remain hidden from the world' (1964 [1863]: 9).

Once it was the flâneur who 'made a study of the physiognomic appearance of people in order to discover their nationality and social station, character and destiny, from a perusal of their gait, build, and play of features' (Benjamin, 2002

[1982]: 430). But now it is *she* and *he* who today are surveilled by their environment. Whereas the flâneur enjoyed 'botanizing on the asphalt' (ibid: 372), revelling in his role as observer of urban flora and fauna, sensualist and environmental scholar, it is the flâneur who is now studied. By means of a historical and poetic rear-view glance, we see that the use of empathic media raises all sorts of questions, but perhaps foremost about the desirability of altering the relationship between citizens' private bodies and the public environment.

Conclusion

This chapter has discussed the ways in which emotions and the biomedicalised body are imbricated in advertising and retail processes. This is far from new in that the use of technology to understand attention and emotion is as old as consumer psychology itself. In the context of empathic media and emotional AI, at the most basic descriptive level what is taking place is the quantification and commodification of emotion. However, the significance of this process is deepened through Martin Heidegger's observations about standing reserves and the stockpiling of all aspects of human life to be mined for value. This point is not lost on a variety of critical and Foucault-inspired biopolitical analysts, who have spoken about the ongoing appropriation of subjectivity and emotional life by the advertising industry. From the advertising industry's point of view, the argument is mixed: one corner speaks of liberalism, rationality and mutual satisfaction of interests, but the other (more influential voice) speaks with a libertarian paternalist voice about behaviour change, social engineering and the acceptability of using behavioural and biometric data to give us what we 'really' want. The outcome of this view is that commercial surveillance and control architectures exist to serve our best interests.

Exploring retail and advertising, this chapter depicted multiple applications of empathic media. Collectively, this entails the datafication of emotions, attention, physical spaces, augmented space and creative processes. Looking forward, critical attention is required regarding the capacity of programmatic exchanges to harness data from all possible networked sources. However, foresight should also be balanced with present-day realism in that establishing baselines, terms of exchange and the nature of emotions is problematic. Nevertheless, by revisiting Baudelaire and the Paris Arcades, we see a clear arc of change. Whereas chroniclers of urban life once botanised and classified the dream machine, it is increasingly we who are captured and studied in order to gauge what we think, see, feel and do.

Notes

1   Tachycardia means increasing adult heart rates over 100bpm.
2   Available from http://hyper-reality.co/

3   I was asked to join the ethical advisory group for this project in 2016. Unpaid, I agreed on the basis that the project was closely aligned with the wider research project that informs this book. I concluded that as a landmark project it was better to be part of the discussion in a non-profit capacity rather than simply an external observer and critic (see http://sensingfeeling.com/).

4   Available from www.youtube.com/watch?v=V3s2zUvuM1g

5   Instead, it is the father figure situated in the kitchen who has turned the engine on remotely with an electronic key.

6   Rinna's blog is available from http://blog.rinna.jp/

7   This was later edited by Rolf Tiedemann and published in 1982.

9

PERSONAL TECHNOLOGIES THAT FEEL: TOWARDS A NOVEL FORM OF INTIMACY

Wearable gadgets, Internet of Things (IoT) devices and the wider subject of self-tracking have received significant scholarly attention, but here I will focus on a specific aspect of bodily sensing: personal devices that feel-into emotional life. This chapter first outlines the historical, conceptual and technical contexts to these technologies. It then explores these in relation to health, wellbeing, work and sex. To account for these topics I draw upon case examples and interviews from Verily Life Sciences (of the Alphabet/Google group), Emotiv (an EEG headset manufacturer), SharpBrains (that researches neuro-technology), Spire (a developer of emotion-sensing wearables for work), Mysteryvibe (a sex-tech developer), RealDoll (a sex robot manufacturer) and a professional psychosexual therapist. This wide-ranging chapter is conjoined by the principle of intimacy. Early sections focus on self-understanding, middle parts consider organisational knowledge of emotions and vulnerabilities, and the final part assesses human–technical intimacy. I conclude by highlighting the conditions through which new forms of intimacy might emerge.

Health: Self-care

Wearable and IoT objects that track emotional states and bodies have a history that precedes the sensors and software discussed in this book. The history of self-care is portrayed by Foucault (1988), who begins his account with Ancient Greece and the practice and philosophy of being 'concerned with oneself'. The necessity of caring for oneself, for Foucault, permeates Greco and Roman philosophies, early Christian spirituality and later periods of the Roman Empire (400–500 AD). This view of care transcends instrumental and mechanical views of the body to include the soul. The connection with empathic media is that these ancient practices were not simply about self-understanding, but about the production of data. Foucault highlights that the Roman author Pliny (the Elder) advised reflection and retreat into oneself to study, read, prepare and meditate. Writing was a key means of generating self-understanding. This was not just about expression, but about generating information that could be shared and studied by oneself or others later. This self-tracking, recording, externalisation and analysis gave rise to a new temporal sense of introspection. Foucault notes that the relationship between writing and self-vigilance attended to behaviour, nuances and moods (among other factors). He gives detailed examples of self-analysis, self-care and record-keeping, including one from a letter by the Roman emperor Marcus Aurelius. In what today would be termed life-logging, Aurelius charts the ins and outs of his day, but also goes into detailed self-analysis about self-care of his health, gargling techniques, food and lunch, bathing, and more food, as well as how he felt about these to stay abridge of trends in his mental wellbeing.

What Foucault allows us to see is that our modern interest in the medicalised self-tracking of our body, mind and emotional life has a long history in Western culture. He finds this in Ancient Greece and in Plato too, who advises that individuals become a doctor of oneself and that self-care is a *perpetual* activity. Likewise, the Stoics developed gymnasia, which means 'to train oneself'. While modern gyms *are* places we visit before and after work, the root meaning is slightly different: gyms are *in* us. Indeed, in the context of wearables and self-tracking they are *on* us. The key principle here is care through permanent self-examination. Today this takes all sorts of forms, such as self-tracking by bathroom scales (Crawford et al., 2015), an interest in Buddhism and Eastern traditions (Ahmed, 2010; Andrejevic, 2013), and courses on positive psychology and mindfulness. Each of these is symptomatic of modern 'healthism', which locates health management with the individual rather than with the collective (Crawford, 1980; Rose, 1999; Neff and Nafus, 2016).

The principle of empathic media as a route to emotional self-knowledge (and help) was a recurrent one in interviews. For example, Kim Du, Vice-President of Corporate Development from Emotiv (that makes wearable EEG headwear to understand mental states), emphasised that consumer-level EEG technology is about 'collecting and exploring data to help you understand yourself'. Recognising the initial oddness of self-tracking the brain, she says that while people who are currently mentally and neurologically healthy might consider the use of personal EEG detection to feel-into one's own brain data as strange, when ageing and development of cognitive and memory problems are factored for, one can appreciate the product and the desire to self-improve.

Personal technologies that feel are made possible by developments in how we interact with computer technologies. Chronologically, line-driven commands gave way to the graphical user interface, and point-and-click was joined by wearable, haptic and tactile interfaces that provide more natural means to interact with computers. Implicit in wearables and other affect-sensitive technologies is a progression from linguistic and screen-based inputs to technologies that *feel* our bodies. This is not meant metaphorically, but literally, to refer to sensing, touching, detecting, perceiving, observing and identifying. In addition to consumer-level EEG, popular methods include the following:

- *Galvanic Skin Response* (GSR): sweat pores on the hands and feet are triggered by emotional stimulation. Whenever we are aroused or stressed GSR sensors may detect distinctive patterns. These are caused by changes of balance in the positive and negative ions in our sweat, which in turn dictate skin conductance. This measure can then be benchmarked against emotional states.
- *Electromyography* (EMG): sensors attached to muscle regions measure muscle activity or the frequency of muscle tension, which has been shown to differentiate positive and negative emotional states.
- *Blood Volume Pulse* (BVP): present on many wrist-based wearables, this sensor bounces infra-red light against a skin surface and measures the amount of reflected light to assess heart rate. Heart rate increases with negatively valenced emotions, such as anxiety or fear.
- *Skin temperature* (ST): sensors measure skin temperature because a change in emotion is associated with an increase and decrease in temperature.
- *Electrocardiogram* (ECG): sensors measure the heart's beats and rhythms by means of its electrical conduction. Changes in rhythm are associated with a change in emotional states.
- *Respiration rate* (R): spirometers measure inhalation and exhalation. Changes in respiratory behaviour correlate with emotional states.

Today, such sensors and wearables are emblematic of the interest in decentralised healthcare. This shifts the onus of care from the collective back to the individual. However, this discourse is present at an institutional level too. For example, the UK's health authority claims that information technologies 'will give patients and citizens more control over their health and wellbeing, empower carers, reduce the administrative burden for care professionals, and support the development of new medicines and treatments' (HM Government, 2014: 3). Through personal sensing, recording and collecting data from self-monitoring, the shift is towards preemptive measures, medical interrogation of the self in real-time and 'in the wild' remote care.

Corporate enabled self-care

Derek Dunfield of Verily Life Sciences of the Alphabet/Google group echoes this (Interview, 2016). He defines Verily's approach to modern health management as preemptive and focused on behaviour change rather than curative products.

Although much of our conversation focused on behaviour tracking (and less on questions of affect and emotions), Dunfield provided useful insights. He expects wearables for wellbeing to be increasingly legally medicalised and eventually to come with approval from the Food and Drug Administration (FDA). With formal recognition come difficulties, not least that 'Privacy concerns and regulation slow us down'. Beyond data protection there are further questions that Verily are dealing with, such as validating phones as health devices, and medical and legal liability regarding data accuracy.

He also observed that despite high sales of wearables, there is little evidence that trackers actually produce behaviour change. Dunfield attributes this to low motivation, a lack of useful feedback from devices and the need for these to be charged. Another reason suggested for dearth of behaviour change is absence of clear incentives or financial reward. He says that if wearables were linked with health insurance the outcome would be different. However, he adds, 'Most extrinsic rewards backfire, producing cheating behaviour, or stopping doing the activity because you haven't hit the target'. Overall, Dunfield argues that to generate a meaningful impact there needs be an increase in value for the wearer. This was recognized in numerous interviews with wearables firms that highlighted poor consumer experience and issues with the technique of wearing, aesthetic appeal, connectivity to other devices and cloud services, battery life and limitation of purpose (a device that only does one thing quickly becomes boring). An additional issue for Verily was embarrassment, especially when devices are used for conditions such as glucose management. Dunfield says, 'For instance it suggests you're fat, sad – a lifestyle stigma. So if there are visible wearables that suggest you're diabetic, this could be a stigma. So we're careful not to make the apps too visible or recognisable' (Interview, 2016).

Given Google's dependence on advertising, I asked Dunfield about the connection between Verily's self-care products and Google's revenue model. He answers saying that one reason Alphabet was started is because Google wanted to separate medical developments from advertising. This is because they have different privacy concerns. Yet providing orienting insight into his personal views and perhaps those of his Verily colleagues, he adds 'I'd love Google to have my medical data so they could tell me and advise me if I'm being unhealthy', and that 'I would opt-in if Google could predict the big things in my life'. Along with other interviewees in this book (notably from the advertising industry), he asserts generational differences towards privacy. Citing the popularity of Facebook, he says younger people have grown up with it (with the inference being that they are more used to living publicly). He also cites low readership of end-user licence agreements, saying 'I don't think people care'.

Against the context of conversation about Dave Eggar's novel *The Circle* (that examines Silicon Valley's impetus to make all aspects of life open and transparent), and responding to a question on whether emotional transparency might be a good thing, he says 'If it's accurate, then it's not bad'. His explanation is that 'Most people can't recognise their emotions and don't have the vocabulary. If my watch could tell me why I feel bad and what to do about it, we would have a better society'. On whether this is at all desirable, as a self-described libertarian paternalist, he believes it is simultaneously possible to respect freedom of choice, but that it is acceptable for private and public institutions to affect behaviour, particularly if people are making poor choices (see Thaler and Sunstein, 2003). While Dunfield is not concerned about corporate influence over behaviour and emotional life, or data privacy, he maintains libertarian unease about state access to this data. He says, 'The main problem is if governments get this data. There are lots of good reasons for why governments shouldn't have it'.

Industrial wellbeing: surveilling emotional labour

We now turn to the second case example of this chapter – work. Industrial psychology is the attempt to understand, measure, inscribe and act upon behaviour, attitudes, personality, or what is broadly a person's subjectivity. In other words, it analyses human behaviour not only to help managers handle workers, but also to assist workers in managing themselves. The point about self-management is an important one because emotional labour demands self-monitoring and self-inspection. In the case of work, this frequently entails living up to brand and reputational standards prescribed by others (Hochschild, 1983; Grandey et al., 2013).

While work may be seen in mechanical exchange terms (labour for wages), closer consideration shows deep psychological components. For the individual, this may be camaraderie, pleasant conditions, life-purpose and progression routes. At an institutional level, Rose notes that 'business success lies in engaging the employee with the goals of the company at the level of his or her subjectivity' (1999: 56). The point about alignment is key, as industrial psychology does not just manage our material bodies. Instead it includes the experiences, motives and make-up of individuals and inter-subjective dynamics in the workplace. A significant landmark study of industrial relations and subjectivity is Elton Mayo's (1933) observation that psychological and social factors play a larger role in productivity than physical elements. Whereas Taylorism focused on how an individual's performance could be improved, Mayo studied the individual in a social rather than solely physical context. He found that when management listened, learned and displayed care about workforce wellbeing, productivity rose. Mayo also points out that managers should research the workforce by interviewing staff to identify their likes/dislikes, correct negative feedback, and conduct studies on employee relations, fatigue and efficiency. The consequence from the point of view of empathic media is the recognition that – contra to Frederick Winslow Taylor's time and motion studies – emotions and feelings matter, and they should be researched and thoroughly understood.

In 1921 in the UK, this was formalised as Charles Myers co-founded the National Institute of Industrial Psychology (NIIP). The aim was to employ scientific methods to harness human energy, yet also provide higher standards of comfort and welfare for workers. This involved understanding intelligence and aptitude (to make sure people were suitably placed in the right job), but also workers' emotions due to observations that emotional make-up had industrial significance in terms of performance measures. This reflects an interest in 'mental hygiene', which entailed the diagnosis and treatment of minor mental troubles, the promotion of a correct version of mental life, and the organisation of the work environment in such a way as to minimise emotional and mental instability. This sanitisation points to a conception of workers as site of emotions, affects and instincts, to be nurtured, modulated and in the jargon of today – 'nudged' (Thaler and Sunstein, 2008). This emotionalisation of the workplace is nothing less than an attempt to make human industrial processes transparent. Again, this is achieved through experimental psychology, the charting of experience, understanding the emotional impact of buildings and workplaces, and the nature of attachment that people have to these sites, the objects therein, managers and co-workers. The links and potential of modern empathic media in this context could not be clearer, especially in terms of transparency of emotional life employed to detect and reduce fatigue, identify stress and sickness, and reduce accidents and long-term absence.

On modern wellbeing initiatives in the workplace *The Economist* (2016) suggests that 'Only happy fools would take that at face value'. The reason for their scepticism is that wellbeing programmes have less to do with an interest in individual welfare than net productivity and resilience. These agendas also assume that if wellbeing is absent in a person it is the individual who is at fault. This ignores or plays down internal (within the workplace), external and structural reasons for unhappiness, such as unreasonable workloads or wider social factors. Rather, the wellbeing agenda requires that the worker 'reframe' the pressures they are feeling. There is an insidious aspect to this in that responsibility for happiness is placed on the individual, rather than on those who have influence over the structural and environmental circumstances in which people find themselves. In other words, happiness becomes a choice rather than an outcome of circumstance (see also Davies, 2015).

The rationality behind the wellbeing agenda emerges in part from early definitions of stress. Hans Selye (1938, 1978) theorised stress as that which makes people less adaptable. For Selye it is a 'nonspecific response of the body' in that a stressor may have an overall impact on a person. Others later defined stress in terms of the responses and reactions of a person, rather than the situation itself, that produced them (Lazarus, 1991). This shift from the objective to the subjective continues, with other stress researchers arguing that various situations are not objectively stressful, but are socially or psychologically defined as such by individuals in terms of social and cultural norms (Levine and Scotch, 1970).

This means that personal technologies that feel are being utilised in the workplace, on the understanding that workforce problems are not issues of structural conditions, but worker coping mechanisms.

Take a deep breath: wearables and work

Developed by Neema Moraverji and Jonathan Palley, Spire was catalysed by mediaX, a start-up incubator at Stanford University. Specifically, it arose out of the Knowledge Worker Productivity research and innovation theme that asks '*What insights about people and technology are needed to develop metrics that can be used to measurably increase the productivity of knowledge workers?*' (mediaX, 2015; original emphasis). The final product is a clip-on wearable technology that monitors body position, activity and respiration to remind users to be mindful of their breathing. Notably, in contrast to trackers that measure steps and distance, Spire seeks to chart qualitative experience by quantitative means. In addition to having a standalone app for iPhone 5s onwards, the device interacts with Apple's Healthkit, which facilitates highly detailed self-tracking of diet, exercise, behaviour and the body. Breathing is visualised on smart phones to give the user insight into their 'state of mind' and to let them know whether they are calm, focused or tense (Spire, 2017). It focuses on breathing because this action indicates heart rate and muscle tension, and that respiration may influence the mind.

By definition, self-tracking is markedly different from covert data tracking because it is consciously done to the self (Lupton, 2016), although (as argued below) there is scope for coercive demands to wear trackers at work. The norms of self-care through wearables characteristically entail self-monitoring, self-disciplining and maintenance of the self as a productive unit (for instance, 'What have I achieved today, have I reached my targets and how can I do better tomorrow?'). Indeed, the Spire branding and aspirational personalities on its landing webpage are reminiscent of Silicon Valley ideals of people around their mid-30s, heterosexual (the male is holding the female to his chest), healthy, happy, successful, well-presented, confident enough to hold the camera's gaze and not appearing to have deviant or difficult political views. Wearable technology such as Spire's and motivations for their use sit well within a broader discussion of how to brand and present the self, neoliberalism, media technologies, self-improvement and self-governance (Marwick, 2010). Such self-investment and self-directed monitoring are particularly salient for knowledge workers because people paid to create, think and deal with information tend to experience high levels of autonomy in their professional lives. Indeed, this class of workers is required to engage in high levels of self-management, because work conditions in the Silicon Valley region are typically unstable and precarious. In general, the logic and language of wearables have uncanny parallels with the vernacular of business, not least through self-regulation, achievement, progress, goals, efficiency, optimisation and self-management.

Spire's activity tracker is worn on the hip of pants (trousers in the UK) or brassieres. The unit is 14 mm wide, 44 mm long and 32 mm thick. The clasp that attaches the grey semi-soft granite-looking body of Spire to a person is 12.5 mm wide and 52 mm long. The Spire app displays a user's respiration and appears on the smart phone screen in real-time (pulsating to represent an expanding and contracting diaphragm). As shown in Figure 9.1, it also displays a wearer's dominant state – calm, focused or tense.

Together the wearable and the app track respiration, physical movement of the body and its position to indicate physiological condition and mental states, and make recommendations, particularly when a person is feeing stressed. Over time, it senses a person's baseline respiration rate and consistency of breathing, with Spire claiming that algorithms become personalised to evolve in relation to the behaviour of the wearer. Spire's tracker is one of the few that monitors breathing

Figure 9.1 Dominant states with 'Tense' clicked upon to show statistics

patterns (others include Prana and OMsignal), although to date Spire has received by far the most coverage on Google.[1] According to Spire's homepage, 'Spire detects when you're tense … and reminds you to take a deep breath. Spire tracks your breathing patterns and activity for real-time insights into your state of mind'. Spire also 'sees moments of tension, focus, calm and activity and provides feedback for a better day'. A mediaX (2015a) webpage for an earlier iteration of the product is tellingly titled 'The Utility of Calming Technologies in Integrative Productivity'. Combining work and wellbeing, the page states that the breath sensor is a tool that assists knowledge workers' self-regulation to optimise their psycho-physiological state. It claims that by sensing, reading breathing patterns, and providing feedback, the product promotes focus and calm, and reduces tension through the principle of mindfulness, or being attentive to the present moment.

The particulars of the patent are for its sensing modules, the product housing and the system that converts breathing patterns into electrical signals (Google Patents, 2014). It gauges inspiration and expiration, and evaluates breathing by measuring the movement of the chest and abdominal wall. The patent goes on to detail a wide range of breathing factors, including the following: respiration rate (for instance, breaths per second); depth of breath; shallowness of breath; inhalation-to-exhalation ratio; thoracic variations (that differ by age, sex and race); estimation of tidal volume (the volume of air moved in and out of the lungs); inspiratory and expiratory flows (such as peak and mean value); fractional inspiratory time (calculated by dividing inspiratory time by the sum of inspiratory and expiratory times); work of breathing (effort required to inspire air into the lungs); phase angle (that involves difficulty in breathing); and respiration waveform morphology (ways of expressing and modelling breathing patterns). The significance of this detail is that it provides a close-up example of affective behaviour and machinic empathy. The unit registers these different types of respiration by means of force-sensing resistors. With pressure on resistors converted into electrical signals, these can be processed as patterns. Converted into information, each behaviour pattern can be classified into Spire's categories of calmness, focus, tension and activity. This example of empathic media can be reduced to body > behaviour > pattern capture by device > pattern matching > classification of emotion > feedback to person wearing the device.

Articulating emotions at work: some issues

However, perhaps the key issue when considering wearables at work is when insights into emotions are fed back not only to the wearer but also to organisations. Wearables are growing in prevalence at work, with one respected market analyst suggesting that by 2020, 40 per cent of employees may use fitness trackers to increase health and lower healthcare costs (Gartner, 2016). At an industry technology conference, GITEX 2016 in the United Arab Emirates (UAE), Daniel Leitao (Head of Product at Vinaya) responded to a question I asked about emotion capture in relation to wearables at work. Arguing for this as a positive development, Leitao cited suicide as a leading cause of death for men in the UK and the scope for employers to intervene. However, recognising the privacy implications he asked 'At what point can you use emotion tracking to see when people are treading into a bad area and need help? It's one of the big questions in the workplace'. He followed this asking 'If you [as an employer] see this, who do you tell, because you are invading their privacy?'.

Pointing to the ubiquity of heart rate sensors and Vinaya's development of galvanic skin response sensors to help manage stress at work, he also said that their corporate service also generates contextual clues if a person gives consent. This takes the form of mining employees' emails to provide increased understanding of emotion and mood trends. For employers and employees alike, Leitao says that this would grant rich insight into a person's character by understanding the tasks demanded of a person and their responses. By means of an example, he adds 'The biosensor might tell you something and then [by means of access to emails and calendar] you understand they were in a meeting with their boss, making them stressed'. While this chapter is ostensibly interested in devices that are worn or used in an intimate capacity, contextual insight is a recurring theme in workplace analytics. For example, Humanyze states that it seeks to 'humanise' the workplace. This is achieved by monitoring internal communications, networks, relationships, location and individual biometrics through smart phones, wearables and voice. The stated objective is to make inferences about how happy and productive a person is at work. Without naming companies, Humanyze lists client case studies that derive from the financial, oil, travel, pharmaceutical and technology sectors (Humanyze, 2017). In effect, this represents the automation of industrial psychology and forced workplace transparency to passively analyse employees on an ongoing basis. For managers, data and insights are now conveniently viewable on digital dashboards.

In a 2016 interview Ben Waber, Humanyze's CEO, recognised the scope for dystopian interpretations (Bloomberg Businessweek, 2016). He made what is at first a curious argument: more regulation is needed. He says that it should be used on an opt-in basis, and that while individuals can access their own behaviour, companies should only receive aggregate statistics. This leads him to argue that people may learn how to improve themselves while the company possesses insight into overall performance. He also reasons that in the future all companies would use this type of technology. This is an important theme common to empathic media developers that we will return to in Chapter 11. That is, profiting and making human physiology and emotional life 'machine-readable' is morally justifiable as long as the data collected cannot be linked to an individual.

A number of named companies, including JPMorgan Chase and Bank of America, are reported to be exploring systems that monitor worker emotions to boost performance and compliance (Bloomberg Businessweek, 2016). In the financial sector, one approach is to use wristwatch sensors to measure pulse and perspiration to warn traders to take a break from their desks when their arousal/emotions are too high. Similarly, Behavox – founded by a former Goldman Sachs employee – uses voice analytics of telephone conversations. Describing itself as a 'holistic employee surveillance solutions' company (Behavox, 2017), it analyses deviations from established patterns, such as shouting at someone they have traded with when previous conversations were calm.

Echoing the discussion about the emotionality of finance in Chapter 3, it is notable that the ability to control and calm emotion is a seen as a requirement for trading. This is because people who can understand and harness their own emotions are less likely to panic, react poorly to market volatility and make impulsive decisions (Ameriks et al., 2009). The reason why this matters is that emotions contribute to how decisions and choices are framed, and why certain options may feel more desirable than others, even when the options have equal logical merit, or may even be illogical (Kahneman and Tversky, 2000). Might it be in both the employee's and employer's self-interest that the trader wears wristwatch sensors to measure their pulse, perspiration and stress? Read positively, transparency and monitoring of emotion in the workplace may grant insight into whether employees are undergoing emotional and physical difficulties, identification of when people are in need of support, mental and physical stresses, illnesses and conditions, and anger flashpoints. Prosaically, those of us who are outside of finance might also appreciate a practical prompt to take a break, breathe deeply or go for a short walk. This might save us from email regret about a hastily and tetchily written memo, or in finance, a spectacularly bad investment.

There are, of course, ethical questions here. Regarding stress – should a financial company have a *duty* to track employees given that they are handling large amounts of a client's money? The same might be asked of public sector employees – as raised in Chapter 7, should police officers prone to stress and over-reactions be allowed to carry guns? However, in reverse, and at a more basic level, on what basis does the average employer have access to their physical and mental states? What of dignity and respect? Alvaro Fernandez from SharpBrains cites one example of a discussion he had with an entrepreneur who has 'a solution to improve employees' mental health' (Interview, 2016). The question is: 'Would you use it if you were an employee – what if my boss realises I have this cognitive problem – will they fire me?' He argues that 'When people realise what is going on, privacy will be a main concern', but also that 'I haven't seen any systematic effort to have privacy standards'.

Next is that while empathic media developers share broad agreement that emotional life may be inferred through biometric devices, they do not share a common language of emotions. Kim Du, for example, says there are no agreed standards for emotion, intention or attention tracking, and that 'there's no clear dictionary or signatures in EEG'. The consequence of a lack of agreed standards about personal biofeedback signals is twofold: the default logic of empathic media privileges universality, basic emotions and biological programs (as opposed to a more eth-nocentric account), yet there is no common standard that people may measure themselves by between devices and sensing types (see also Arroyo-Palacios and Romano, 2008). The issue of standards is significant if organisational decisions are made about employees and citizens on the basis of this data.

We can add coercion to the list of concerns. Even hypothesising that an employer is 100 per cent trustworthy, that the data collected is true to emotional states, and that meaningful assurances can be given that personal data and aggregated information from devices may be kept entirely separate from personal data, the principle of volitional consent is deeply problematic in a workplace context.[2] Although an opt-in option may be provided as described by Humanyze and Vinaya, will new employees who have landed their dream job at JPMorgan Chase or Bank of America be able to say 'no'? The problem of coercion lingers because even in the happiest of workplaces, those who reject the offer of wearables to track wellbeing are likely to feel that they have been placed on a real or mental list of non-participative employees (that may come to mind when making decisions about redundancies, career progression and offering opportunities).

Sex Objects

Empathic media and 'technologies that feel' not only enhance wellbeing, health, self-care activities and productivity, but also sexual pleasure. This is achieved through IoT devices that are sensitive to bodily reactions and discern a person's preferences. In an interview in 2016, Soumyadip Rakshit, co-founder of MysteryVibe, explained the scale of the 'sex-tech' industry, depicting $20bn reported sales of sex toys globally.[3] Rakshit added that this figure could be larger because many sales go unreported. He attributed this growth to online retail and that as a consequence many entrepreneurs are gravitating towards the sex-tech sector.

MysteryVibe allows users to personalise their masturbation as the device, Crescendo, bends to reach various spots. By means of software on a user's phone, Crescendo's vibrations alter to match levels and stages of a person's arousal. MysteryVibe's business plan is to expand the capacity of the software so a device can discern the context in which sex is taking place, engage with room temperature settings, lighting, music and television, and modulate them 'during play' to compliment and heighten the pleasure experience. The goal for MysteryVibe is a 'seamless experience where things just happen'. Rakshit says:

> Imagine you walk in to your bedroom and your room is cold. You were hoping on having an intimate time but you don't feel aroused in the cold anymore. You switch on the heating but it takes a while to get warm and you are asleep by then. If only the temperature had been pre-set to the right one, that would have been one less thing to plan or

worry about. The same goes for other experiences in the bedroom – lighting, music, videos. This is what excites us – being able to create that immersive bedroom experience by understanding our body's arousal. (Interview, 2016)

On what happens with the data, the scope for privacy breaches was clear to Rakshit, not least because of widely reported problems and hacks of vibrators. For example, in 2017 We-Vibe were ordered to pay customers up to $10,000 because they collected information about their toy usage without users' knowledge and left them prone to hacking. Also, at Def Con 2016 in Las Vegas (a hackers conference), two hackers named 'goldfisk' and 'follower' live-hacked Standard Innovation's Bluetooth controlled vibrator. It is notable too that these devices are relatively popular, with over 2 million people using Standard Innovation's devices. In Standard Innovation's case, data about the temperature and intensity settings of the device is sent back to Standard Innovation, which tells the firm (and anyone able to hack the connection) how and when the device was used.

The significance is that users can be targeted with ransomware as data about targets is sold through the dark web.[4] (This also raises other matters, not least that if a device is attacked while in use, can a remote sexual assault be said to have taken place?) Rakshit states that no personal, identifiable or device-level data leaves the smart phone.[5] MysteryVibe plan to allow anonymised data to be shared with researchers in the same way that the Google Genome Project grants open access to a mass repository of data. For Rakshit, this will allow sex researchers, doctors, sex experts, and other companies involved with sex-tech 'to better understand arousal and maybe even support bigger things like helping people get pregnant or simply live happier lives' (Interview, 2016). On whether data would be shared with marketers he replied that it would, because the dataset would be open and available for everyone to use. He suggests that Chanel might, for example, create a new perfume based on arousal data. Similarly, erotica makers might use such data to create better movies. Genuinely open, egalitarian and friendly in interview, he says that 'Our objective is to support everyone to create more pleasure objects and services so we can all enjoy that'.

I also spoke with Kate Moyle, a sex therapist and partner in Pillow, an app that encourages greater intimacy between lovers. She explains that separate from her work with Pillow, as a therapist, the subject of technology frequently arises when counselling couples. This includes partners' *not* picking up the phone, but also never being away from their phone. In general, she observes that technology can get in the way of relationships and create barriers. She also notes that dating apps have a tendency to make people more consumable and disposable, akin to the pick-and-choosing of shopping. On MysteryVibe and similar products, Moyle broaches privacy and (indirectly) the somewhat Heideggerian principle of 'making-present', saying:

> I think people are scared about what can be known about them, e.g. MysteryVibe can tell us lots about the female orgasm. I think that's great. But it does highlight the idea that nothing is secret any more – nothing is unseen.

We also discussed SexBit, which is a Fitbit for sex that tracks male thrusts and even allows men to share their performance online. This for Moyle is not healthy because if 'people are publishing that sort of information, then that's it, if it's out there. It's like educating young people not to put sexy pictures of themselves online'. However, she cites what she sees as more positive examples of self-monitoring, such as an app called Edge by Tracey Cox[6] that helps couples struggling with rapid male ejaculation.

On wider developments in sex-tech, moods and emotions, Moyle notes the rise of robots, but remarks that while the sex-tech industry is enthused and prone to excitable claims about this emergent sector, she does not think they can be argued to be emotional creatures. Given that a recurrent theme of the research informing this book is the principle of intimacy, I was interested in how Moyle would respond to the question 'What is intimacy?'. Her response was 'I get asked this all the time', and she answers 'In-to-me-see': this means 'allowing a person to see you in a way that is closer or different to how others might see you. And you connect intimately on different levels, e.g. sexually, emotionally, intellectually and physically'. She adds that 'It's about what makes one relationship different to another'. From the point of view of empathic media this is telling, particularly if intimacy is judged through strength of emotional connection, bio-arousal and emotion type, cognition and the contextual factors known about a person or group, and the extent to which empathic media provide feedback in unique, resonant and physically appropriate ways. However, if the criterion of intimacy is a quality and form of understanding different from that maintained with other people, can sex robots and empathic media be said to be capable of intimacy? I suggest the answer is 'yes with caveats' on the basis that empathic media may feel, learn, remember, understand factors about selfhood missed by other people, and measure and react to uniquely personal biometric traits.

Modern sex robots are affectively capable humanoids. For example, RealDoll's Jessica is 165 cm, 80 pounds and made of soft, durable and realistic silicon skin. Like a person, the joints of her skeleton are flexible. RealDoll claims she is capable of simulating complex programmed female sexual acts. Online promotional material claims that these programs are based on the Kama Sutra and that a pornography star 'taught' her techniques. In addition to possessing highly realistic body parts, RealDoll's sex robots contain sensors that respond to touch, scope for speech and verbal response. Others employ sensors and behavioural response mechanisms that are dependent upon the chosen characteristics of the sex robot. These include wild, experienced, ready to provide pain fantasies and also, somewhat disturbingly, 'frigid' (True Companion, 2017).

Interviewed by *The Sun* newspaper, Matt McMullen, the CEO of RealDoll, says 'I want to have people actually develop an emotional attachment to not only the robot but the actual character behind it – to develop some kind of love for this being' (Birchall, 2016). Connecting with the discussion in Chapter 6 on realism and domestic voice assistants, RealDoll's intention is not an attempt to fool a person into questioning whether a doll is a real person. Instead it is to create new experiences that are distinctively meaningful, entertaining, enjoyable and believable. In an interview with *Vice*, McMullen explains that their AI has 'a needs system and the experience is game-ified. So the AI has desire—or at least the illusion of desire—and there are goals, and if you meet them you're going to get some kind of reward, be that verbal, visual, or in sexual movements' (Anderson, 2016). He adds 'It's far more than sexual entertainment. People really zero in on, "Oh, you're making a sex robot." I'd say we're making a robot that can have sex. Although it's a very different, very intimate way that you can connect with something that is robotic and has AI technology built in'. On relationships and emotion, McMullen questions whether a person would fall in love with his robots. Rather, he seeks to facilitate bonds and relationships previously unseen in other machine–human relationships. One would be correct to reason that this is a somewhat unidirectional relationship, but McMullen reasons that the capacity to robotically express and feel-into emotion (through facial coding, heart rate, breathing and sweat) has the scope to initiate new forms of connection. This is debatable, not least because the scope of the relationship is functionally limited. However, realism should not be the primary criticism. As discussed in Chapter 6, lessons from Joseph Weizenbaum's 1960s *Eliza* might be born in mind, when Weizenbaum (1976) found strong emotional responses, suspension of disbelief and anthropomorphic behaviour to Eliza's conversation, even when patients were aware they were conversing with a machine. Related, Darling (2014) found that when people were asked to strike a bug-like robot they were less likely to want to strike the robot when it was given a name or backstory. This led Darling to suggest this is human empathy, rather than hesitation due to perceived value of the robot. The key to this is in anthropomorphic framing of the robot, even if the robot is otherwise unlifelike.

This raises notable ethical questions, perhaps overall about the potential loss to authentic human relations (Turkle, 2010). There is also the issue of the nature of intimacy. While machines may feel and see into people's bodies, Moyle's point about sexual, emotional, intellectual and physical connection remains. This leads us to the caveat alluded to above, because without the fullness of these channels, sex arguably becomes pornographic due to the likely absence of care. Then there is the existence of child sexbots – which raises the subject of the status of prostituted robots (Richardson, 2016). Are they tools or actors, and do we gauge the status (and rights) of this in reference to the object itself, the connection a person has with it, or what a person's intent is? Cases are also emerging of robots such as True

Companion's *Roxxxy* that is arguably constructed to fulfil rape fantasies. As noted above, one of her personalities is programmed to be 'frigid' and unappreciative of advances. This signals an absence of consent to simulate her resistance to sexual advances (Sharkey et al., 2017).

What sex robots illustrate is that our relationships with technology are becoming increasingly entangled, co-constituted and quite literally 'coupled'. Indeed, Realbotix sell an app called 'Harmony' that is said to 'learn' about a person as they converse with it. This software can be connected with physical robots and virtual companions. While it remains to be seen how many of these robots will be ordered by ordinary people, Szczuka and Krämer (2017) asked 229 heterosexual males (with 53.3 per cent in a relationship) whether they could imagine buying a sex robot now or within the next five years. Surprisingly, 40.3 per cent indicated that they would. At a minimum, what these robots signify is complication of a conception that frames them as constituted by traditional tool-based 'in order to' characteristics. While 'sex-bots that feel' certainly involve objectifying practices, there are complicating inter-agent factors, such as anthropomorphic behaviour, projection, dignity, language practice, and whether the principle of electronic personhood applies.

Conclusion

The focus of this chapter has been the significance of personal technologies that use biofeedback to interact with arousal, affective life and emotions. We have considered cases of health, work and sex. Early sections identified that self-care, sensing, recording and analysing physical and mental life have a long cultural history. In a modern decentralised and pre-emptive health setting, self-tracking also involves varying degrees of corporate access to this data. In the case of Verily, the interviewee (speaking of his own views rather than Verily's) saw no ethical problem with allowing an advertising company (Google) to access data about users' health and emotional life.

In the context of work, I first identified longstanding interest in the psychological and emotional dimensions of the workplace. To explain how personal technologies gauge emotions at work I assessed the Spire unit. At a physical level this illustrated the connection between bodily behaviour and emotions. At a social and more discursive level it connected self-care with the neoliberal politics of self-regulation, achievement, progress, goals, efficiency, optimisation and self-management. I then assessed the institutional application of wearables-at-work. This involves what Foucault (1988) designates 'technologies of power', or the scope to monitor and determine people's conduct. While companies spoke of choice and consent, it is hard to avoid the issue of coercion (both implicit and explicit). This also invokes the question of workplace rights, the law and employee access to the terms by which decisions have been made about them. Related is the question of liability:

does an employer have a responsibility to tell a wearer if they have biological information that could save them from harm? Also, might employers themselves be made accountable for poor employee wellbeing?

The final case example considered personal technologies in terms of pleasure and sex. While high sales of sex robots remain a prediction, the wider sex-tech sector is growing rapidly. Given that developers are keen to engage with a person's life context, devices and home networks, the privacy implications are clear. What is perhaps more interesting is the nature of intimacy in relation to empathic media. While few people would argue that technologies have sufficient scope for human interpersonal intimacy, there is an argument for an emergent and not-yet-defined type of intimacy. Technically this is based on feeling-into human physiological behaviour, measuring and reacting to affect, memory, learning and feedback. What remains to be seen is what social, projective, anthropomorphic and imaginary qualities people will bring to these human–technical relationships.

Notes

1   Search conducted in March 2015 using the search term 'wearables breathing'.
2   A point recognised by Europe's data protection instruments. See for example Article 29's Opinion 2/2017 on data processing at work.
3   In 2016 *Forbes* recorded it as $15bn: see www.forbes.com/sites/janetwburns/2016/07/15/adult-expo-founders-talk-15b-sex-toy-industry-after-20-years-in-the-fray/#775dce2e38a1
4   This contains websites only accessible using non-standard communications protocols, ports and browsers, particularly Tor that facilitates anonymous behaviour online.
5   I did not inspect the device or software so cannot confirm whether this is correct.
6   Available from https://itunes.apple.com/gb/app/edge-stamina-by-tracey-cox/id869274903?mt=8

10
EMPATHIC CITIES

Readers will know that a utopia is a vision of a society that is desirable and approaching perfection for its citizens. What is less likely to be known is that the capital of the island of Utopia is Amaurot; a town square in shape, roughly two miles in either direction and adjacent to a river. Protected by high and thick fortified walls, towers and forts, on three sides of the perimeter is a deep ditch. On the fourth is a river. The town has drinking water delivered through earthen pipes, and for areas where pipes cannot reach there are cisterns to collect rainwater. Streets allow all sorts of vehicles, and the adjacent buildings are uniform. This means each side of a street appears to be one long house. Individually, the houses themselves are three storeys high, make good use of glass, have front doors to the street and back doors into well-tended gardens. There are no locks and every person may enter freely into any house, although each house typically contains 10–16 adults – assisted by two slaves. Agriculture is Utopia's most important industry and source of work, although jobs such as carpentry, metal-smithing and masonry are also vital. As there is no private property and all able-bodied people work, citizens only labour for six hours a day. Hospitals are free and there is a welfare state. Politically, regional and national representatives of the island are elected; but once elected the head of Utopia, the Prince holds the post for life – assuming there is no attempt to enslave the people. Meals are taken in public community dining halls, but there are no pubs, taverns or licentious places (such as brothels) for private gatherings. This keeps citizens in full view, so that they are obliged to behave well.

This vision is, of course, Thomas More's *Utopia*, first published in 1516. Just over five hundred years later, we still like to think of future cities. Many of the themes introduced remain: questions of security, work, architecture, public services, sanitation, municipal management, health, and questions about surveillance and citizen privacy. Today's experimental utopia is 'smart cities', 'future cities', 'sentient cities', 'senseable cities', 'conscious cities', and what is here termed 'empathic cities'. Each is enabled by connectivity, widespread use of low-cost sensors, ambient awareness, adaption to conditions, feedback and increased monitoring of citizenry. Key areas of interest for new city developers include: using sensors to monitor and improve traffic flow and parking; water and waste management; logistics, mobility and autonomous cars; adaptive lighting in buildings and public spaces; energy management; drone and freight logistics; surveillance cameras to monitor non-policed areas; body cameras and local area networks for police; and collection of wearable, smart phone, social media and retail data by city departments.

Such developments in modern urban, municipal and commercial planning also represent the scope to sense moods, emotions and the perspectives of a city's inhabitants. This is based on device and sensor feedback, and measurement of experience. Analytics range from sentiment analysis to understanding brain behaviour. Although smart cities are not fictional, they are conceptual, ideological, technocratic and too often hyper-sterile orientations to the future. The impetus is improvement, intelligence, management and control over urban life, things, processes and people. In theory, control through connectivity is a two-way process. It grants a top-down understanding of the civic infrastructure, the impact of decision-making about public resources, efficiency gains, and citizen and consumer moods. In terms of a bottom-up component, smart cities involve the use of communications technology to increase citizen engagement, and to identify and react to complaints. While these are largely schematic rather than implemented, the vast scale of research, development and investment by behemoths such as Siemens, Microsoft, Phillips and Cisco should not be overlooked. Nor should the fact that the most significant developments are taking place not in the West, but in Africa, India and other regions often overlooked by Western books on technology and digital politics.

Against this connected context, this chapter accounts for the emotional dimension of networked cities and the ways by which they may feel-into the moods of their citizenry. To do this I draw upon conversations and interviews with stakeholders including Siemens (that is developing smart city 'solutions'), Philips (that provides intelligent lighting), KM4CITY (an Italian public–private partnership), Repustate (a sentiment analyst), Smart Dubai (a political initiative to raise happiness levels), State of Green (a Danish public–private partnership) and Mosaico Digitale (that makes a product capable of displaying digital images in public spaces). Specifically, this chapter explores the proposition that it is possible to both manufacture and gauge the emotional life of cities, and that this simultaneously has socially beneficial and negative consequences. I conclude by assessing what it means to live in cities that simultaneously have utopian and dystopian characteristics.

Emotionality of Space

Cities are emotional places containing elements that have been created by people for specified objectives and to generate prescribed affects. Interactions with people, groups, organisations, companies, authorities, buildings, transport infrastructure, parks and other elements all generate emotional responses within urban contexts. Indeed, architecture itself is never neutral because its objective is to stimulate emotions and moods. This might be a sense of reverence, playfulness, studiousness, gravitas, care, power or ostentatiousness. However, developers recognise that a city is much more than its infrastructure. It includes its psycho-geography and how that is engaged with and experienced.

This entails what Palti and Bar (2015) account for as 'the city's awareness of the motives, personalities and moods of its inhabitants', which consists of con-scious streets, buildings and municipal spaces that are sensitive 'to the mood and context of their users'. Factors used to feel-into citizen experience include assessment of online sentiment, spending trends, cameras, citizen mobility and how people engage with urban objects. The emotional experience of cities is also tracked through in-house techniques and questioning within research facilities. This includes not only the application of market research techniques such as EEG and facial coding, but also mapping of the 'emotional topography of cities' to pro-vide an emo-geography of sorts. This involves understanding citizen experience of the buildings, urban design, parks, paths and layout of cities. This is not just about tracking mobility, but about how the brain comprehends and orients itself in space and the objects therein. Responses to architecture and urban environments can be measured by wearable biometrics (such as mobile EEG, GSR and heart rate capture) and connecting this data with geographic information. One way of doing this is to take people on tours of a city, to ask questions about what they see, feel and remember, and then to measure the arousal rates of their brain and body against parts of the city. Psychologists of urban geography can topographically link arousal reactions with elements of the city and thereafter use this data to plan for future design (Ellard, 2016). Indeed, there is no reason why emotional topog-raphies cannot be linked with publicly available online maps.

Between surveillance and efficiency

We should not hold back from using the correct word to identify these develop-ments. They are utterly based on surveillance, and what's more their developers are not afraid to use this word, not least because it refers to what they do – namely, architecting data-oriented situations whereby authorities may manage, influence and control citizenry. In 1992 Giles Deleuze published 'Postscript on the Societies of Control', a classic essay about the shift from 'discipline' to 'societies of con-trol'. This depicts a scenario of new social arrangements that promise freedoms and hope, but are imbued with the mechanisms of citizens' own confinement. To put this in terms of Amaurot, Utopia was the brochure to sell Dystopia. Indeed Deleuze – some years ago now – discusses a scenario where an identity card is required to navigate elements of the city. This also tracks and effects a 'universal modulation' (Deleuze, 1992: 7). Today this oblique Deleuzianism is clarified by city apps for location tracking, big data techniques that provide municipal author-ities with dashboard visualisations of social sentiment, flow of citizens through urban space, feedback from sensors on buildings, and prescriptions on which civic decisions should be made on the basis of incoming information. Whereas the language of surveillance once appeared excessively critical, today it is readily used at events championing smart cities.

The word is accurate in that the objective of smart city management is control over large and small objects, systems, people and all things that flow throughout spaces. Moreover, biometric measures are increasingly relied upon to make what are seen as evidence-based municipal, urban planning and city investment decisions. This means that the focus on cities as sites of engineering prowess, networking and sensing is to miss the point: the real issue of ubiquitous sensing technologies is not technology, but phenomenology, psychology, biology and emotion (also see Weiser, 1991).

The use of biometrics to understand psycho-geography and research citizen experience of place is not inherently unethical, nor is use of digital platforms to enable more direct communication with governments and registering of negative (and positive) feedback. In principle it binds citizenry and municipal and political decision-makers more closely. However, the thin line between surveillance and efficiency is expressed well by the director of KM4CITY (a public–private partnership based at the University of Firenze, Italy) that uses sensors and sentiment analysis so that municipal authorities and managers of public services may use data to make more effective decisions about resources in Florence (Italy). On emotions and feeling-into civic moods, he explains that they capture information from citizens because 'It is so important to understand the mood of citizens' (Interview, 2016). Open social media data is analysed in relation to public services and amenities: for instance, 'we had a broken pipe and the mood of the people went down'. Interested in what their promotional literature terms as 'virtuous behaviour', I asked my interviewee when this monitoring tips into surveillance. He explains that 'In reality it is surveillance from the start because data is used for both', on the basis that the municipality uses data about people to manage infrastructure. On influence and controlling factors of surveillance, he remarks that virtuous behaviour not only addresses criminality; it could also be used to encourage behaviour change, such as citizens using buses rather than cars to improve air quality. I asked how citizens feel about the overall increase in monitoring of public spaces and he admits that 'Some aren't happy' and they know there are monitors that use face recognition. He explains that this is not switched on at all times, but only when deemed necessary. The resolution is dropped down after a few hours if that level of data is not needed, but if a criminal situation arises, the authorities are authorised to use facial recognition for a longer period.

Florence's citizens are also encouraged to use official city apps. These have the capacity to be useful in that they can send geo-located descriptions of problems (such as a broken street light) to the appropriate government department. They also provide a great deal of information about who, where, and what is being said. The implication is significant because the potential exists to turn the city into an advertising platform. This is a dramatic extension of modern 'audience as commodity' critiques (McStay, 2011; Fuchs, 2016), which diagnose how interactions with online services and content are tracked, commodified, and used to target advertising and create revenue for ad networks, publishers and app developers. By treating the 'citizen as a commodity' and cities in terms of sensors and connectivity, urban life effectively becomes a digital advertising opportunity. Underpinning this is sophisticated data: public sensors, device data, location, sentiment, emotion, screens and augmented reality components. Indeed, in principle, real-time dynamic data could be readily augmented by research data about the emotional topography of cities. Revenue from public–private partnerships and advertising networks would service city development.

This is reminiscent of online programmatic platforms used in advertising (discussed in Chapter 8). These also make use of data from diverse sources (such as web cookies, app data, data owned by brands and purchase data) to advertise more effectively. Applied to the city, this suggests a publicly owned advertising platform that interacts with people in public spaces in real-time as they move throughout networked spaces. This is not idle speculation because the director of KM4CITY sees this as a realistic revenue stream for authorities, although he also says 'the user must be capable of deciding what data to leave'. I asked if this was opt-in or opt-out but the answer was unclear (my Italian is poor and my interviewee's English was less than perfect). Nevertheless, he says 'It is a trade-off, you have to agree. If I want a book from Amazon I have to give them my behaviour so they can recommend a better book' and 'This is not a big problem, but it will become more aggressive in coming years'.

Algocracy: feeding emotion into policy

Another question that needs to be answered is whether data about citizen feelings, moods and emotions inform policy. Do policy-makers simply cherry-pick the feedback that serves their interests and quietly ignore feedback that is difficult or controversial? Citizens may give direct feedback through city apps, social media and e-mail, and data generated through passive tracking of infrastructure and services. Yet do decision-makers simply select elements of the data to justify policies that they have already implemented or want to implement? The aforementioned director of KM4CITY told me that data is not used by the top political strata of the city, but by those at the municipal level just below the political level. He explains that these are the people technically responsible for Florence – rather than the elected officials. This leads him to argue that data *is* directly acted upon. In November 2016 I also spoke with representatives from Siemens. Among other services, they provide policy-makers and municipal authorities with easy-to-understand dashboards of real-time data about their cities. This gives an overview of how the city infrastructure is coping and whether the authorities are on course to meet their targets.

Indeed, the dashboards themselves should not be overlooked. These are subject to testing to understand the mental effort required by a user. For example, Deloitte customise their dashboards to their client. This includes the specifics of their business or municipal department, and their cognitive capacities (such as the ability to read and process charts, models and displays of data). User experience of dashboards is tested by implicit reactions (i.e. no self-reporting), galvanic skin responses, eye-tracking and facial coding of emotional reactions to dashboard screen interfaces (Deloitte, 2013).

Siemens' dashboards not only model incoming data, but they also offer a means of modelling the *impact* of municipal decisions. Although the city-as-ecosystem is an arguably over-used metaphor, it becomes quite real when considering the knock-on effects of decisions. For example, while there may be a political and citizen motivation to target and reduce air pollution, if the authorities simply ban cars, this has an impact on how to provide public transport and what to do with city car parks that are no longer needed. What Siemens offer is a means of algorithmically displaying the outcomes of what-if scenarios on the basis of sensors, and passive and active citizen feedback (the latter gained from social media posting and city apps).

Given the capacity to model the impact of decisions, I asked a representative of Siemens 'Who would you trust more to make a citizen-centric decision: a roomful of politicians or an AI that has learned through machine learning what a citizen and city needs?'. His reply was 'In all honesty, the machine'. The take-home point here is that a high-level employee developing contextually-aware decision-making agents suggests that an *algocracy* is better able to serve the needs of citizens than politicians (Aneesh, 2006). However, it would be remiss to leave the point at that. The context of the conversation was not one where my interviewee seriously suggested abandoning the role of politicians, but it was one based on having faith in the data and efficiencies of automation, and that in many cases algorithms would demonstrate significantly better judgment than people. On the extent to which decision-makers actually listen to advice from machines, the answer from Siemens has two parts: that 'it depends on which policy-makers and at what level', and that 'it differs between region'.

The context of algocracies, or where algorithms guide political rule and decision-making, is old. It connects with the logic of cybernetics, the science of feedback, maintenance of norms, homeostasis and self-regulating systems (Ashby, 1956; Beniger, 1986). As with cybernetics, algocracies require goals. In the context of politics this involves 'desired outcomes' and agreed aims (O'Reilly, 2013). On the face of things a drive towards socially positive outcomes is a good thing. Health, safety, fairness, education, happiness and citizen wellbeing are not controversial. The problem is that algorithmic regulation promises to achieve these goals without debate and clashes of worldviews. This is a form of governance in which *how* we do politics is worryingly deteriorating. The idea of a dispassionate 'Great Machine' that is not susceptible to feeling-into party politics, voter baiting, confirmation bias and granting caveats to external lobbying influences has some immediate appeal, but it is not realisable. This is because politics cannot be transcended. Even if turned over to a Great Machine, this has either been programmed with, or has learned, a set of values by which it makes decisions – just as is the case with human bureaucracies and political parties. Ultimately, there is no 'outside' of politics. Moreover, we should be sceptical of decision-making processes and systems that are closed to public inspection.

Measuring Happiness: Smart Dubai

So far we have touched upon some of the key issues surrounding so-called smart cities. These include questions of feedback, sentiment, governance and the somewhat utopian parcel wrapping that smart cities are presented in. Dubai is a city in the United Arab Emirates (UAE) that has taken the rhetoric of smart cities seriously. Indeed, as accounted for below, they also build them for others. A key interest of Dubai is to use sensors, analytics and empathic media to understand feelings and emotions to promote happiness. As we know, emotions can be tracked by means of what people do and how they behave, by tracking online sentiment, and through use of psycho-physiological measures. Use of these approaches tells city analysts how residents, visitors, daily commuters and tourists alike feel about municipal matters. Use of emotion-sensitive technologies at a city level is increasing as Dubai and other cities around the world vie to be seen as happy cities – ostensibly to attract talent and investment. Martin Ostrovsky of Repustate, a Canada-based sentiment analysis company, also recognises this picture, observing interest in the use of affect and mood-sensitive technologies to discern the emotional understanding of cities. Important too, he notes that while there is a great deal of industrial conversation about sentiment and smart cities, the most tangible implementations are taking place where Westerners might not expect them. He gives the examples of the Middle East and Asia where Repustate sees 'a lot of engagement from ministries to data-mine and react to citizens to see what people think about specific laws'. He also gives the example of Singapore where they work with the Ministry of Information and Ministry of Public Education. He adds, 'We don't see that much in North America and Europe. I don't know why, but it very much is a thing in those other countries'.

The exemplar effort to track and measure happiness is Dubai. In addition to use of emotion tracking to feel-into the city, at the time of writing it has gone furthest in bringing together the various strands of smart city initiatives. Dubai is also significant because Dubai Holding, an investment company, is signing deals and building smart cities in Lagos (Nigeria), Kochi (India), Malta (Europe) and South Korea. In Dubai itself, the interest in tracking emotions in cities fits within a wider initiative branded Smart Dubai. The objective of this is to digitise its public services. This is championed by its political elites, not least the Ruler of Dubai, Sheikh Mohammad Bin Rashid Al Maktoum, who is also Vice-President and Prime Minister of the UAE. On Twitter he reflects the practical nature of Smart Dubai when he states 'National happiness isn't a wish. Plans, projects, programs, indices will inform the work of our ministries to achieve happiness'.[1] For Dubai, their happiness agenda 'is a globally unique, science-based approach to measuring and impacting people's happiness, fuelling the city's transformation' (Smart Dubai, 2016). Smart Dubai is part of a series of major reforms in the UAE's government strategy to make the UAE 'One of the best countries in the world' by 2021. Since February 2016 the UAE has had a Minister of State for Happiness, Ohood bint Khalfan Al Roumi, who I also met briefly in the course of researching this book.

In 2016 I attended the GITEX Technology Week (16–20 October) in Dubai, where I had an opportunity to meet and interview a range of people working on smart city initiatives. Speaking with one of the architects of the happiness agenda within Smart Dubai, he tells me that the UK and the West in general are not seen as competitors to Dubai. This is curious because European cities lead the Happiness Index. (In 2017 Norway retook the title of 'world's happiest country', beating Denmark into second place. Both were followed by Iceland, Switzerland and Finland.) Echoing the earlier interviewee from KM4CITY, the Smart Dubai architect likened it to Amazon's platform in that incoming data from multiple sources is used to make recommendations about policy, infrastructure and investment. Where non-sensitive, the data is made open across all components of Smart Dubai in the form of dashboards and key performance indicators. This grants those charged with executive decision-making a real-time overview of the state of the city. He added that use of sensors in the city and centralisation of this information will improve customers' transit experience (such as cars or public transport) and thereby happiness. Thus, by providing passive and direct feedback to Smart Dubai by sensors, social media and city apps, they claim to be able to record, respond to and increase the overall happiness quotient through more efficient services.

Centralisation: the city-as-platform and the Data Law

The principle behind Smart Dubai is that it is a centralised monitoring and management layer to understand all goings-on in the city. Devistat provides Smart Dubai with its 'dashboard solution' that allows real-time and retrospective modelling of how the city is functioning and how people feel. It also predicts issues and problems. A representative from Devistat I spoke with gave travel as an example in that they can use sensors to track busy roads and emergent parking difficulties, and although a problem might not yet exist, they can detect that one might arise and take pre-emptive measures (thereby raising infrastructural happiness). This means that past as well as real-time data can be used to understand all dimensions of Dubai. This entails not only all areas of public policy and spending (such as education, roads, health, policing, transport and borders), but also citizens' reported sentiment within Dubai in the form of complaints, citizen feedback, spending, location tracking, health records, and use of sentiment analysis.

There are multiple access levels: open to all citizens, shared (mild restrictions), confidential, sensitive and secret. The belief is that when 'data silos' are open to authorities, services can be run more efficiently and new forms of value can be extracted from open data. When asked how comfortable he is with this, my interviewee said 'Why not, if it's useful? *If* [emphasis stressed] you get a better service or easier life, why not give your data or information?'. He followed this by also saying that they are developing another project connecting businesses with the public whereby use of the city app on their phones can be used to receive adverts and discounts. There is a range of socio-technological discourses feeding into Smart Dubai and their endeavours to surveil and centralise information. These include 'big data', or the intention to maximise the variety, volume and velocity of data to identify patterns and react quickly (Laney, 2001). Smart Dubai itself also speaks of 'rich data' – or that which helps deal with 'why' questions. Another is platform logic: here the city is digitally and physically a 'walled garden', in that the platform provider has control over the applications, content and media that are carried on its infrastructure (Gillespie, 2010). The city app in this case is the software upon which significant elements of everyday life are carried out. With advertising interests added, this sees citizens subjected to commodity logic.

For Smart Dubai, the city-as-platform has the following structure: 1) infrastructure layer (city IoT, sensors and city data sources); 2) data orchestration layer (data ingestion, storage and transformation); 3) services enablement layer (security data governance, payment, location and platform-as-service); and finally 4) the application layer (personal dashboards, district data dashboards, applications, a unified control centre and city open data dashboard). Reminiscent of the Internet Protocol stack, Smart Dubai begins with the fundamentals of networks and ends in applications that users can see (Smart Dubai, 2015).

For the city-as-platform to work, legal structures need to be in place to facilitate this open data structure. In the case of Dubai, access to diverse information sources is made possible through the Dubai Data Law (The Supreme Legislation Committee in the Emirate of Dubai, 2016). This has been in force since 27 December 2015. More formerly known as 'Law No. (26) of 2015 Regulating Data Dissemination and Exchange in the Emirate of Dubai', the aim for this is clearly stated in Article 4(1) which says that this law serves to 'enable the fulfilment of the Emirate's vision of turning Dubai into a Smart City'. The law achieves this through the language of integration, synergy, optimisation, transparency, dissemination, exchange, speed, competitiveness, streamlining, support of decision-making processes, creativity, welfare and community.

Dubai does this by effectively claiming ownership of 'any data related to the Emirate of Dubai and available to data providers' (Article 3(3)). As is often the case with legislation, socially significant points are buried in its dry language. In this case 'data providers' could mean anything from individuals to establishments and companies who would be required to grant access to the city because the data has been deemed an asset to Dubai. This means they are unable to delete or dispose of data, as they will be required to classify sets as 'open' or 'shared'. This is echoed in Article 4(11), which highlights that data can be provided to 'non-government entities with a view to supporting the development and economic plans of the Emirate', although Article 4(10) says that this is to be balanced with confidentiality and privacy. Taking this at face value, the problem is that while individual elements of data might not identify a person, when data from different sources are correlated the scope for identification is significantly increased. Also, as further evidence of the Amazon-like platform logic, what is immediately notable about the privacy discussion is that citizens are presented as customers, and on reading the law in full there is no mention at all of the word 'citizen' or rights in relation to citizens. Indeed, given that its political system is a constitutional federation (and each of its emirates have dynastic rule) there is not even a mention of people as subjects. Instead, in this important piece of legislation for a state that would be a template for smart cities around the world, people are constituted as consumers.

In addition to the said data, data providers are required to hand over *all* information about how their systems work, including all security (and privacy) protocols (Article 10). Furthermore, the only entities to have rights are intellectual property owners. This is expressed in Article 9 but so far it is unclear what this might mean in practice, and while this *may* provide organisations some protection it does nothing for residents and visitors to Dubai. And while Article 13 mentions privacy, this should be understood in relation to the fact that residents and visitors do not have privacy rights anything like those that have been legislated for in Europe. Notably, there is no data protection regulator.

However, the UAE constitution grants a general right to liberty for citizens under the UAE Constitution (Federal National Council, 2010). Article 26 says a person may not be arrested, searched, detained or imprisoned except in accordance with the provisions of the law. Article 31 of the Constitution also provides for a general right of 'freedom of corresponding through the post, telegraph or other means of communication and the secrecy thereof shall be guaranteed in accordance with the law'. Although this broadly entails an individual's general right to privacy (although the word is not mentioned), that right is limited to citizens of the UAE. This is a very small percentage of the population living in the UAE (around 8 to 12 per cent of the total population). While these constitutional qualifications are important, they do not apply to what in Europe and elsewhere we would term 'personal data'. Indeed, any notion of control or ownership of personal data (sensitive or otherwise) is lost on identification of the fact that according to Article 15 of the Dubai Data law, 'Dubai Data is deemed to form part of the assets of Dubai Government'.

In sum, the city-as-platform is technical, industrial, legal and political. It is also nothing less than the forced transparency of public and private life. On the chapter's core interest of feeling-into citizenry, surveillance and use of data about emotions, the city-as-platform is pivotal. This is because the removal of separations between data silos is a core pillar of the campaign to detect emotion and civic mood and brand Dubai the happiest city on the planet.

Social engineering

The term 'social engineering' broadly means influencing attitudes and behaviours on a large scale to produce desired characteristics in a target population. It connects with definitions from the politics literature that sees social engineering as 'the designing and erecting of structures and processes in which human beings serve as the raw material' (Alexander and Schmidt, 1996: 1). What is characteristic of both general and specific definitions is that they reflect a grand vision for society. Applied to Smart Dubai, this is not innately bad (it is hard to argue that genuine happiness is undesirable), but the concern comes from the all-embracing nature of such visions and the close parallels with totalitarianism (which stems from the Latin word *totus*, or 'all-embracing'). Further, such social engineering initiatives tend to start off as utopian projects, which in turn require control over social life. The nature of control in the Smart Dubai context occurs through political processes, legislation, the application of commercial tracking technologies, empathic media, and as we will see, applied neuroscience. On speaking with a representative of Smart Dubai, he recognizes the social engineering critique, but explained that the intention is to create a happier society. He admits that steering residents to share data about themselves is social engineering, but challenged me to identify the problem with this, asking 'If society is happier, and if talent and investment flow into Dubai, where is the harm?'.

For the social engineering of happiness to occur, it first has to be quantified. This is done at both macro- and meso-levels. Macro-level dashboard-based appraisal is done through an assessment not only of infrastructure and public services, but also of complaints, citizen feedback and spending. At the meso-level in Dubai, 'the Happiness Agenda sets forth a series of programs designed to discover, influence and satisfy individuals' affective, basic, cognitive and deeper needs – the essential ingredients for happiness' (Smart Dubai, 2016). In addition to an assessment of the efficiency of city functioning, and spending patterns and commercial data, is the Happiness Meter. This is a real-time citywide sentiment capture engine. Data for this is obtained from physical stands, screen and web tools asking whether people feel satisfied, neutral or dissatisfied with either a public or commercial service.

More granular analysis is done through in-house EEG tracking and assessment of skin responses to gauge how people feel about given propositions. The representative of Smart Dubai I spoke with explained that EEG skullcaps (provided by Emotiv) and finger monitors that measure galvanic skin responses are used to detect emotions. Pre-empting the spectre of lie detection, he says this is not how it is intended: the idea is to truly understand how people feel about the city, policies and its infrastructure to measure happiness. The context for this is (again) the disavowal of self-reporting common to nearly all proponents of empathic media, which is based on the belief that what a person says and what they actually do are often at odds with one another (McLure et al., 2004; Satel and Lilienfeld, 2013).

Bentham's Happiness Economics with a Twist

As discussed in Chapter 2, for Bentham and his forerunners, happiness is core to how a society should be run. It is based on the idea of a common good that eschews self-realisation in favour of social policy based on a common goal and a common good: happiness. Bentham's task was answering how to make happiness transparent so that policy-makers would make decisions that promoted overall net happiness. His solution, the utilitarian doctrine, is implicitly fundamental to the Smart Dubai enterprise. The intention is clear: to use modern data collection techniques about happiness and emotion, remove any barriers that impede this goal, and then use these insights to inform evidence-based policy-making. Smart Dubai takes it's cue from Richard Layard's (2005) *Happiness* that sees it as uncomplicated. There is a spectrum of either happy or not: there is no sophisticated bittersweet happiness, but simply happy through to unhappy. Furthermore, it is expressed in purely physical and neuroscientific terms. This means there is no qualitative difference between the happiness that comes from reading highbrow Greek literature and that which is felt from eating pizza.[2]

A little thing called democracy
As Bentham depicts and Layard updates, happiness economics and policy-making is, in theory, based on a citizenry that have equal rights. Each person should have an equal right to attain happiness and each person's happiness should count equally. Happiness through the principle of utility is a teleological moral philosophy that, in essence, means trying to make the world better for the greatest amount of people possible. There is simultaneously brutality and beauty in its simplicity. Irrespective of the particular individuals in question, it seeks to maximise societal happiness and reduce suffering. This is achieved by ensuring laws and policies are based on the doctrine of utility: to simultaneously produce happiness and reduce unhappiness. Layard's (2005) book *Happiness* is an important one in that it is was recommended to me by my Smart Dubai contact as *the* book to read on the topic. In his book Layard points to the need for neuroscience, sociology, economics and philosophy to all play their part in encouraging happiness, but to this list we can add empathic media. The capacity to sense, track and analyse a spectrum of emotions adds depth to the Smart Dubai initiative.

Despite numerous mentions of the American Declaration of Independence, Layard makes a curious claim in his book when he says that 'there is more to life than prosperity and freedom' (2005: 7). In relation to prosperity this is relatively uncontroversial (many are not rich yet are quite happy with life), but the freedom dimension causes one to pause, particularly when one considers that the most famous sentence of the Declaration says 'We hold these truths to be self-evident, that all men are created equal, that they are endowed by their Creator with certain unalienable Rights, that among these are Life, Liberty and the pursuit of Happiness'. This does not easily apply to Dubai that is both an autocratic society ruled by the Al Maktoum family and a state in which migrant workers are heavily exploited. This is the foreign underclass from South East Asia that built the city, and are visible during the day in their blue uniforms and at night getting on buses that remove them from the city. Human rights organisations such as Human Rights Watch argue that many of the 250,000 foreign labourers for the city live in inhumane conditions, and are prone to abuse because they do not have the minimal protection afforded by the UAE's labour laws. Layard, and indirectly Bentham, are clear on this: happiness means the removal of misery as well as the promotion of happiness. Indeed Layard (2005: 231) says that it is morally right to give extra weight to removing misery, and elsewhere he links happiness to compassion. It is clear then that Dubai does not consider the foreign workers who build its cities as having the same rights to happiness. It is not the aim of this chapter to list the various practices that would be intolerable under Western standards (such as gross worker abuses, the criminality of sexual relations outside of marriage and the death penalty for homosexuality), but the political interest in happiness branding raises immediate questions: is one person's happiness the same as that of others; what of the malcontents; what of people who have different perspectives; and what of those who do not want to share intimate dimensions of themselves and take action to stop this?

Whereas most liberals will suggest that freedom, autonomy and health are paramount, Layard argues that these are 'instrumental goods' and a means of reaching happiness, which is the real objective. He states:

And that is why we are sometimes willing to sacrifice one of these goods for the sake of another. To provide security on the streets, we lock up criminals (balancing the autonomy of the citizen against the freedom of the criminal). To reduce illiteracy, we levy taxes (balancing accomplishment against economic freedom). (2005: 113)

What he does not say is how much liberty he is willing to exchange to obtain maximum security and thereafter happiness. One begins to see how Layard's work has been embraced by Smart Dubai: by prioritising happiness over freedom, and arguing that security leads to happiness, this provides sufficient license (if it were required) to instigate practices that would not be possible in societies that put freedom before happiness. One sees this elsewhere in Layard (2005: 145) where he argues that public policy is mistakenly dominated by an understanding of people as self-determining agents. Instead he argues this needs to be combined with knowledge from other social sciences. His point is that a model of citizenry based on human rationality alone does not best deliver a good society, but rather that quantified happiness should be the goal of policy. Societal happiness is clearly a good thing if reached, but one can also see the appeal for an autocratic government: the agenda has a convenient singularity of purpose and vision.

Politics of Happiness: Beyond Dubai and Bentham

Having spoken with people from Smart Dubai who have so extensively implemented tracking of infrastructure, public services and citizenry with the expressed aim of increasing happiness, I was keen to speak with representatives of other countries interested in happiness. In 2016 Denmark came top of the annual World Happiness Report to be declared the planet's most contented country. This is benchmarked according to factors such as equality, GDP per capita, social support, life expectancy, perceptions of corruption and freedom to make life choices.[3] This seemed a good place to start and I was able to interview Anne Vestergaard Andersen from Denmark's State of Green (views not representative of the organisation). This is a public–private partnership ostensibly designed to attract investment and promote Denmark as a brand that signifies it as a green economy. On being asked why Denmark is the happiest country in the world, she says 'I don't know why, but it's probably because of the welfare society, good gender equality, free education, healthcare and roads', and that 'we pay 40–60 per cent tax which provides a great safety net'. She also adds that they emphasise the need to balance work and other life activities, noting they have the lowest working hours in Europe: 'It's not prestigious to be a workaholic. It's not cool. To be cool you need to be a good mum, do sport, have a social network and travel' (Interview, 2016).

I was particularly interested in whether happiness extends in practice to all citizens, or whether the happiness levels of some groups are valued more than others. Although she highlighted that not everything is perfect (and we should keep in mind that Andersen is, to an extent, a brand manager for Denmark), her answers are noteworthy: social integration is a priority; ghettoisation is shunned on the basis that it does not serve society's long-term interests; they take a holistic approach to urban development; and the livability aspect is high on the political agenda. This includes many green areas, outdoor activities *in* the city, a clean harbour where people can swim and a good cycling infrastructure.

Although there is much work being done with sensors and the datafication of Denmark's environment (air quality, waste, bin usage, trees and more), Andersen was unable to speak about citizen analytics. However, citizens can post messages to the city on social media, although she does not know whether municipal agents are responsive. On policing, security and intelligence agencies' use of data about citizens, Andersen's colleague who joined the conversation said 'We have a general trust in authorities and neighbours' and that 'we trust our authorities are using our data well and not giving it to other parties'. In contrast to Dubai that promotes happiness as a result of police and security services, she says, 'I don't feel safe in Denmark down to police surveillance, but because of trust generally. I do trust the police would do their job, but it's not because of the police that I feel safe'. Andersen echoes this, saying that 'It's the most livable and very safe' and that 'there must be a link … I can leave my house without locking the door. There's a high level of trust. We don't expect lies or cons from our fellow people, it's a trust-based system – but not naïve'.

This suggests a utopia of sorts, but Andersen clarifies that 'politicians are hated, as in other countries', and that 'we have huge public budgets and there's always debates about how well money is spent, but we know they wouldn't be corrupt'. Most telling is emphasis on transparency, freedom of speech, and that at school from an early age 'we're educated to be critical, to teachers and to theorists, whereas in Sweden, for example, they are shy of conflict, but that's not so in Denmark. We can speak freely in Denmark and we feel very free generally'. I ask if people who are not affluent and in less well-off parts of society would agree with her, to which she answers 'No, but they are better off than other countries' poor. And they know they will be OK'.

Lightening Public Moods

As introduced in Chapter 8, the flâneur was a leitmotif and chronicler of Parisian modernity. In 19th-century Europe emergent city life was inextricably connected with innovation – not least the gas lighting of the city's boulevards. This served many practical functions in terms of visibility, combatting criminality and creating a feeling of security. It also profoundly altered the emotionality of urban space and buildings. Light is not simply functional or binary (on/off), but qualitatively contributes to human experience. When lighting flickers or is too bright, it is painfully noticeable, but when employed sensitively, it has subtle effects on our moods and practical benefits. In hospitals it helps patients to recover, but also night staff and nurses to keep their body clocks in line with daylight trajectory. Similarly, it can be tweaked and optimised to alter behaviour – such as calming children after playtime. Just as with home, school, hospital, retail, work, restaurant or airplane environments, we can also speak of lighting as a key enabler of the emotionality of cities. I explored this with a senior representative of Philips at the Smart Cities World Congress Barcelona (Interview, 2016).

For Philips, lighting does not simply illuminate or even evoke moods. The physical infrastructure of city lighting can also be used to measure pollution and sense noise, such as when children leave school, and low frequency noise when a truck comes along. My interviewee explains that whereas many aspects of smart cities are quite utilitarian (such as sensor-augmented traffic management, pothole awareness and disposal of rubbish before bins overflow), Philips think a lighting company has an emotional role in smart city infrastructure. Examples include making people feel more secure, improving their interaction with spaces (such as subways, parks and plazas), generating civic pride, heightening their aesthetic experience and assisting in the regeneration of public spaces. My interviewee continues, 'Philips thinks you can make people happy with lighting – that a well-lit space generates a joyous response. You can't get this with rubbish collection or sewerage', also adding 'When someone walks into a beautifully-lit space, they are uplifted, but they are often not aware that it is the technology and lighting that is generating this'.

This is reminiscent of the Heideggerian (2011 [1962]) phenomenology of moods and experience. His point is that moods are a way of being-in-the-world. They represent an attunement that characterises being-there and the disclosure of how and what things are. The practical significance of this is they also create new social vectors and behavioural possibilities. Again, I asked if this applies to less salubrious parts of towns, as well as the gentrified safer areas. The Philips interviewee says 'yes', claiming that lighting has contributed to urban regeneration and that areas that are made appealing through changes in ambience will attract people. She cites Newcastle (UK) and a range of cases in the Netherlands where lighting was used to renew and reenergise buildings, districts and urban spaces.[4] Eindhoven's Catharinaplein square for example had recently been refurbished, yet was failing to attract visitors or customers to local stores. This was attributed to a lack of atmosphere and being potentially unsafe through being poorly lit. New lighting where each LED could be individually controlled meant that the mood and ambience could be modulated according to day and season. The result was a quantifiable change in behaviour that recorded people returning to the city centre. This example from Philips (and there are many more on their website) serves to illustrate that we should be careful in simply seeing sensors, the engineering of emotion and increased control of elements of cities in negative terms. Rather, the question is the extent to which developments genuinely serve the needs, wants and welfare of its citizenry.

Pro-social psycho-geography

In 2016 I interviewed Salvatore Pepe, CEO of Mosaico Digitale, also at the Smart Cities World Congress in Barcelona. Mosaico Digitale's product is based on mosaic tiles that are capable of displaying digital images and patterns on walls and floors. While the product was interesting and I outline this below, what was more notable was Pepe's attitude to the culture of discussion of smart cities.[5] In general, for Pepe, the emotionality of cities is facilitated by good design. He cites Barcelona as a good example where once, in crossing the city, one would inevitably get stuck in traffic, but through public infrastructure developments, authorities created a street under the bridge without traffic lights (on the Gran Via de les Corts Catalanes, or known to locals as the Gran Via). By building a multi-levelled infrastructure and lowering car traffic, this allowed new public buildings, metro stations, paths and cycle lanes, plazas, playgrounds and green spaces.

As with the Philips lighting discussion above, infrastructure plays a fundamental role in the emotionality of space. For Pepe, 'people changed this via using their brains. Political attention was given to the problem. You must put soul, not just the technology. Technology already exists. We need humanity and love of the city and citizen', also adding that 'I saw an old person sitting on a bench reading the newspaper and pumping a machine with his foot – foot exercises. *This* is a smart city. The policy approach that drives the city is paramount' (Interview, 2016). Thus while smart city discourse is typically either utopian or one based on a surveillance dystopia, Pepe's attitude was a refreshingly citizens-first approach – perhaps one that recognised the soul of a city is not found in feedback loops, but in its messiness, surprise, unpredictability, idiosyncrasy, and an element of secrecy that separates citizens from the state. Indeed, this is reminiscent of Guy Debord's (1955) pro-social account of psycho-geography in which he urges attention to be paid to 'the precise laws and specific effects of the geographical environment, consciously organized or not, on the emotions and behavior of individuals'. Indeed, Debord sought to awaken the masses 'to the conditions that are imposed on them in all domains of life, and to the practical means of changing them'. In a modern context, Debord may have seen the potential for empathic media to be a critical method and means of resistance.

The point here is about understanding people's experience of urban spaces as a means to improve life for the many. This is in contrast to seeing sensors as an opportunity to construct 'cities-as-platforms' to mine the 'citizen-as-commodity'. On the question of emotion, surveillance and the city, Pepe says that it is not the existence of the data itself that is the problem, but the intentions of the policy-makers. He says 'If the policy-maker loves the citizen, then there is no problem. But if they want to control the citizen, then that is a problem'. Pepe's citizen-first approach is where the city is not just created *for* citizens (as with the Philips and Dubai examples), but to an extent *by* citizens. In contrast to techno- and municipal-determinism he points to both a resistive and aesthetic dimension. On the former, speaking of Taranto, the coastal city in Apulia, Italy, he says:

> In southern Italy there is a famous harbour dominated by a long-standing polluting company. People have developed cancer there. We put a sensor on the harbour that senses pollution and, through an app, immediately told the citizens once it was over a certain level. For the first time in fifty years, the people knew what the pollution was from this big company.

On aesthetics and civic life, he says:

> We can use technology and art to attract people and change the flow in a city. Art can change people's minds and perception, and can make people live better. Technology is not just for control and monitoring people and for the police. Control is bad for freedom. Technology can also deliver freedom. The city should go in the direction of freedom, services for the city, traffic management, beauty, such as citizen-centric wants, beauty, cleanliness, freedom. There are choices to be made.

I asked Pepe to elucidate on positive uses of technology and its creative potential as he offered a strikingly less sterile and surveillent account of smart cities to others present at the Smart Cities World Congress trade conference. He said 'Art and design for big data – you can attract people via art, not because of the sensors but because of the art, the beauty'. He continued, 'Without that people won't come for a coffee in a bad part of town like Mina. People move around the world in order to see art. Until now we had a one-to-one relationship between the artist and the artwork, such as a sculptor who creates a statue in a certain location'. Beginning to outline and market his own product (digital tiles that carry digital imagery that build to mosaic scales), he says 'Digital art changes this physical locative relationship … Now we can have thousands of lives changed with an app. It's a new opportunity'. One application of Pepe's tiles is to allow citizens to upload images to public digital displays through Pinterest: 'If people who hate the art want to destroy it, scratch it out, they can.' In addition to uploading and replacing imagery, citizens can download, share and comment on the work. Artists (or just enthusiasts), visitors and interested parties such as local authorities also know how many people interacted with the work. This leads Pepe to designate it as 'social art'. He also posits that 'with augmented reality, who knows what will happen in the future' – noting the capacity for AR to allow novel forms of informatising and understanding physical space.

Conclusion

It would have been easy to depict smart cities simply as assemblages employed for societal surveillance and control. Indeed, such accounts are not wrong – but they are incomplete. Both the rhetoric and material manifestations of smart cities have positive attributes, such as ecological improvements and enhanced experience of cities. Developing the idea of 'empathic cities', this chapter focused on the emotional dimension of increased sensing of public and private spaces. This is achieved by a mediation and quantification of feeling at macro- and meso-levels. Although this chapter has been critical of the city-as-platform, it has not rejected psycho-geography, or even the datafication of emotional life. Rather, its concern is about motivations that do not genuinely put citizens first or respect human rights. The scope to map, improve material space, raise wellbeing for poor as well as wealthy citizens, emotionally annotate city features, leave biometric markers of experience, tell stories, enrich and co-create citizen-led digital emotional art is possible. All of these provide positive uses of psycho-geographic sensing technology. This is a city that invites us to feel good.

Notes

1   Available from https://twitter.com/HHShkMohd/status/697434334563852290
2   Interestingly, J.S. Mill (1962 [1859]), Bentham's protégé, debated this point when he argued that people have faculties more elevated than those derived from sensation.
3   It is notable too that the runners-up include countries from the same region, namely Switzerland, Iceland, Norway and Finland.
4   Multiple case studies are available at www.lighting.philips.co.uk/cases/cases#page=1
5   Although Pepe is Italian the interview was conducted in English, and while his English was good, some of the expression was unusual (although Pepe has read and agreed the transcript notes).

11

POLITICS OF FEELING MACHINES: DEBATING DE-IDENTIFICATION AND DIGNITY

This book is of a critical disposition, but it does not argue that novel modes of human–machine interaction should be forbidden, nor that media content that makes use of insight into emotions be prohibited. Instead it sees potential benefits for people in terms of novel experiences, valuable learning, ease of interaction with technology and health. However, this should be balanced with recognition that there is something fundamentally important about emotional life and its centrality to human experience. We should also remember that what is in hand is not simply our web browsing history and online searches (important as these are), but the body itself. Any neo-behaviourist proposal to render human physiology and emotional life 'machine-readable' needs to be treated with caution. The task for all stakeholders is to find appropriate means of living with emotion-capture technologies in a way that respects the dignity of human life, rather than approaches that treat people as emotional animals to be biomedically mapped and manipulated. To reach suggestions about how this can be achieved, this chapter investigates the ethics of emotion detection technologies, but I pay specific attention to processes based on techniques that *do not* make use of personal data.

By 'personal' I refer to the legal sense of the word whereby a person is either identifiable or singled-out in some way for differential treatment. The reason why this matters is because while personal data and sensitive data (which is personal but with extra consequences if misused) are subject to data protections, non-personal data is typically not – even if it involves emotions and intimate information. Phrased otherwise, the question is this: is it acceptable for an organisation to passively collect, process and gain value from data about human emotions when that information is not legally personal? This is important because non-identifying usage underpins many of the applications of empathic media and emotional AI discussed in this book. To begin to answer this, I delineate industry, policy and citizen perspectives on non-identifying emotion capture. The first two sets of insights derive from interviews, and the third from a UK survey I carried out with ICM Unlimited to identify UK attitudes to the possibilities of empathic media in situations and technologies they are familiar with. Armed with these insights I progress to consider the ethical factors of using non-personal data about emotions, paying particular attention to classical liberalism, pragmatism, questions of the body, and factors unforeseen by individual organisations developing empathic media. I conclude with tangible suggestions about how to manage this situation at a regulatory level.

Industry Perspectives

Many technologies, developers and end-user organisations extract value from data about emotions on the basis that it can be done without identifying people. Although I primarily have economic value in mind, this principle applies to policing, surveillance, workplaces and cities, which entail understanding group emotions for specified ends. This is a paradigm shift from what once appeared to be an inexorable tendency towards personalisation, identification and audiences of one. Non-identifying data is useful to organisations because (foremost in an advertising and marketing context) a message does not need to directly address a person to resonate, but it does need to be targeted at a profile that is *like* a person. This means that the communication can feel relevant, meaningful and direct without the communicator actually aiming a message at a particular person. The task for organisations using emotion-sensing technologies is to find the smallest possible groups without possibility of identification, or separating out an individual from a group for unique treatment. Related are uses, such as within cities, retail or the workplace, where the analyst seeks to understand reactions to given prompts and general *overall emotion* (whether this be annoyance, pleasure or stress).

A key reason that underpins small-group targeting is that organisations seek to stave off regulation. This point emerged in my discussion with John Taysom, a founder and angel investor in a wide range of technology start-ups in the UK and US (Interview, 2015). On data that is identifiable, he says this is 'toxic' because it requires data managers to treat it differently and pay extra care to it when it provides no functional benefit. His logic, along with that of other industry figures I spoke with, is that commercial value can be leveraged with no harm to the individual. The question for this chapter is whether this is correct in relation to empathic media: does passive use of non-identifying data about emotions equate to being privacy-friendly? On this issue, an interviewee from Facebook who preferred anonymity said that the moral question of emotion detection is 'whether it is done *for* people or done *to* people', also posing the question 'are people in control ... am I in control?' (Interview, 2016). There is irony here in that Facebook is routinely accused of unclear consent mechanisms and opaque terms and conditions, and of capturing and manipulating moods without users being aware of their experiments (see Chapter 3). What is valuable to take away is that individuals in positions of influence believe that user-centred control is a good baseline and the right thing to do.

Moving from the level of philosophical principle to personal devices, inter- viewees from the wearables sector and those developing emotion-enhanced applications for mobile phones (such as mood self-trackers) said the only way to ensure user control is through device-level processing. This recommendation contrasts with services where analysis of biometric data for indication of emo- tion takes place on a computer other than a person's own devices (or when it is shared with 'the cloud'). This closely aligns with the issue of proximity. This has two dimensions in that for IoT and wearable devices to work properly, it is preferable to put as much intelligence as close to the device as possible because of latency. This is a technical and functional matter, but it has another dimension: users should be sceptical of retaining meaningful control over data when it is processed in the cloud and away from a person's own device. The significance of this is that the possibility of privacy-by-design in emotion-based technolo- gies is raised when processing takes place on a person's device, and decreased when not. Thus, when considering use of emotion capture to enhance device or content interaction, it is preferable that processing takes place locally to avoid an after-market in data about emotions (whether this be advertising, insurance, data brokerage, human resources, workplace surveillance measurement, or use by police and intelligence agencies).

While all interviewees agreed that high levels of consent are required when data about emotions may be linked with identifiable information, many were less strident about non-personal data. For example, Gabi Zijderveld of the facial cod- ing company Affectiva recommended that:

> The opt-in should always be there. So if I'm using an app or walking in the store, there should always be a way for me to get out of having *my face recorded.* There should always be the option to turn the cam- era off. *The data should always remain anonymous.* (Interview, 2016; emphasis added)

The reason for that emphasis is that Affectiva's products are often used in a way that people do not have a choice about. For example, working with the retail ana- lytics firm Cloverleaf, shelf-level cameras recognise emotions in faces. The face itself is not recorded, but instead the relevant action units are detected and logged. Even companies such as the emotion-based market research firm Sensum, that have meaningfully engaged in public discussion about the ethics of empathic media and emotion-capture technologies (we have co-hosted events), paused on the question of regulating and controlling use of non-identifying data about emotions. On being asked about whether legal controls are required, Sensum's CEO Gawain Morrison says:

> Yes, for trial cases kicking it off … to make people feel comfortable that there is a duty of care. If we jump straight in, there will be a PR backlash. We need a stepping-stone, testing and rolling it out, opening it up for feedback. (Interview, 2016)

The industrial assumption is that emotion capture in public spaces can be made acceptable, but that citizens need to be familiarised with the practice. Although Morrison expresses the socialisation theme well, it occurred in other interviews too. The 'PR backlash' is also important because this reflects a concern that it will not only be citizens who will reject emotion capture in public spaces, but advertisers and clients too. In an interview in 2016, Kim Smouter of the World Association for Market, Social and Opinion Research (ESOMAR) said that for emotion detection in a market research context to scale, this requires careful management not only of 'prior notification, but also expectations and willingness to share'. For Smouter there is a social inevitability because 'emotion recognition is a natural conclusion' and 'the Holy Grail [for marketers] is real-time information about customer needs and emotions', although he too adds that application of emotion-sensitive technologies should be done *with* rather than *at* people.

Other industry representatives highlight that although they care about morals and ethics, at the time of creating products and attempting to win investor funding, the full consequences of innovations are not considered. In 2016, Jesse Robbins of Orion (who makes a voice-based wearable) says: 'It's complicated. You don't hold global policy implications in your head when you decide to build a device.' Speaking in reference to the 2013 Snowden leaks, that involved intelligence agencies using telecommunications corporations' platforms to surveil citizens, Robbins' comments illustrate that ethical decisions about product development should be seen in terms of the pressure to develop effective services, competition and functioning technology. Jane Frost of the Market Research Society (an organisation that regulates and advises marketers) makes a related point, saying we should be mindful 'of the geek who wants to do it because they can', and also adding that 'just because they can – it doesn't mean they should' (Interview, 2016). She continued by pointing out that 'in the rush to do it' we should not only ask 'should we do it?', but also subscribe to the 'cock-up, not conspiracy thesis' in that harms are brought about by 'ordinary people doing things they shouldn't'.

Identification

What the passages above tell us is that there is keen interest in using emotion-capture techniques, and while the industry recognises qualms about linking data about emotions with personal data, it sees little problem with non-personal data about emotions. To clarify what personal data is, the Article 29 Working Party (a group of representatives from the data protection authority of each EU Member State) states that 'a person can be considered identifiable when, within a group of persons, they can be distinguished from others and consequently be treated differently' (2015: 5). This includes recognition of a person, but also means that a person can be said to receive individual treatment even if they are not recognised in the sense that we usually understand the term. This is because a person may be singled out for special treatment through a unique code, string, mark or identifier that distinguishes a specific unit from a group. Recital 26 of the General Data Protection Regulation (GDPR) advances this when it says:

> The principles of data protection should therefore not apply to anonymous information, namely information which does not relate to an identified or identifiable natural person or to personal data rendered anonymous in such a manner that the data subject is not or no longer identifiable. This Regulation does not therefore concern the processing of such anonymous information, including for statistical or research purposes.

This means that if the empathic media practice does not involve information that connects in some way with an 'identified or identifiable natural person', then data protection regulations do not apply – nor does regulation of sensitive personal data, because although data about the body and emotions is sensitive, it is not necessarily personal. Paradoxically, the regulations on identifiying biometric data are stringent, as evidenced in Article 9(1). This says that biometric data should not be used to uniquely identify a person or data concerning health or sex life and sexual orientation. If this information is required, consent is of a higher level, demanding explicit consent. A customary way of meeting this standard is by ticking an unchecked tick box.[1]

The explicit form of consent applies to data listed in Article 9(1) that reveal 'racial or ethnic origin, political opinions, religious or philosophical beliefs, or trade-union membership, and the processing of genetic data, biometric data for the purpose of uniquely identifying a natural person, data concerning health or data concerning a natural person's sex life or sexual orientation'. The test, then, of whether a person is identifiable or not is whether any of the following questions are answered in the affirmative: is a person identifiable from the data; is a code attributed to a person; is the person singled out in some way, even if this 'singling' cannot be obviously linked back to a real living person? If not, data protection rules do not apply and organisations are free to use biometric and emotion-capture technologies without regulation. However, as GDPR takes root, case law develops and emotion detection becomes more widespread, one can envision interesting cases being brought. Non-identifying emotion capture is legal territory that has not been explored in case law, nor have other relevant areas of law been applied, such as health and safety law (in workplaces) or consumer protection law that addresses deceptive and abusive practices.

For example, in being interviewed in 2016 about out-of-home emotion-enhanced advertising that is said not to identify a person, Ashley Roughton from the law firm Nabarro made a noteworthy counter-argument. He reasoned that if only one person had waited for a bus during a given period, then the data used to feed the emotion-sensitive out-of-home billboard advert at the bus-stop is unique and therefore under the remit of data protection regulations. Recognising that this is somewhat hypothetical (but not impossible), he also argued that 'consent is always required because identification is always possible'. This reflects understanding among privacy specialists that recognises anonymisation is a fraught issue (Ohm, 2009; Kaye, 2015; McStay, 2017). The issue is that while a handful of data points might not identify a person, people can always be identified when enough data is combined with the original data (in our case data about emotions).[2] This is known as the jigsaw or mosaic argument.

Roughton says that while some countries such as the UK may have a more laissez-faire interpretation of European data protection regulations, their law firm (Nabarro) needs to ensure that business activities will not fall foul of tougher data protection enforcement in countries such as Germany. In general, any business working in this area needs Europe-wide consent. However, my interview with an anonymous senior member of the Directorate General for Communications Networks (DG Connect) of the European Commission disagreed, saying:

> Even under the hypothetical condition that only one person has been scanned [by means of grid points assigned to a person's facial features that move as a person changes emotional expression], if the data does not provide enough information for it to identify a person it may be legal, without the need for consent. (Interview, 2016)

Further, she added that publishers who own poster sites, who would naturally be interested in collecting data to know how their poster site is performing, would not be breaking the law. We also discussed retail possibilities where I explained camera-enabled in-store screens that track people for their gender, age, emotion and eye movements. These are used to track the attention given to different elements of a screen, to understand brand preferences, store names, goods and other elements of an interactive display. She says that although this begins to move closer to constituting personal data, the principle remains the same. The information is legally not personal data if no picture is taken and the information cannot be used to search other databases (such as images collected from social media sites where people post photos). To ensure no ambiguity, we concluded by underlining the fact that in reference to out-of home-advertising that scans faces, assigns pixels to facial features, and infers emotions, it is legal if:

1. no personally identifiable information is collected – this means that no code is generated about an individual that either temporarily or permanently identifies a person and no photo is taken/stored;
2. no data about a person's facial expression can be used to search other databases, for example data from Instagram posts or fire hose data of images from other social media/self-publishing sites.

At the time of meeting in 2016, we both agreed that if facial coding technologies do become widely used by advertisers and marketers, this is not something the GDPR has envisaged. The result is a regulatory gap about data that is intimate (emotions), but not necessarily personal. This applies in other contexts too: in the UK, for example, the Information Commissioner's Office (2012) states that data protection codes for workplaces are built on the premise of identifiability. Thus, although workers have both legitimate expectations to keep their personal lives private and are entitled to some privacy in the work environment, data protection only applies when data about a person either identify them or single them out in some way. If the data is demonstrably aggregated, it is legally arguable that it falls outside of the codes' strictures. One might argue that mental and physical health data has special provision, but while true, this is again premised on being able to link this sensitive information with an individual and data deemed to be personal. In general, the UK codes consistently suggest that employers anonymise data, and that if they do so the employer is legally compliant because the data protection rules do not apply.

Lack of Suitable Legislation

On outlining the key features of empathic media for Gus Hosein, Executive Director of Privacy International, Hosein (speaking of his own views rather than those of the organisation) recognised that 'we don't have the legal frameworks' to deal with this. On ethics and emotion detection that does not make use of personal data, he said that 'it is still taking something from me … it is still interacting with me … it is interfacing without my say-so'. The key factor here is 'control' and a 'say on outcomes' and processes (Interview, 2015). Other NGOs made similar points: for Jeremy Gillula of the Electronic Frontier Foundation 'there should also be an opt-out mechanism' and 'people should have a choice about this'. On advertising itself, without my prompting, Gillula said that, while it would look creepy, advertising would probably be the first driver of a wide adoption of affective computing in public spaces. However, he was less concerned than other NGO groups about the use of non-personal data about emotions, saying 'it's harder to make the case that there's significant harm if you can't trace back to a person'. His next point is an important one: that law enforcers might say 'everyone's fine with sensors everywhere, so we're going to deploy our own too'. There is a precedent for this in an online context, as the US National Security Agency (NSA) via its XKeyscore surveillance program piggy-backed on advertisers' tracking cookies to trace information such as names, dates of birth, where people live, occupation, the sites they have visited, what they searched for, and their interests (The Intercept, 2015).

An interviewee from the ethical hacking community was sceptical about claims that facial data collected by cameras could be processed and discarded in a way that renders the data non-personal. Jamie Woodruff, a world-renowned ethical hacker from the UK, says 'From my ethics perspective, when you scan a face you scan not just the emotions but features. How does the data get stored?'. This means that increased cameras in public spaces are essentially surveillance devices used to understand not only emotions, but also personal profiles. Woodruff cites Trapwire, a system that came to prominence in 2012 when Wikileaks released a bulk load of leaked emails. TrapWire works by collecting data from security cameras at potential terrorist targets and analysing that data for patterns that indicate planning for a terrorist attack or other criminal activity. In essence this automates the role of a human surveillance camera operator. For Woodruff, he sees a clear connection between cameras used in out-of-home interactive advertising (whether emotionally enabled or not) and the extension of surveillance.

On the use of non-personal data and empathic media at live events using facial coding and voice detection (as used at the Wimbledon tennis championship in 2015), Becky Kiely from F-Secure (a data security company that sponsors campaigns for digital rights) says people must be able to decline or opt-out. She adds, 'if attending a sporting event that cost £100, a person cannot be reasonably expected to leave the event where facial coding is taking place' (Interview, 2016). This contrasts with retail examples where one might decline to enter a store without significant penalty. In the context of IoT and sensors placed in environments to track people through location and facial expressions, she says that 'start-ups are rushing to develop products, but are not paying enough attention to security' and that 'security is just not a priority'. Jim Killock and Javier Ruiz from Open Rights Group (ORG) made similar points. ORG are not currently campaigning on emotion detection issues. Nevertheless, they compared these anonymisation claims to those encountered from defenders of the UK's governmental bulk data collection of citizens' digital communications.

On the use of emotion detection when matched with identifiable data, Killock made an interesting point about 'legitimate services'. He said that there is potentially an argument to be made for emotion detection and first-party relationships with services and vendors. This is a notable point that aligns with Hosein's above, in that Killock finds emotion detection in first-party relationships acceptable (but not re-selling and sharing with after-market third-party trackers). In summary, the NGO data protection community is certainly wary of non-identifying emotion capture techniques and third-party data trading, but they are not completely against emotion detection. Rather, with varying degrees of emphasis, they insist on awareness and consent – even if the data is not personal. We might note at this point that industry as well as the NGO community has highlighted a control-based approach to empathic media. Although I expected a more critical response from the NGO community to the 'creepy' notion of emotion detection, instead they were broadly accepting on the basis that it enhances first-party relationships and that a person is in control of what happens with their data.

Satellite issues

The emphasis on privacy-as-control should not be surprising, as it is perhaps *the* dominant way of conceiving of privacy and how people manage relationships with other people, organisations and machines (Altman, 1975; Gavison, 1984 [1980]; Privacy International, 2013; McStay, 2014, 2017). Underpinning this is a highly liberal approach to privacy based on non-interference and active control over one's life (Mill, 1962 [1859]). Note that this is not a negative view of privacy based on security, hiding or seclusion, but a positive assertion of rights, sovereignty of the self and demand for a basic level of respect. At its simplest, it is the demand of an individual to be seen as a subject rather than an object. Bloustein (1984 [1964]), for example, sees privacy in terms of dignity and spiritual values, rather than the impersonal discourse of property, reputation and – as recognised here – identification. To expand, dignity and recognition of subjectivity means acknowledging the autonomy of others, and their capacity and desire for self-control, self-guidance and choice. This is a classical liberal argument that is based on a view that people should have a minimum area of personal freedom that should not be violated. Applied, personal freedom in relation to empathic media is the right not to have our emotional life surveilled, even if the data being collected is not personal or identifiable. This right to self-governance argument has two branches, discussed below in turn: first is the use of data about emotions to manipulate choices, and second is the body itself.

Manipulating choice

As discussed in Chapter 8, the value of collecting data about emotions is crystallised when we consider the role of behavioural sciences (that encompass psychology, psychobiology, social neuroscience and cognitive science). In a commercial context this is about architecting choices and steering decision-making (Thaler and Sunstein, 2008). The problem here is simple: people do not like being duped or used as puppets (Wilkinson, 2013). Best expressed by Isaiah Berlin, this is classic liberalism in that a person wishes '[...] to be somebody, not nobody; a doer–deciding, not being decided for, self-directed and not acted upon by external nature or by other men as if I were a thing, or an animal, or a slave incapable of playing a human role' (2006 [1958]: 44). In the context of an unsolicited application of empathic media, this is characterised by a lack of transparency about manipulative techniques.

To be clear, the problem is not with the premise of 'nudging' or 'choice architecture' itself. People may be prompted to learn and make rational choices about preferences. It is not even with the premise of manipulation itself, because we are faced with it throughout everyday life. Indeed, sometimes we will enjoy it (surely everyone has one ad they like?). Sunstein (2016) frames the problem of manipulation in terms of context, and the expectations we have of places and people's roles therein. He gives two criteria for ethical objections to the use of behavioural sciences:

1. When the manipulator's goals are self-interested or venal.
2. When the act of manipulation is successful in subverting or bypassing the chooser's deliberative capacities. (ibid: 86)

Empathic media in a commercial setting would frequently fall foul of this because the applications are inherently self-interested and they exceed the expectations of that scenario (such as shelf-level cameras). Also, when employed in retail and marketing contexts, the function of empathic media is to influence a chooser's deliberative capacities. This is because data about emotional states has scope to inform how choices are presented to a person without that person being aware. We might note at this point that identification and singling out does not occur as a criterion for Sunstein. Furthermore, individual companies cannot be relied upon to behave ethically because competition for attention and customers will eventually mean that they will be at a disadvantage if they do not use more invasive tracking techniques. Given this, there is a need for greater regulation to ensure dignity. The question, then, is not 'should there be more rules?', but rather 'who should set them?'.

The body
The second point about governance is more corporeal than the issue of manipulation. Although data protection regulations are based on identification, the principles they are informed by are more expansive in nature. Article 8 of the European Convention on Human Rights (EHCR) places a broader emphasis on respect and dignity, rather than the identity-based account of privacy presented in GDPR and early drafts of the e-Privacy directive available in 2017. To ground this point, in an interview in 2015, Daniel Tench, partner at the media law firm Olswang, said that 'privacy law has some flexibility' and there is a case to be made about emotion-sensitive technologies. He highlighted not only that empathic media do not have precedent in UK law and are therefore on the cusp of British

legal protection, but also that recent case law has placed emphasis on the 'respect' part of Article 8 of the European Convention on Human Rights, and its demand for 'Respect for private and family life'. This can be applied to emotions, which opens up the possibility for a case to be made on the basis of violation and feeling aggrieved.

Another key issue is that the matter in hand is not just about identification, but about the intention to make the body 'machine-readable'. This invites a different set of privacy considerations from relatively straightforward questions of identification, to include the right to control who is able to see and touch a person's body. In a different but relevant capacity, Lynskey (2015) suggests that we compare Article 8 of the ECHR to the protection offered by data protection law. She notes, for example, that data protection law has little to say about an intrusive strip-search, but this is very much accounted for by Article 8 of ECHR that demands respect for private and family life.

Again, dignity is the defining element. This is implicit in questions of data privacy (not least through informational self-determination), but a rightful emphasis on the body, respect and not to be treated as an object presents a different picture from identification as the primary concern. Indeed, empathic media span both interests (data + body) because emotions are indivisible from physiology, yet also entail its 'datafication'. However, to account for empathic media in terms of data tracking is to offer a limited account. In looking at empathic media this way we should be careful not to demean traditional questions about privacy and bodily rights, particularly in relation to feminist campaigning (Allen, 1988, 2003; MacKinnon, 1989; McStay, 2017). Nevertheless, with the introduction of technologies that feel, the objectification of emotional life though computer vision and intrusion upon intimacy, we are able to elevate empathic media from routine questions of data privacy. In practice, this means that with the exception of sentiment analysis, any ethical, legal and regulatory assessment of empathic media must ask whether the body is being intruded upon in any way – regardless of whether a person can be identified or singled out for unique treatment.

Citizen Perspectives

Having explored industry, policy and NGO accounts, what of how citizens feel about the emotion capture of non-personal data? In November 2015 I carried out a UK-wide and demographically representative online survey with ICM Unlimited. I asked 2067 adults across the full age, gender, social class and region spectrums about their attitudes towards the potential for emotion detection in a range of then-nascent everyday uses of empathic media. These were sentiment analysis, out-of-home advertising, gaming, interactive movies, and voice-based capture through mobile phones. UK citizens had mixed and mostly negative feelings about emotion detection (for the full results see Appendix 2).

179

My overall findings were not significantly different between each of the proposed emotion detection methods. The overall figures derived from reactions to each method are:

- 50.57 per cent of UK citizens are 'not OK' with emotion detection in any form;
- 30.67 per cent are 'OK' with emotion detection if they are not personally identifiable;
- 8.32 per cent are 'OK' with having data about emotions connected with personally identifiable information;
- 10.45 per cent do not know.

In relation to the ethics of collecting non-identifying information, the significance is that just under 39 per cent of UK citizenry surveyed can be said to be 'OK' with having any data about emotions collected about them. Also of interest is age, and while gender, social class and region did not produce noticeable variances from their respective mean averages, age did produce significant deviations. Younger people (18–24) were more likely than any other age group to be 'OK' with some form of emotion detection in the digital media and services they use. To illustrate, the mean average of 18–24s 'not OK' with *any* form of emotion detection is only 31.43 per cent compared with the overall figure for all age groups of 50.57 per cent. Central to this chapter that is exploring emotion detection that does not make use of personal data, young people were most likely to be 'OK' with non-identifying emotion detection. They were the highest of all age groups, with over 65s being least likely to be 'OK' with it. This can be seen in Table 11.1 below.

The creepy factor

There is a range of methodological issues with surveys trying to gauge how people feel about technologies that they are unlikely to have experienced and have not had explained to them. The survey results warrant both further qualitative and

Table 11.1   Percentages of UK citizens OK with non-identifiable emotion detection (November 2015)

Total number of people sampled per age group	Age	Percentage
248	18–24	56.57
331	25–34	49.35
393	35–44	40.71
351	45–54	40.33
310	55–64	28.54
434	65+	25.70

quantitative research, but also suggest the need for reflection by policy-makers and industrialists alike. Although it is problematic to attribute motives for why, overall, citizens are 'not OK' with having non-identifying data about emotions collected about them, what is clear is that social values are misaligned with technological capabilities. This is what Tene and Polonetsky (2014) define as the 'creepy factor', or when new technology and corporate behaviour are accused of being creepy, yet do not breach any of the recognised principles of privacy and data protection law.

This signals a variance between the norms of technologists, the marketing industry and citizenry. Indeed, with just under 39 per cent of UK citizenry comfortable with any form of emotion capture, this leaves just over 61 per cent potentially at odds with technologists and marketers. However, perhaps more significant than the imbalance between technologists and those seeking to put these innovations to work in a marketing context, is variance with the law. This chapter has shown a clear imbalance between social values and data protection laws that focus on *identification* as the defining criterion for citizen protection. As it stands we have a legal lacuna, and while proponents and critics of the technology industry may debate the motive for making use of this lacuna (in one corner we have 'harm free' versus 'exploitative' in the other), we can certainly infer that there is a strong mismatch between what people want and what the law is.

There is scope here for correction. With apologies to non-European readers as I address an important technicality, Article 6(2) and Article 9(4) of the GDPR leave the door open to new conditions and limitations: the latter says that 'Member States may maintain or introduce further conditions, including limitations, with regard to the processing of genetic data, biometric data or health data'. Although the GDPR cannot be weakened, it can be nationally strengthened. As a minimum I suggest a new class of privacy considerations based on *intimacy* rather than solely identity. This has clear roots in the European Convention on Human Rights and the convictions that inform European regulations (and those of other jurisdictions), but recognises that human dignity can be undesirably impacted upon by unconsented-to emotion detection practices. The reason why this is necessary is because by making emotional life and the body 'machine-readable', the terms by which data protection harms are considered are different from what is usual. To reiterate, this is because when biometric technologies are used to identify people they are considered as making use of sensitive data, yet when information about the body is used without identifying the person, they are left with no protection at all. This is an important oversight, especially given that EU privacy law sets the highest standards of data protection in the world.

While privacy has come to be synonymous with identification, it has not always been this way. Indeed, in what is widely accepted among privacy scholars to be the first essay on this, two lawyers named Samuel Warren and Louis Brandeis (1984 [1890]) wrote 'The Right to Privacy'. Not without conceptual flaws, it nonetheless provides fertile thinking for legal and regulatory remedies for empathic media. The authors argue that 19th-century US common law provided a person self-determination on 'to what extent his thoughts, sentiments, and emotions shall be communicated to others' (ibid: 198). Although they were writing about published emotions in the form of writings, photos, paintings, diary entries, poems, and the level of control a person should have when others seek to publish these without the consent of the author, their arguments apply here. To repurpose Warren and Brandeis, the principle of self-determination of the communication of sentiments, moods and emotions is useful for empathic media (sentiment analysis excluded). Updated, this means the following:

- A person should never be compelled to express emotions, or have data about emotions collected without their consent.
- Even if a person has chosen to give data about their emotional expressions, they should retain the power to fix the limits of the publicity.
- The existence of this right does not depend upon the particular method of expression adopted.
- The existence of the right does not depend upon the nature or value of the thoughts or emotions.
- Meaningful consent is required so in every such case the individual is entitled to decide whether that which is his or hers shall be given to the public.

The legal right to our own emotions not to be read in public falls under the principle of what Warren and Brandeis term 'inviolate personality', which is part of 'a general right to one's personality' (ibid: 195, 215). This is based on the desirability of peace of mind that is attained with such protection. Today this applies to the right not to undergo discomfort in public spaces due to emotion tracking. Again, the matter is one of dignity. This protects against emotional distress even when no material harm has taken place.

Conclusion

The founder and executive chairman of the World Economic Forum, Klaus Schwab (2016), depicts the modern and nascent technological environment as one based on networks, machine learning and intelligence, intimate human–computer relationships, and closer technical inter-relationships with the body. Scant on detail, he argues that we should restructure our social and political systems to take advantage of these technologies. He also notes that our regulatory structures are not able to able to cope with these emergent technologies. Speaking to fellow business leaders, he urges 'Let us together shape a future that works for all by putting people first, empowering them and constantly reminding ourselves that all of these technologies are first and foremost tools made by people for people' (2016: 114). I say let us take this fine sentiment at its word and hold the technology industry to it. As Schwab says, this means putting the public interest first, ensuring that development is sustainable, and that new technology should improve rather than exploit human life.

There is nothing innately wrong with technologies that capture data about emotion, and those practices that do identify people are already subject to high levels of regulation in Europe. The lacuna and problem are with practices that are not based on identification. The technology and marketing industries have seen an opportunity here, but this chapter argues that ethical questions need to be asked by national regulators regarding the desirability of non-identifying emotion capture. At a minimum they should take seriously findings from this chapter that suggest a creepy variance between social values, technological capacities, use of behavioural sciences and the laws that guide these.

It is relatively early days for emotion capture technologies, but as other chapters have shown, these are developing in scope and rollout. At present we have a window to consider the desirability of what are currently unrestrained practices and what, if anything, we should do about them. In considering this we should pay attention to the fact that it involves questions of manipulation, dignity and datafication of the body. We should also attend to outcomes unanticipated by any start-up or established business seeking to make use of intimate data. This is two-fold in that their systems have sufficient scope to be hijacked and repurposed for biometric surveillance, as is the case with web technologies. It also entails the recognition that if allowed in a commercial setting, then policing and intelligence organisations will see this as a license to employ similar sensors, if not to directly use those employed by commercial actors. This is backed up by a comment in my interview with David Omand (ex-Director of GCHQ), who remarked that, in theory, if the technology is there someone will exploit it – and that this was true in Marconi's time (with radio), in Turing's (with thinking machines), and today. One can see the logic: if the technology is being used to increase sales, than why not safety? The question of course is whether this is a desirable world to live in.

Notes

1   The legislation on the difference between explicit and routine consent (for non-sensitive personal data) is far from clear, but we can summarise that it requires both explicit *and* affirmative consent. For example, as noted, the requirements of explicit consent can be met by ticking an unchecked tick box. The requirement for routine personal data is vague and subject to debate. While GDPR rejects pre-ticked boxes and inactivity as a means of gaining consent, Recital 32 of GDPR says consent can be given through 'another statement or conduct which clearly indicates in this context the data subject's acceptance of the proposed processing of his or her personal data'. Controversially, if notices and the context of which personal data is required are deemed to be clear, an opt-in box is not required.

2　This argument is not without its critics. For example, Lafkey (2009) draws on a study by the US Department of Health and Human Services' Office of the National Coordinator for Health Information Technology to argue that re-identification is not as straightforward as critics suggest. The UK's ICO applies the 'likelihood test' as certainty of what data controller B may or may not have in their possession cannot be guaranteed.

12

CONCLUSION: DIGNITY, ETHICS, NORMS, POLICIES AND PRACTICES

This book has accounted for the ways in which media technologies are showing qualities of 'empathy'. That is, they have the capacity to gauge emotions, intentions and attention through analysis of writing, images, speech, voice, facial expressions, bodily movement and physiology. Although some of the technologies in question pre-date the 1990s, the subject of empathic media is indivisible from technical developments in 'affective computing'. This involves computational processes that sense and respond in kind to people's emotions (Picard, 1995, 1997, 2007). The purpose of this brief final chapter is to recap the key themes of the book, clarify its ethical position, consider future research questions, and state what needs to be done immediately at a policy level.

The Arguments

On beginning the research for this book, I began with two propositions. These were:

1. We increasingly 'live with' technologies that feel and these are sensitive to human life in ways hitherto not seen.
2. Empathic media provide opportunities for new aesthetic experiences that not only draw upon information about emotions, but also provide new means for people to 'feel-into' aesthetic creations.

Throughout the course of interviewing industry, legal, policy, intelligence and NGO stakeholders from multiple regions of the world, these propositions became arguments. To address proposition 2 first, the aesthetic dimension of empathic media entails a *communion* between content, object and person – a phenomenon often discussed in terms of immersion, flow and presence. This most obviously applies to gaming and VR, but the principle applies to other mediated experiences augmented by emotion tracking. Beyond entertainment, the aesthetic aspect of empathic media encompasses the ways by which we may feel-into places, periods, cultures, objects, and real and fictional worlds. While it encompasses visually oriented, narrative-driven content, it is not synonymous with it. In VR and education for example, this includes historical reconstruction as well as visualisation and interaction with representations of elements of the brain. Other once-unlikely domains where people 'feel-into' aesthetic creations include mental health, journalism, marketing and policing. This is enabled by stimulation of sensation, interaction with emotion, recording of attention and gauging intention. Other factors are feelings of authenticity, presence, immersion, insulation within mediated environments, inclusion, ease of interactions, in-world control, movement, realistic images, fluidity and the capacity to interact with others.

Living with empathic media

There is more to be said about proposition 1 because it requires we confirm that it is sensible to say that we 'live with technologies that feel'. It also obliges us to consider the significance and implication of this notion. First, some theoretical caveats are required. At a general level it is sensible to say that we increasingly live with technologies that interact with people by means of biometric data, expressed feeling and the capacity to interact with emotional life. Indeed, given the very ubiquity of smileys and emojis, it is easy to miss that this has been routine for some time. However, we must also pay critical attention to the terms by which emotional life is gauged and understood. Although we are increasingly living with technologies that feel, emotional life is being defined in biomedical terms that suit technology, industrial categorisation, ranking systems, commercial culture, surveillance and political interests in happiness. These are all factors that impact on the Foucauldian question of why emotions are defined the way they are, and whose interests are being served. Looking forward, these constructions will have consequences for a) how decisions are made about us, and b) how people develop understanding of their own emotional lives and affective states. What might empathic media based on other approaches to affective and emotional life be like, particularly ones that admit constructionist critique and the social and cultural contexts that emotions are experienced in?

It is tempting to say that because machines are irritating and often quite stupid (I have Amazon's Alexa in mind), people will always have the upper hand in empathy due to their sensitivity to social context, cues, norms and performativity. An eyebrow raise at an inappropriate moment is a physically small act, but communicatively may be very significant. The capacity to intuitively derive meaning from such an act in the context of a dynamic social situation is something people mostly excel at. However, machines have strong cards of their own. Beyond micro-expressions they can sense, capture, process and interpret public detail that is inaccessible to people. They can also compare and remember in ways that people cannot. Given these properties, it is entirely reasonable to argue that we are increasingly 'living with' technologies that present a form of emotional intelligence. This is the capacity to detect emotions, categorise behaviour, learn to recognise these in new settings, adapt and respond appropriately. These systems also qualify as empathic on the basis that empathy and sympathy are different. This understanding means that both people and machines 'theorise' emotion through observation. Further, like people, machines may also draw upon prior knowledge of a person, a group, a situation, interactions and other contextual clues. These allow them to make judgements and predictions about people.

The point is perhaps better made when we consider the failure of empathy. After all, people will often misread, misinterpret and fail to understand the context that informs a person's behaviour. Indeed, like machines, people will also approximate, draw upon experience and use past learning to work out where other people are coming from and what they will do next. In fact they will often do this to influence their decisions. My argument is not to suppose that machines and people are equivalent, but that the affordances of empathic media and emotional AI are novel and socially significant. As these technologies become more capable and embedded in devices and environments, we need to directly address the implications of living alongside systems that feel.

Dignifying norms

We should educate and challenge those who seek to advance and exploit the affordances of new technologies without caring about the implications. What is required is responsible innovation that displays a meaningful commitment to people, lived environments, the future and socially desirable outcomes. This is achievable because the technologies that underpin empathic media have significant scope for pleasure, entertainment and health. As Koops (2015) highlights, the notion of responsible innovation is far from new, but draws from science and technology studies (STS), questions of value-sensitive design, privacy-by-design and the wider domain of applied ethics. Each recognises that technologies are not socially neutral and that the nature of how technologies are designed, rolled out and employed has social consequences. A responsible approach to innovation embeds positive social values into technology. These values derive from legal and ethical norms, but in the case of empathic media and affective computing the academy has a role to play in studying the terms and contexts in which people are happy to engage with these technologies.

Particularly in the case of empathic media that are at early stages of development, there is scope for a wide range of actors to advance an ethically-led approach. This includes regulators, data protection bodies, research funders, start-up incubators, industry and corporate leaders, smart city vendors, municipal managers, NGOs and universities through both teaching and research. Regulators and data protection authorities, for example, might interact at early stages, offer advice and guide innovators on what their stance is likely to be.

187

Research funders can incentivise scientists and innovators to insist that data ethics are meaningfully built into funded design processes, and universities can insist that technology courses contain ethical considerations. Similarly, incubators and corporate leaders (from regional innovators to large bodies such as the World Economic Forum) may advise on thinking through the potential social consequences of technological development. This is certainly not a silver bullet solution, but by initiating a conversation about the implications of mining highly personal and intimate data, we improve our chances of these technologies being individually and socially beneficial.

In fact, an ethically-led approach to this sector may be the one that succeeds in the marketplace. As discussed in Chapter 11, according to surveys I carried out for this book many citizens are not against the principle of emotion tracking and new modes of interactivity, but they appear to be rightfully wary. Rather than relying on citizen habituation to uncomfortable and unwanted conditions, a responsible approach is one that promotes creativity, fun, reward, benefits, and a very upfront approach to why data is being used and what happens with it. Of course, the collection and use of this data should not begin without meaningful consent. Indeed, in 2016 I organised and co-hosted an event with the emotions company Sensum. Titled 'Emotion Capture and Trust Workshop', and held at Digital Catapult in London, this featured a range of stakeholders. They included emotions companies (including Realeyes, Sensum and CrowdEmotion among others who preferred anonymity), the UK's Information Commissioner's Office, the UK's advertising self-regulator (the Committee of Advertising Practice), multi-national advertising agencies, security companies, civil liberties organisations, psychologists, legal ethicists, and surveillance experts. The objective was to find out what ethical guidelines for start-ups and innovators these actors would design and allow to be published online. The full report of the event is available online (McStay, 2016b), but after presentations to introduce ethics and emotion-capture practices, I split all the participants into groups to consider 'do's and don'ts' for those working with data about emotions. There was a remarkable convergence of ethics on liberal principles of autonomy, consent, control, empowerment, freedom, transparency and trust. Collectively the room agreed a set of guidelines for those working with data about emotions (see Table 12.1).

In addition to the positive do's list, the shorter don'ts list is also highly significant. Here the group shunned covert tracking and deceptive practices. In the context of this book, this has implications for emotion tracking in public places (such as adverts and retail) and through devices where it is not clear that data about emotions are being collected. Given that a key reason for the use of empathic media is that they can generate emotional insights that bypass self-reporting about how a person feels, delegates were wary of passive tracking and collection when there is no clear consent mechanism. Indeed, what was most telling about the event was the degree of ethical convergence.

Table 12.1 Stakeholder created guidelines for working with data about emotions

Do	Don't
Put the person first	Be covert
Put them in control	Use emotion as the be-all and end-all of profiling
Abide by external and internal guidelines (laws and norms)	
Facilitate user autonomy	
Grant meaningful choice	
Ensure the data used is proportionate to the goal	
Ensure users' benefit trumps commercial gain	

The scope for privacy-washing and moderator bias should not be missed, nor should the fact that the event was framed around ethics, which undoubtedly influenced the design of guidelines. However, it remains valuable that CEOs and business leaders conceived, created and agreed these codes that are published on the Digital Catapult website.[1] Useful for further research and development of responsible innovation in the empathic media sector, delegates at the workshop suggested further conversations about 'what actors from specific "verticals" think' (such as business, government and citizens), 'more work on clarifying what the norms generated might mean in practice', and a 'greater clarity and application to specific forms of emotion-capture techniques and empathic media practices'.

Future Research Questions

So far this concluding chapter has reflected on the utility of the propositions established early in the research process for this book, scope for responsible innovation, and areas for further social conversations between interested stakeholders. I now turn to academic questions, the answers to which will further knowledge about the emergent field of emotion tracking, empathic media and novel ways in which people are being datafied. Although this book has provided quantitative information about how people in the UK feel about the potential for emotion capture in technologies they are familiar with, there is an urgency here with regard to a qualitative assessment of how people feel about growth of these technologies. The focus should be on social media services, apps, home AI agents, smart televisions, games, retail spaces, out-of-home adverts, wearables, VR/AR units, cars and toys.

As these technologies mature and become more routine, it will be important to assess how people engage with these technologies and potentially use them to make sense of their own emotional lives. This is problematic in that the articulation of emotional life offered by affective technologies does not reflect what emotional life is, but instead it reflects only a portion of the science and learning about what emotions actually are. Conveniently, the science chosen for development is that which works best with biomedical datafying technologies and AI systems predicated on a symbolic abstraction from the messy world of relations, context, environment and social life. Given that most of the technical approaches to emotions have united behind what is broadly an Ekman world-view, what in effect is happening is the deterritorialisation of emotional life; that is, astute ambiguity about the fluidity, continuous, situated and contextual nature of affect and emotional life is displaced by a veneer of metric-based certainty about what emotions are. The seductive biomedical account of emotional life is also amplified by attractive interfaces that clearly describe what a person is feeling and how much they are feeling it.

This raises the issue of scientism or the problem of reducing what exists to what can be measured. Ultimately, are we set to internalise an account of emotional life that appears quantifiable and true, but which is based on foundations that are employed because they are expedient rather than accurate? With this premise it is difficult to avoid the gravity of Foucault (1988) and his argument that we should study the terms by which knowledge about life (and emotions) is produced, mediated, internalised and acted upon. Emotional accuracy is arguably not especially significant for the average user of mood-sensitive wearables. Although clients should disagree, it might not even be considered that important in advertising, marketing and retail. However, it certainly begins to matter if this information is used to make decisions about a person. As we have seen, this might involve their mental health, insurance, effectiveness at work, and other forms of automated psychological profiling.

Immediate Action

The Collingridge dilemma is when the impact of a technology cannot be easily predicted until the technology is extensively developed and widely used (Collingridge, 1980). This is the classic problem of when regulators should intervene (if at all) in a nascent technology. If done too early promising developments can be crushed, but if left too late technologies can become so firmly embedded in social life that this is painful or impossible to correct. The use of third-party cookies and illogical consent mechanisms in online behavioural advertising is a relevant example of this premise. While undoubtedly organisations will push to link biometric information about emotional life with identifying data, there is a more immediate concern. This is the need to tackle the fact that legal consent is not required to capture data about emotions if it is not possible to identify or single-out a given person for differential treatment. This is a lacuna that will be exploited, perhaps especially by 'choice architects' in retail and advertisers using computer vision techniques in public and quasi-public spaces (such as shopping malls). Data protection authorities and industry self-regulators across diverse sectors (such as advertising, consumer protection, retail and marketing) need to tackle the following question: are citizens and the reputations of industries best served by this passive surveillance of emotional life?

If the answer is no, codes of practice should be amended and meaningful sanctions created. Legislators should also pay close attention and consider regulating the emergent empathic media sector. The reason is that questions of ethics, emotion capture and machine-readable bodies are not contingent upon identification, but on human dignity, choice, and civic decisions about what kinds of environments we want to live in. While we cannot yet be sure of the final impact of emotional AI and empathic media, what is clearly visible is that commodity logic is pushing at moral limits. This should be guarded against because, at a fundamental level, the ongoing commodification of human existence is a form of corruption that undermines the relationship between the individual and public life.

Note

1   Available from https://pdtn.org/emotional-ai-dos-donts/

APPENDIX 1

TABLE OF ORGANISATIONS AND NUMBERS OF PEOPLE INTERVIEWED

Organisation	Type	No. of people interviewed from organisation
1. 11KBW	Law	1
2. Adform	Advertising/marketing	1
3. Affectiva	Market research	4
4. AXA Insurance	Insurance	1
5. Azure	Market research	2
6. B-alert	Brain technology	1
7. B-reel	Advertising/marketing	1
8. Beyond Verbal	Voice technology	1
9. Bioresentile	IoT	1
10. Bondara	Sex technology	1
11. Comm of Advertising Practice	Regulator	2
12. Confirmit	Market research	1
13. Crimson Hexagon	Sentiment analyst	1
14. CrowdEmotion	Market research	1
15. D2Emotion	Technology	1
16. DataXu	Advertising/marketing	2
17. David Omand	Ex-GCHQ speaking personally	1
18. Digital Catapult	Government to stimulate business	2

(Continued)

(Continued)

Organisation	Type	No. of people interviewed from organisation
19. Dubai Health	Health/technology	1
20. Electronic Frontier Foundation	NGO	1
21. Emblematic Group	VR	1
22. Emoteyourday	Mobile technology	1
23. eMotion	Wearable technology	1
24. Emotiv	Brain technology	1
25. ESOMAR	Market research	1
26. eXelate	Audience/market research	1
27. Exterion	Advertising	1
28. European Commission	Law/policy/regulation	3
29. Facebook	Technology	1
30. F-Secure	Online security	1
31. Gartner	Market analyst	1
32. Ghostery	Web technology	2
33. Havas	Advertising/marketing	1
34. HW Communications	Technology	1
35. i2mediaresearch	Retail technology	1
36. IAB Europe	Advertising/marketing	1
37. IAPP	Association for privacy practitioners	1
38. IBM Watson	Technology	2
39. ICO	Regulator	3
40. Innovate UK	Technology/innovation funder	1
41. Jamie Woodruff	Ethical hacker	1
42. Jennifer Chenoweth	Artist	1
43. John Taysom	Investor	1
44. Kate Moyle	Sex therapist/Pillow	1
45. Kantar	Audience/market research	1
46. Kinetic	Advertising/marketing	1
47. KM4 City	Smart city developer	2
48. Marketing Research Society	Audience/market research association	1

Organisation	Type	No. of people interviewed from organisation
49. M&C Saatchi	Advertising/marketing	1
50. MediaRebel	Law/facial coding	2
51. Motorola Solutions	Security/policing	2
52. MyVessyl	IoT	1
53. Nabarro	Law	2
54. Nevermind	Games/technology	1
55. nViso	Technology	1
56. Ocean Outdoor	Advertising/marketing	1
57. Ogilvy & Mather	Advertising/marketing	3
58. Orion Labs	IoT	1
59. Philips	Smart cities/IoT	1
60. Planet Labs	Space and technology	1
61. Player Research	Games technology	1
62. Privacy International	NGO	3
63. Quell	Health technology	1
64. Realeyes	Audience research	2
65. Repustate	Sentiment analyst	1
66. Portal	Media	1
67. Olswang	Law	1
68. Sensum	Audience/market research	1
69. Sharpbrains	Brain technology	1
70. Siemens	Technology	2
71. Smart Dubai	Government technology	1
72. Somatic	Wearables technology	1
73. Spire	Wearables technology	1
74. State of Green	Denmark government	1
75. Steve Mann	Technologist and academic	1
76. Strap	Technology and advertising	2
77. Thales	Policing	1
78. This Place	Technology and marketing	1
79. Teleplan	Policing	1
80. Valve	Gaming	1

(Continued)

(Continued)

Organisation	Type	No. of people interviewed from organisation
81. Volker Hirsch	Investor	1
82. WayRay	Technology in-car displays	1
83. Verily (Alphabet/Google)	Technology, biosciences and health	1
84. VTT Technical Research	Technology	1
		Total 108

APPENDIX 2

TABLES OF RESULTS FROM UK NATIONAL SURVEY ON EMOTION DETECTION IN EXISTING AND NASCENT MEDIA TECHNOLOGIES

Question 1 (Social media)

Table 1.1   Headline results (UK sample excluding Northern Ireland)

Statement	Number of people (n=2067)	Percentage
Statement 1 (Not OK)	1050	50.79
Statement 2 (OK/no PI)	650	31.45
Statement 3 (OK/PI)	151	7.31
Statement 4 (DK)	216	10.45

Table 1.2   Gender

Statement	Male (n=1013)	Female (n=1054)
Statement 1 (Not OK)	512 (50.56%)	538 (51.02%)
Statement 2 (OK/no PI)	319 (31.51%)	331 (31.38%)
Statement 3 (OK/PI)	81 (8.01%)	70 (6.64%)
Statement 4 (DK)	100 (9.92%)	116 (10.96%)

Table 1.3 Age

Statement	18–24 (n=248)	25–34 (n=331)	35–44 (n=393)	45–54 (n=351)	55–64 (n=310)	65+ (n=434)
Statement 1 (Not OK)	74 (29.88%)	131 (39.48%)	198 (50.53%)	175 (49.87%)	204 (65.73%)	268 (61.71%)
Statement 2 (OK/no PI)	110 (44.23%)	119 (36.05%)	111 (28.19%)	111 (31.48%)	73 (23.69%)	126 (29.10%)
Statement 3 (OK/PI)	29 (11.54%)	38 (11.41%)	45 (11.45%)	23 (6.67%)	8 (2.44%)	9 (2.01%)
Statement 4 (DK)	36 (14.36%)	43 (13.06%)	39 (9.83%)	42 (11.98%)	25 (8.14%)	31 (7.18%)

Table 1.4 Social class

Statement	AB (n=558)	C1 (n=599)	C2 (n=434)	DE (n=476)
Statement 1 (Not OK)	301 (54.00%)	300 (50.00%)	210 (48.29%)	239 (50.31%)
Statement 2 (OK/no PI)	180 (32.30%)	191 (31.90%)	135 (31.21%)	143 (30.09%)
Statement 3 (OK/PI)	41 (7.32%)	48 (8.00%)	26 (6.03%)	36 (7.59%)
Statement 4 (DK)	36 (6.38%)	61 (10.10%)	63 (14.46%)	57 (12.00%)

Table 1.5 Region (UK excluding Northern Ireland)

Statement	South East (n=525)	Midlands (n=546)	North England (n=519)	Wales/South West (n=298)	Scotland (n=179)
Statement 1 (Not OK)	275 (52.40%)	271 (49.60%)	256 (49.40%)	150 (50.35%)	98 (54.51%)
Statement 2 (OK/no PI)	156 (29.74%)	166 (30.37%)	178 (34.24%)	105 (35.31%)	45 (25.27%)
Statement 3 (OK/PI)	49 (9.36%)	48 (8.85%)	26 (4.96%)	17 (5.80%)	11 (5.92%)
Statement 4 (DK)	45 (8%)	61 (11%)	59 (11%)	25 (9%)	26 (14%)

Question 2 (Outdoor ads)

Table 2.1 Headline results (UK sample excluding Northern Ireland)

Statement	Number of people (n=2068)	Percentage
Statement 1 (Not OK)	1028	49.72
Statement 2 (OK/no PI)	687	33.22
Statement 3 (OK/PI)	163	7.78
Statement 4 (DK)	190	9.19

Table 2.2 Gender

Statement	Male (n=1013)	Female (n=1054)
Statement 1 (Not OK)	484 (47.79%)	544 (51.57%)
Statement 2 (OK/no PI)	342 (33.75%)	345 (32.71%)
Statement 3 (OK/PI)	92 (9.05%)	71 (6.73%)
Statement 4 (DK)	95 (9.41%)	95 (8.98%)

Table 2.3 Age

Statement	18–24 (n=248)	25–34 (n=331)	35–44 (n=393)	45–54 (n=351)	55–64 (n=310)	65+ (n=434)
Statement 1 (Not OK)	85 (34.22%)	137 (41.54%)	191 (48.51%)	163 (46.47%)	187 (60.21%)	265 (61.06%)
Statement 2 (OK/no PI)	107 (43.25%)	113 (34.12%)	118 (30.11%)	124 (35.43%)	95 (30.68%)	129 (29.64%)
Statement 3 (OK/PI)	32 (13.06%)	41 (12.40%)	43 (10.88%)	28 (7.97%)	11 (3.53%)	8 (1.73%)
Statement 4 (DK)	23 (9.46%)	39 (11.94%)	41 (10.50%)	36 (10.13%)	17 (5.59%)	33 (7.57%)

Table 2.4 Social class

Statement	AB (n=558)	C1 (n=599)	C2 (n=434)	DE (n=476)
Statement 1 (Not OK)	290 (52.01%)	314 (52.34%)	192 (44.23%)	232 (48.75%)
Statement 2 (OK/no PI)	189 (33.85%)	193 (32.20%)	153 (35.24%)	152 (31.93%)
Statement 3 (OK/PI)	43 (7.63%)	51 (8.47%)	34 (7.92%)	35 (7.34%)
Statement 4 (DK)	36 (6.50%)	42 (7.00%)	55 (12.62%)	57 (11.99%)

Table 2.5 Region (UK excluding Northern Ireland)

Statement	South East (n=525)	Midlands (n=546)	North England (n=519)	Wales/South West (n=298)	Scotland (n=179)
Statement 1 (Not OK)	267 (50.81%)	255 (46.60%)	248 (47.77%)	168 (56.35%)	90 (50.37%)
Statement 2 (OK/no PI)	161 (30.71%)	187 (34.30%)	186 (35.86%)	98 (32.75%)	55 (30.41%)
Statement 3 (OK/PI).	50 (9.51%)	46 (8.47%)	36 (6.89%)	17 (5.69%)	14 (7.68%)
Statement 4 (DK)	47 (8.97%)	58 (10.54%)	49 (9.48%)	16 (5.21%)	21 (11.53%)

Question 3 (Gaming)

Table 3.1 Headline results (UK sample excluding Northern Ireland)

Statement	Number of people (n=2067)	Percentage
Statement 1 (Not OK)	978	47.30
Statement 2 (OK/no PI)	631	30.51
Statement 3 (OK/PI)	192	9.27
Statement 4 (DK)	267	12.92

Table 3.2 Gender

Statement	Male (n=1013)	Female (n=1054)
Statement 1 (Not OK)	447 (44.15%)	531 (50.33%)
Statement 2 (OK/no PI)	337 (33.24%)	294 (27.89%)
Statement 3 (OK/PI)	103 (10.18%)	89 (8.40%)
Statement 4 (DK)	126 (12.44%)	141 (13.37%)

Table 3.3 Age

Statement	18–24 (n=248)	25–34 (n=331)	35–44 (n=393)	45–54 (n=351)	55–64 (n=310)	65+ (n=434)
Statement 1 (Not OK)	76 (30.47%)	110 (33.31%)	167 (42.59%)	155 (44.13%)	177 (57.13%)	292 (67.40%)
Statement 2 (OK/no PI)	104 (41.96%)	120 (36.19%)	123 (31.26%)	118 (33.64%)	75 (24.22%)	91 (20.91%)
Statement 3 (OK/PI)	42 (16.84%)	56 (16.97%)	54 (13.87%)	24 (6.97%)	8 (2.66%)	6 (1.50%)
Statement 4 (DK)	27 (10.73%)	45 (13.53%)	48 (12.28%)	54 (15.26%)	50 (15.98%)	44 (10.91%)

Table 3.4 Social class

Statement	AB (n=558)	C1 (n=599)	C2 (n=434)	DE (n=476)
Statement 1 (Not OK)	290 (51.94%)	274 (45.68%)	196 (45.20%)	218 (45.82%)
Statement 2 (OK/no PI)	170 (30.52%)	192 (32.07%)	139 (32.02%)	129 (27.16%)
Statement 3 (OK/PI)	47 (8.35%)	64 (10.73%)	32 (7.27%)	49 (10.32%)
Statement 4 (DK)	51 (9.18%)	69 (11.53%)	67 (15.51%)	79 (16.68%)

Table 3.5 Region (UK excluding Northern Ireland)

Statement	South East (n=525)	Midlands (n=546)	North England (n=519)	Wales/South West (n=298)	Scotland (n=179)
Statement 1 (Not OK)	246 (46.92%)	253 (46.46%)	233 (44.92%)	157 (52.55%)	88 (49.14%)
Statement 2 (OK/no PI)	157 (29.88%)	160 (29.32%)	168 (32.37%)	96 (32.16%)	50 (27.88%)
Statement 3 (OK/PI)	51 (9.75%)	57 (10.41%)	49 (9.43%)	19 (6.32%)	16 (8.85%)
Statement 4 (DK)	71 (13.45%)	75 (13.83%)	69 (13.28%)	27 (8.96%)	25 (14.14%)

Question 4 (Smart-device entertainment)

Table 4.1   Headline results (UK sample excluding Northern Ireland)

Statement	Number of people (n=2067)	Percentage
Statement 1 (Not OK)	1067	51.63
Statement 2 (OK/no PI)	623	30.12
Statement 3 (OK/PI)	180	8.73
Statement 4 (DK)	197	9.52

Table 4.2   Gender

Statement	Male (n=1013)	Female (n=1054)
Statement 1 (Not OK)	486 (48.02%)	581 (55.10%)
Statement 2 (OK/no PI)	322 (31.84%)	300 (28.48%)
Statement 3 (OK/PI)	109 (10.76%)	71 (6.78%)
Statement 4 (DK)	195 (9.39%)	102 (9.64%)

Table 4.3 Age

Statement	18–24 (n=248)	25–34 (n=331)	35–44 (n=393)	45–54 (n=351)	55–64 (n=310)	65+ (n=434)
Statement 1 (Not OK)	82 (33.11%)	133 (40.19%)	188 (47.89%)	165 (47.03%)	196 (63.13%)	303 (69.84%)
Statement 2 (OK/no PI)	110 (44.43%)	114 (34.51%)	114 (28.98%)	117 (33.36%)	76 (24.63%)	91 (20/93%)
Statement 3 (OK/PI)	30 (12.14%)	51 (15.49%)	49 (12.36%)	32 (9.15%)	13 (4.06%)	6 (1.34%)
Statement 4 (DK)	26 (10.33%)	32 (9.81%)	42 (10.77%)	37 (10.45%)	25 (8.17%)	34 (7.89%)

Table 4.4 Social class

Statement	AB (n=558)	C1 (n=599)	C2 (n=434)	DE (n=476)
Statement 1 (Not OK)	304 (54.53%)	303 (50.57%)	220 (50.63%)	240 (50.48%)
Statement 2 (OK/no PI)	162 (29.11%)	190 (31.70%)	137 (31.60%)	133 (27.97%)
Statement 3 (OK/PI)	52 (9.28%)	54 (9.02%)	28 (6.43%)	47 (9.82%)
Statement 4 (DK)	39 (7.08%)	52 (8.71%)	49 (11.34%)	56 (11.74%)

Table 4.5 Region (UK excluding Northern Ireland)

Statement	South East (n=525)	Midlands (n=546)	North England (n=519)	Wales/South West (n=298)	Scotland (n=179)
Statement 1 (Not OK)	259 (49.27%)	273 (49.98%)	266 (51.28%)	167 (55.88%)	103 (57.49%)
Statement 2 (OK/no PI)	168 (31.98%)	154 (28.25%)	165 (31.82%)	88 (29.55%)	47 (26.43%)
Statement 3 (OK/PI)	50 (9.43%)	62 (11.29%)	38 (7.39%)	22 (7.33%)	9 (5.11%)
Statement 4 (DK)	49 (9.31%)	57 (10.48%)	49 (9.51%)	22 (7.24%)	20 (10.98%)

Question 5 (Voice)

Table 5.1   Headline results (UK sample excluding Northern Ireland)

Statement	Number of people (n=2067)	Percentage
Statement 1 (Not OK)	1104	53.42
Statement 2 (OK/no PI)	579	28.03
Statement 3 (OK/PI)	174	8.40
Statement 4 (DK)	210	10.15

Table 5.2   Gender

Statement	Male (n=1013)	Female (n=1054)
Statement 1 (Not OK)	507 (50.03%)	597 (56.67%)
Statement 2 (OK/no PI)	321 (31.70%)	258 (24.51%)
Statement 3 (OK/PI)	102 (10.09%)	71 (6.78%)
Statement 4 (DK)	83 (8.18%)	127 (12.04%)

Table 5.3 Age

Statement	18–24 (n=248)	25–34 (n=331)	35–44 (n=393)	45–54 (n=351)	55–64 (n=310)	65+ (n=434)
Statement 1 (Not OK)	73 (29.46%)	129 (38.89%)	209 (53.25%)	186 (52.85%)	197 (63.71%)	310 (71.46%)
Statement 2 (OK/no PI)	103 (41.47%)	121 (36.66%)	103 (26.34%)	97 (27.64%)	70 (22.61%)	85 (19.49%)
Statement 3 (OK/PI)	37 (14.94%)	43 (12.95%)	40 (10.12%)	33 (9.35%)	13 (4.20%)	8 (1.87%)
Statement 4 (DK)	35 (14.13%)	38 (11.49%)	40 (10.28%)	36 (10.16%)	29 (9.48%)	31 (7.18%)

Table 5.4 Social class

Statement	AB (n=558)	C1 (n=599)	C2 (n=434)	DE (n=476)
Statement 1 (Not OK)	317 (56.73%)	314 (52.44%)	225 (51.76%)	249 (52.29%)
Statement 2 (OK/no PI)	150 (26.85%)	177 (29.60%)	133 (30.61%)	119 (25.09%)
Statement 3 (OK/PI)	49 (8.81%)	53 (8.90%)	29 (6.57%)	43 (8.97%)
Statement 4 (DK)	42 (7.61%)	54 (9.06%)	48 (11.06%)	65 (13.65%)

Table 5.5 Region (UK excluding Northern Ireland)

Statement	South East (n=525)	Midlands (n=546)	North England (n=519)	Wales/South West (n=298)	Scotland (n=179)
Statement 1 (Not OK)	278 (52.86%)	276 (50.64%)	277 (53.32%)	163 (54.75%)	111 (61.59%)
Statement 2 (OK/no PI)	152 (28.92%)	150 (27.57%)	153 (29.59%)	87 (29.22%)	37 (20.38%)
Statement 3 (OK/PI)	52 (9.82%)	53 (9.71%)	33 (6.45%)	20 (6.83%)	15 (8.52%)
Statement 4 (DK)	44 (8.40%)	66 (12.07%)	55 (10.64%)	27 (9.21%)	17 (9.51%)

REFERENCES

Aarseth, E. (1997) *Cybertext: Perspectives on Ergodic Literature*. Baltimore, MD: Johns Hopkins University Press.

Ahmed, S. (2010) *The Promise of Happiness*. Durham, NC: Duke University Press.

Ahmed, S. (2014) *The Cultural Politics of Emotion*, 2nd edn. Edinburgh: Edinburgh University Press.

Ailon, G. (2008) Mirror, mirror on the wall: Culture's consequences in a value test of its own design, *Academy of Management Review*, 33 (4): 885–904.

Akerlof, G. and Shiller, R. (2015) *Phishing for Phools*. Princeton, NJ: Princeton University Press.

Aletras, N., Tsarapatsanis, D., Preoţiuc-Pietro, D. and Lampos, V. (2016) Predicting judicial decisions of the European Court of Human Rights: A natural language processing perspective, *PeerJ Computer Science,* 2: e93. https://doi.org/10.7717/peerj-cs.93 (accessed 27/10/17).

Alexander, J. and Schmidt, J.K.H.W. (1996) 'Social engineering: Genecology of a concept', in A. Podgórecki, J. Alexander and R. Shields (eds), *Social Engineering*. Ottowa: Carleton University Press. pp. 1–20.

Allen, A.L. (1988) *Uneasy Access: Privacy for Women in Free Society*. Tutowa, NJ: Rowman & Littlefield.

Allen, A.L. (2003) *Why Privacy Isn't Everything: Feminist Reflections on Personal Accountability*. Lanham, MD: Rowman & Littlefield.

Altman, I. (1975) *The Environment and Social Behavior: Privacy, Personal Space, Territory, Crowding*. Monterey, CA: Brooks/Cole.

Ameriks, J., Wranik, T. and Salovey, P. (2009) *Emotional Intelligence and Investor Behaviour*. Charlottesville, VA: The Research Foundation of CFA Institute.

Anderson, G.L. (2016) Is RealDoll Close to Delivering Its Promised AI Sex Robots? *Vice*, www.vice.com/en_us/article/dpkypk/real-doll-artificial-intelligence-sex (accessed 27/10/17).

Andrejevic, M. (2013) *Infoglut: How Too Much Information is Changing the Way We Think and Know*. New York: Routledge.

Aneesh, A. (2006) *Virtual Migration: The Programming of Globalization*. Durham, NC: Duke University Press.

Arendt, H. (1962 [1951]) *Origins of Totalitarianism*. New York: Meridian.

Ariel, B., Sutherland, A., Henstock, D., Young, J., Drover, P., Syles, J., Megicks, S. and Henderson, R. (2017) Contagious accountability: A global multisite randomized controlled trial on the effect of police body-worn cameras on citizens' complaints against the police, *Criminal Justice and Behavior*, 44 (2): 293–316.

Aristotle (2008 [350 BC]) *Physics*. London: Penguin.

Arroyo-Palacios, J. and Romano, D.M. (2008) 'Towards a standardization in the use of physiological signals for affective recognition systems', in *Proceedings of Measuring Behavior 2008*. Maastricht: Noldus. www.noldus.com/mb2008/program/Proceedings_Measuring_Behavior_2008_web.pdf (accessed 27/10/17).

Ashby, W.R. (1956) *An Introduction to Cybernetics*. London: Chapman and Hall.

Bachelard, G. (1994 [1958]) *The Poetics of Space*. Boston, MA: Beacon.

Baldwin, R.C. (1940) The meeting of extremes in recent esthetics, *Journal of Philosophy*, 37 (13): 348–58.

Baron-Cohen, S. and Tead, T.H.E. (2003) *Mind Reading: The Interactive Guide to Emotion*. London: Jessica Kingsley.

Barrett, L.F. (2006) Solving the emotion paradox: Categorization and the experience of emotion, *Personality and Social Psychology Review*, 10: 20–46.

Barrett, L.F. (2006a) Are emotions natural kinds? *Perspectives on Psychological Science*, 1: 28–58.

Barrett, L.F. (2014) What Faces Can't Tell Us, *New York Times*, www.nytimes.com/2014/03/02/opinion/sunday/what-faces-cant-tell-us.html?_r=0 (accessed 27/10/17).

Baudelaire, C. (1964 [1863]) *The Painter of Modern Life*. New York: Da Capo Press.

BBC News (2009) HP Camera 'Can't See' Black Faces, http://news.bbc.co.uk/1/hi/technology/8429634.stm (accessed 04/10/17).

Beer, D. (2016) *Metric Power*. Basingstoke: Palgrave Macmillan.

Behavox (2017) Behavox Partners with Cloud9 to Provide Comprehensive Monitoring for Voice Trading in the Capital Markets, https://behavox.com/release_mar.html (accessed 05/10/17).

Bell, C. (1824) *Essays on the Anatomy and Philosophy of Expression*. London: Murray.

Beniger, J.R. (1986) *The Control Revolution: Technological and Economic Origins of the Information Society*. Cambridge, MA: Harvard University Press.

Benjamin, W. (2002 [1982]) *The Paris Arcades*. Cambridge, MA: Harvard University Press.

Bentham, J. (2000 [1781]) *An Introduction to the Principles of Morals and Legislation*. Kitchener, Ontario: Batoche Books.

Berardi, F. (2009) *The Soul At Work: From Alienation to Autonomy*. Los Angeles, CA: Semiotext(e).

Bergson, H. (1999 [1913]) *An Introduction to Metaphysics*. Indianapolis, IN: Hackett.

Berlin, I. (2006 [1958]) 'Two concepts of liberty', in D. Miller (ed.), *The Liberty Reader*. Edinburgh: Edinburgh University Press. pp. 33–57.

Bernhaupt, R., Boldt, A. and Mirlacher, T. (2007) Using emotion in games: Emotional flowers, *Proceedings of the International Conference on Advances in Computer Entertainment Technology*, Salzburg, Austria, 13–15 June, pp. 41–48. https://dl.acm.org/citation.cfm?id=1255056 (accessed 31/10/17).

Beyond Verbal (2014) Moodies – The World's First Emotions Analytics App For iOS Press Release, www.beyondverbal.com/beyond-verbal-launches-patented-technology-that-decodes-human-emotions-through-raw-voice-article-3 (accessed 27/10/17).

Beyond Verbal (2014a) *What We Do*, www.beyondverbal.com/start-here/what-we-do/ (accessed 27/10/17).

Bijker, W.E., Hughes, T.P. and Pinch, T. (eds) (1993) *The Social Construction of Technological Systems: New Directions in the Sociology and History of Technology*. Cambridge, MA: MIT.

Biocca, F. and Levy, M.R. (1995) 'Communication Applications of Virtual Reality', in F. Biocca and M.R. Levy (eds), *Communication in the Age of Virtual Reality*. Hillsdale, NJ: Lawrence Erlbaum. p. 128.

Birchall, G. (2016) ROBO ROMPS Sex Robots with Terrifyingly Realistic Genitalia to Hit the Market NEXT YEAR and Cost £12,000, www.thesun.co.uk/tech/2083660/sex-robots-with-terrifyingly-realistic-genitalia-to-hit-the-market-next-year-and-cost-12000 (accessed 04/10/17).

Bloom, P. (2017) *Against Empathy: The Case for Rational Compassion*. London: Ecco.

Bloomberg (2017) Wall Street Embraces Emotional Trading Surveillance, www.bloomberg.com/news/videos/2016-09-01/wall-street-embraces-emotional-trading-surveillance (accessed 05/10/17).

Bloomberg Businessweek (2016) Startups Wielding Sensors and Algorithms Promise a New Era of Surveillance, www.bloomberg.com/news/articles/2016-09-01/wall-street-s-next-frontier-is-hacking-into-emotions-of-traders (accessed 05/10/17).

Bloustein, E.J. (1984 [1964]) 'Privacy as an aspect of human dignity: An answer to Dean Prosser', in F.D. Schoeman (ed.), *Philosophical Dimensions of Privacy: An Anthology*. Cambridge: Cambridge University Press. pp. 156–202.

Borders (2017) AVATAR – Automated Virtual Agent for Truth Assessments in Real-Time, http://borders.arizona.edu/cms/projects/avatar-automated-virtual-agent-truth-assessments-real-time (accessed 04/10/17).

Bradley, M.M. and Lang, P.J. (1994) Measuring emotion: The self-assessment manikin and the semantic differential, *Journal of Behavior Therapy and Experimental Psychiatry*, 25 (1): 49–59.

Brown, T. (2010 [1820]) *Thomas Brown: Selected Philosophical Writings*. Exeter: Imprint Academic.

Camerer, C., Issacharoff, S., Loewenstein, G., Donoghue, T. and Rabin, M. (2003) Regulation for Conservatives: Behavioral economics and the case for 'asymmetric paternalism', *University of Pennsylvania Law Review*. 151: 1211–54.

Canetti, E. (1981 [1960]) *Crowds and Power*. New York: Continuum.

Castells, M. (2001 [1996]) *The Rise of the Network Society*. Oxford: Blackwell.

Castells, M. (2009) *Communication Power*. Oxford: Oxford University Press.

Cawsey, A. (1998) *The Essence of Artificial Intelligence*. Harlow: Prentice Hall.

Chen, A. (2015) The Agency, *New York Times Magazine*, www.nytimes.com/2015/06/07/magazine/the-agency.html (accessed 27/10/17).

Christianson, S-A. (1992) *The Handbook of Emotion and Memory: Research and Theory*. New York: Psychology Press.

Clarke, A.E., Mamo, L., Fosket, J.R., Fishman, J.R and Shim, J.K. (2010) *Biomedicalization: Technoscience, Health and Illness in the U.S.* Durham, NC: Duke University Press.

Clarke, A.E., Shim, J.K., Mamo, L., Fosket, J.R. and Fishman, J.R (2003) Biomedicalization: Technoscientific transformations of health, illness, and U.S. biomedicine, *American Sociological Review*, 68 (2): 161–94.

Clynes, M. (1977) *Sentics: The Touch of the Emotions*. New York: Anchor Press/Doubleday.

Collingridge, D. (1980) *The Social Control of Technology*. New York: St Martin's Press.

Contagious (2016) eBay/High Intensity Interval Shopping, www.contagious.com/blogs/news-and-views/ebay-high-intensity-interval-shopping (accessed 05/10/17).

Crary, J. (2013) *24/7: Late Capitalism and the Ends of Sleep*. London: Verso.

Crawford, K. (2016) Can an algorithm be agonistic? Ten scenes from life in calculated publics, *Science, Technology & Human Values*, 41 (1): 77–92.

Crawford, K., Lingel, J. and Karppi, T. (2015) Our metrics, ourselves: A hundred years of self-tracking from the weight scale to the wrist wearable device, *European Journal of Cultural Studies*, 18: 479–96.

Crawford, R. (1980) Healthism and the medicalization of everyday life, *International Journal of Health Services*, 10 (3): 365–88.

Crimson Hexagon (2014) Crimson Hexagon Forsight Platform Plots UK Politicians 2013 Tweets on Energy Prices, Syrian Crisis, and the NHS, www.crimsonhexagon.com/business-intelligence/social-analytics/media-research/social-media-reveals-what-members-of-parliament-think (accessed 27/10/17).

Cumberland, R. (2005 [1672]) *A Treatise of the Laws of Nature*. Indianpolis, IN: Liberty Fund.

Damasio, A. (2003) *Looking for Spinoza: Joy, Sorrow, and the Feeling Brain*. Orlando, FL: Harcourt.

Damasio, A. (2011) *Self Comes to Mind: Constructing the Conscious Brain*. London: Vintage.

Darling, K. (2014) 'Who's Johnny?' Anthropomorphic Framing in Human–Robot Interaction, Integration, and Policy, www.werobot2015.org/wp-content/uploads/2015/04/Darling_Whos_Johnny_WeRobot_2015.pdf (accessed 27/10/17).

Dartnall, T. (ed.) (2013) *Artificial Intelligence and Creativity*. Dordrecht: Springer.

Darwin, C. (2009 [1872]) *The Expression of the Emotions in Man and Animals*. London: Harper.

Davies, W. (2015) *The Happiness Industry: How the Government & Big Business Sold Us Wellbeing*. London: Verso.

Davies, W. (2016) How are we now? Real-time mood-monitoring as valuation, *Journal of Cultural Economy*, 10 (1): 34–48.

De la Peña, N., Weil, P., Llobera, J., Giannopoulos, E., Pomes, A., Spanlang, B. and Slater, M. (2010) Immersive journalism: Immersive virtual reality for the first-person experience of news, *Presence*, 19: 291–301.

De Montaigne, M. (1999 [1603]) Montaigne's Essays MICHEL EYQUEM DE MONTAIGNE (1533–1592), trans. J. Florio, *Renascence Editions*, https://scholarsbank.uoregon.edu/xmlui/bitstream/handle/1794/766/montaigne.pdf (accessed 27/10/17).

Dean, J. (2005) Communicative capitalism: Circulation and the foreclosure of politics, *Cultural Politics*, 1 (1): 51–74.

Debord, G. (1955) *Introduction to a Critique of Urban Geography*, http://library.nothingness.org/articles/SI/en/display/2 (accessed 27/10/17).

Deleuze, G. (1992) Postscript on the societies of control, *October*, 59 (4): 3–7.

Deleuze, G. and Guattari, F. (2000 [1972]) *Anti-Oedipus: Capitalism and Schizophrenia*. London: Athlone.

Deloitte (2013) Dashboard of the Future Vision, www2.deloitte.com/content/dam/Deloitte/de/Documents/finance-transformation/Dashboard%20of%20the%20future.pdf (accessed 04/10/17).

Derrida, J. (1996) *Archive Fever: A Freudian Impression*. Chicago, IL: University of Chicago Press.

Dewey, J. (1925) *Experience and Nature*. Chicago, IL: Open Court.

Dimberg, U. (1997) 'Psychophysiological reactions to facial expressions', in U. Segerstråhle and P. Molnar (eds), *Nonverbal Communication: Where Nature Meets Culture*. Mahwah, NJ: Lawrence Erlbaum. pp. 47–60.

Diverge (2017) Ogilvy Launches Center for Behavioral Science, www.ogilvy.com/media-center2017/press-releases/january-26-2017-ogilvy-launches-center-for-behavioral-science/ (accessed 05/10/17).

Dixon, T. (2012) 'Emotion': The history of a keyword in crisis, *Emotion Review*, http://emr.sagepub.com/content/4/4/338.full.pdf (accessed 27/10/17).

Dreyfuss, E. (2017) Silicon Valley Would Rather Cure Death Than Make Life Worth Living, *Wired*, www.wired.com/2017/03/silicon-valley-rather-cure-death-make-life-worth-living (accessed 04/10/17).

Du Plessis, E. (2011) *The Branded Mind*. London: Kogan Page.

Duchenne de Boulogne, G.B. (1990 [1862]) *The Mechanism of Human Facial Expression*. Cambridge: Cambridge University Press.

Duggan, M. (2015) The Demographics of Social Media Users, *Pew Research Center*, www.pewinternet.org/2015/08/19/the-demographics-of-social-media-users (accessed 27/10/17).

Durkheim, É. (1997 [1893]) *Division of Labour in Society*. New York: Free Press.

Easterbrook, J.A. (1959) The effect of emotion on cue utilization and the organization of behaviour, *Psychological Review*, 66 (3): 183–201.

Edge (2011) Biometrics – the Future of Videogames? www.edge-online.com/features/biometrics-future-videogames/ (accessed 27/10/17).

Edgeworth, F.Y. (1881) *Mathematical Psychics*. London: Kegan Paul.

Ekman, P. (1977) 'Biological and Cultural Contributions to Body and Facial Movement', in J. Blacking (ed.), *The Anthropology of the Body*. London: Academic Press. www.paulekman.com/wp-content/uploads/2013/07/Biological-And-Cultural-Contributions-To-Body-And-Facial-Mov.pdf (accessed 27/10/17).

Ekman, P. (1989) 'The argument and evidence about universals in facial expressions of emotions', in H. Wagner and A. Manstead (eds), *Handbook of Social Psychophysiology*. Chichester: Wiley. pp. 143–64.

Ekman, P. and Friesen, W.V. (1971) Constants across cultures in the face and emotion, *Journal of Personality and Social Psychology*, 17 (2): 124–29.

Ekman, P. and Friesen, W.V. (1978) *Facial Action Coding System: A Technique for the Measurement of Facial Movement*. Palo Alto, CA: Consulting Psychologists Press.

Ekman, P., Friesen, W. and Hager, J. (2002) *Facial Action Coding System*. Salt Lake City, UT: A Human Face.

Elias, N. (1987) On human beings and their emotions: A process-sociological essay, *Theory, Culture & Society*, 4 (2): 339–61.

Ellard, C. (2016) *Places of the Heart: The Psychogeography of Everyday Life*. New York: Bellevue Literary Press.

Emerson, R.W. (1984 [1844]) *The Collected Works of Ralph Waldo Emerson: Essays, Second Series vol. 3*. Cambridge, MA: Harvard University Press.

eyeQ (2017) *About eyeQ*, www.eyeqinsights.com/about/ (accessed 05/10/17).

Federal National Council (2010) United Arab Emirates Constitution, www.iedja.org/ wp-content/uploads/pdf/litterature_juridique/EMIRATS%20ARABES%20UNIS/ revision_constitutionnelle_2011.pdf (accessed 05/10/17).

Ferrara, A. and Bessi, E. (2016) Social Bots Distort the 2016 US Presidential Election Online Discussion, *First Monday*, 21(11), http://firstmonday.org/ojs/index.php/fm/ article/view/7090/5653 (accessed 27/10/17).

Finger, S. (2001) *Origins of Neuroscience: A History of Explorations into Brain Function*. New York: Oxford University Press.

Foucault, M. (1988) 'Technologies of the self', in L.H. Martin, H. Gutman and P.H. Hutton (eds), *Technologies of the Self: A Seminar with Michel Foucault*. Amherst, MA: University of Massachusetts.

Foucault, M. (1998 [1976]) *The History of Sexuality Vol. 1: The Will to Knowledge*. London: Penguin.

Freitas-Magalhães, A. (2017) *Facial Action Coding System 2.0: Manual of Scientific Codification of the Human Face*. Porto: FEELab Science Books.

Fridlund, A.J. (1991) The sociality of solitary smiles: Effects of an implicit audience, *Journal of Personality and Social Psychology*, 60: 229–40.

Fridlund, A.J. (1995) *Human Facial Expression: An Evolutionary View*. San Diego, CA: Academic.

Fuchs, C. (2013) *Social Media: A Critical Introduction*. London: Sage.

Fuchs, C. (2016) *Reading Marx in the Information Age: A Media and Communication Studies Perspective on Capital Volume 1*. New York: Routledge.

Gale, H. (1896) 'On the psychology of advertising', in H. Gale (ed.), *Psychological Studies*. Minneapolis, MN: H.S. Gale. pp. 39–69.

Gametrack (2016) GameTrack: Digest Quarter 1 2016, www.isfe.eu/sites/isfe.eu/files/ attachments/gametrack_european_summary_data_2016_q1.pdf (accessed 27/10/17).

Gartner (2016) Gartner Predicts a Virtual World of Exponential Change, www.gartner. com/smarterwithgartner/gartner-predicts-a-virtual-world-of-exponential-change/?cm_ mmc=social-_-rm-_-gart-_-swg (accessed 04/10/17).

Gavison, R. (1984 [1980]) 'Privacy and the limits of the law', in F.D. Schoeman (ed.), *Philosophical Dimensions of Privacy: An Anthology*. Cambridge: Cambridge University Press. pp. 346–402.

Gazzola, V., Aziz-Zadeh, L. and Keysers, C. (2006) Empathy and the somatotopic auditory mirror system in humans, *Current Biology*, 16 (18): 1824–29.

Geertz, C. (1973) 'Thick description: Toward an interpretive theory of culture', in *The Interpretation of Cultures: Selected Essays*. New York: Basic Books.

Gillespie, T. (2010) The politics of 'platforms', *New Media & Society*, 12 (3): 347–67.

Gillespie, T. (2013) 'The relevance of algorithms', in T. Gillespie, P. Boczkowski and K. Foot (eds), *Media Technologies*. Cambridge, MA: MIT Press. pp. 167–193.

Goffman, E. (1990 [1959]) *The Presentation of the Self in Everyday Life*. London: Penguin.

Goldman, A.I. (2008) *Simulating Minds: The Philosophy, Psychology, and Neuroscience of Mindreading*. New York: Oxford University Press.

Google Patents (2014) System and Method for Monitoring Respiration, www.google.co.uk/ patents/US20140228657?dq=spire+health+wearable&hl=en&sa=X&ei=F7D0VNeIIp PtauecgugG&ved=0CDwQ6AEwBA (accessed 17/10/17).

Grandey, A.A., Diefendorff, J.M. and Rupp, D.E. (2013) 'Bring emotional labor into focus', in A.A. Grandey, J.M. Diefendorff and D.E. Rupp (eds), *Emotional Labor in the 21st Century: Diverse Perspectives on Emotion Regulation at Work*. New York: Routledge.

Greenfeld, L. (2013) *Mind, Modernity, Madness: The Impact of Culture on Human Experience*. Cambridge, MA: Harvard University Press.

Gunes, H. and Pantic, M. (2010) Automatic, dimensional and continuous emotion recognition, *International Journal of Synthetic Emotions*, 1 (1): 68–99.

Gupta, O. and McDuff, D. (2016) Real-time Physiological Measurement and Visualization Using a Synchronized Multi-camera System, http://alumni.media.mit.edu/~djmcduff/assets/publications/Gupta_2016_Realtime.pdf (accessed 27/10/17).

Guznov, S., Lyons, J., Nelson, A. and Woolley, M. (2016) 'The effects of automation error types on operators' trust and reliance', in S. Lackey and R. Schumaker (eds), *Virtual, Augmented and Mixed Reality*. Dordrecht: Springer. pp. 116–24.

Habermas, J. (1991 [1962]) *The Structural Transformation of the Public Sphere: An Inquiry into a Category of Bourgeois Society*. Cambridge, MA: MIT Press.

Hao, F., Zhang, H and Fu, X. (2005) 'Modulation of attention by faces expressing emotion: Evidence from visual marking', in J. Tao, T. Tan. and R.W Picard (eds), *Affective Computing and Intelligent Interaction*, First International Conference, October 2005 Proceedings. Berlin: Springer. pp. 127–34.

Hardee, G.M. (2016) 'Immersive journalism in VR: Four theoretical domains for researching a narrative design framework', in S. Lackey and R. Schumaker (eds), *Virtual, Augmented and Mixed Reality*. Dordrecht: Springer. pp. 679–90.

Hardt, M. and Negri, A. (2000) *Empire*. Cambridge, MA: Harvard University Press.

Harré, R. (1986) *The Social Construction of Emotions*. London: Basil Blackwell.

Heidegger, M. (1991 [1939]) *Nietzsche, Vol. IV: Nihilism*, J. Stambaugh, D.F. Krell and F.A. Capuzzi (trans.). San Francisco, CA: Harper & Row.

Heidegger, M. (1993 [1954]) 'The question concerning technology', in D.F. Krell (ed.), *Basic Writings*. New York: HarperCollins.

Heidegger, M. (2011 [1962]) *Being and Time*. New York: Harper & Row.

Herder, J.G. (2002 [1774]) 'This too a philosophy of history for the formation of humanity [an early introduction]', in M.N Forster (ed.), *Philosophical Writings*. Cambridge: Cambridge University Press.

Hinton, G. (2016) Deep Learning, http://deeplearning.net/tag/geoffrey-hinton/ (accessed 27/10/17).

Hjortsjo, C. (1969) *Man's Face and Mimic Language*. Lund, Sweden: Studentlitteratur.

HM Government (2014) Personalised Health and Care 2020 Using Data and Technology to Transform Outcomes for Patients and Citizens: A Framework for Action, www.gov.uk/government/uploads/system/uploads/attachment_data/file/384650/NIB_Report.pdf (accessed 27/10/17).

HMIC (2012) Protecting the Public: Police Coordination in the New Landscape, www.gov.uk/government/uploads/system/uploads/attachment_data/file/263518/28923-R_-_Protecting_the_Public.pdf (accessed 04/10/2017).

Hochschild, A. (1983) *The Managed Heart: Commercialization of Human Feeling*. Berkeley, CA: University of California Press.

Hofstede, G.H. (1980) *Culture's Consequences: International Differences in Work-related Values*. Beverly Hills, CA: Sage.

213

Howes, D. and Classen, C. (2013) *Ways of Sensing: Understanding the Senses in Society*. New York: Routledge.

Humanyze (2017) Customer Spotlight, www.humanyze.com/case-studies (accessed 05/10/17).

Hume, D. (1896 [1739]) *A Treatise of Human Nature*. London: Oxford University Press.

Husserl, E. (1980) *Phenomenology and the Foundations of the Sciences*. The Hague: Martinus Nijhoff.

Husserl, E. (1991 [1966]) *On the Phenomenology of the Consciousness of Internal Time (1893–1917)*. Dordrecht: Kluwer.

Husserl, E. (2002 [1952]) *Ideas Pertaining to a Pure Phenomenology and to a Phenomenological Philosophy: Second Book*. Dordrecht: Kluwer.

Information Commissioner's Office (2012) Anonymisation: Managing Data Protection Risk Code of Practice, http://ico.org.uk/~/media/documents/library/Data_Protection/Practical_application/anonymisation-codev2.pdf (accessed 23/10/17).

Isreal21c (2014) Israeli Research Shows it's the Voice not the Eyes that is the Window to the Soul, www.israel21c.org/people/israeli-research-shows-its-the-voice-not-the-eyes-that-is-the-window-to-the-soul/ (accessed 27/10/17).

James, W. (1884) What is an emotion?, *Mind*, 9 (43): 188–205.

Jamieson, K.H. and Cappella, J.N. (2008) *Echo Chamber: Rush Limbaugh and the Conservative Media Establishment*. Oxford: Oxford University Press.

Jansz, J. (2005) The emotional appeal of violent video games for adolescent males, *Communication Theory*, 15(3): 219–241.

Jasper, J. (1998) The emotions of protest: Affective and reactive emotions in and around social movements, *Sociological Forum*, 13 (3): 397–424.

Jevons, W.S. (1965 [1871]) *The Theory of Political Economy*. New York: Augustus M. Kelley.

Juslin, P.N. and Scherer, K.R. (2005) 'Vocal expression of affect', in J. Harrigan, R. Rosenthal and K. Scherer (eds), *The New Handbook of Methods in Nonverbal Behavior Research*. Oxford: Oxford University Press. pp. 65–135.

Justia Patents (2006) System for Indicating Emotional Attitudes through Intonation Analysis and Methods Thereof, http://patents.justia.com/patent/8078470 (accessed 27/10/17).

Justia Patents (2012) System and Method for Determining a Personal SHG Profile by Voice Analysis, http://patents.justia.com/patent/8768708 (accessed 28/10/17).

Kahneman, D. (2011) *Thinking, Fast and Slow*. London: Penguin.

Kahneman, D. and Tversky, A. (1979) Prospect theory: An analysis of decision under risk, *Econometrica*, 47 (2): 263–91.

Kahneman, D. and Tversky, A. (2000) *Choices, Values, and Frames*. New York: Cambridge University Press.

Kant, I. (1983 [1795]) 'To perpetual peace: A philosophical sketch', in *Perpetual Peace and Other Essays* (T. Humphreys trans.). Indianapolis, IN: Hackett. pp. 107–143.

Kant, I. (1990 [1781]) *The Critique of Pure Reason*. London: Macmillan.

Kaye, D. (2015) *Report of the Special Rapporteur on the promotion and protection of the right to freedom of opinion and expression*, www.ohchr.org/EN/HRBodies/HRC/RegularSessions/Session29/Documents/A.HRC.29.32_AEV.doc (accessed 28/10/17).

Kennedy, R.S., Drexler, J. and Kennedy, R.C. (2010) Research in visually induced motion sickness, *Applied Ergonomics*, 41: 494–503.

Keshavarz, B., Hecht, H. and Lawson, B.D. (2014) 'Visually induced motion sickness: Characteristics, causes, and countermeasures', in K.S. Hale and K.M. Stanney (eds), *Handbook of Virtual Environments: Design, Implementation, and Applications*. Boca Raton, FL: CRC Press. pp. 648–97.

Kleinsmith, A., Fushimi, T. and Takenaka, H. (2003) Towards bidirectional affective human-machine interaction, *Journal of Three Dimensional Images*, 17: 61–66.

Klineberg, O. (1940) *Social Psychology*. New York: Holt.

Knight, W. (2016) Amazon Working on Making Alexa Recognize Your Emotions, MIT Technology Review, www.technologyreview.com/s/601654/amazon-working-on-making-alexa-recognize-your-emotions/ (accessed 27/10/17).

Kollanyi, B., Howard, P.N. and Woolley, S.C. (2016) Bots and Automation over Twitter during the U.S. Election, *Data Memo*, www.politicalbots.org (accessed 28/10/17).

Koops, B-J (2015) 'The concepts, approaches and applications of responsible innovation', in B.J. Koops, I. Oosterlaken, H. Romijn, T. Swierstra and J. van den Hoven (eds), *Responsible Innovation 2: Concepts, Applications, and Approaches*. Dordrecht: Springer. pp. 1–15.

Kozinets, R.V. (2015) *Netnography: Redefined*. London: Sage.

Kramer, A.D.I., Guillory, J.E. and Hancock, J.T. (2014) Experimental evidence of massive-scale emotional contagion through social networks, *Proceedings of the National Academy of Sciences*, 111 (29): 8788–90.

Kurasawa, F. (2009) A message in a bottle bearing witness as a mode of transnational practice, *Theory, Culture & Society*, 26(1): 92–111.

Lackey, S. and Shumaker, R. (eds) (2016) *Virtual, Augmented and Mixed Reality: 8th International Conference, VAMR 2016*. Dordrecht: Springer.

Lafkey, D. (2009) 'The Safe Harbor Method of De-identification: An Empirical Test', ONC Presentation, 8 October, www.ehcca.com/presentations/HIPAAWest4/lafky_2.pdf (accessed 18/04/14).

Laney, D. (2001) 3D Data Management: Controlling Data Volume, Velocity and Variety, http://blogs.gartner.com/doug-laney/files/2012/01/ad949-3D-Data-Management-Controlling-Data-Volume-Velocity-and-Variety.pdf (accessed 15/04/15).

Layard, R. (2005) *Happiness*. London: Penguin.

Lazarus, R.S. (1991) *Emotion and Adaption*. New York: Oxford University Press.

Lazzarato, M. (2014) *Signs and Machines: Capitalism and the Promotion of Subjectivity*. Los Angeles, CA: Semiotext(e).

Le Bon, G. (1896) *The Crowd: A Study of the Popular Mind*. New York: Macmillan.

LeDoux, J. (1999) *The Emotional Brain: The Mysterious Underpinnings of Emotional Life*. New York: Phoenix.

Levine, S. and Scotch, N.A. (1970) *Social Stress*. Chicago, IL: Aldine.

Lewis, S., Dontcheva, M. and Gerber, E. (2012) *Affective Computational Priming and Creativity*, https://egerber.mech.northwestern.edu/wp-content/uploads/2012/11/Gerber_AffectiveComputationalPriming.pdf, accessed 10/12/16.

Leys, R. (2011) The turn to affect: A critique, *Critical Inquiry*, 37 (3): 434–72.

Leys, R. (2012) 'Both of Us Disgusted in My Insula': Mirror Neuron Theory and Emotional Empathy, *Nonsite.org*, http://nonsite.org/article/%E2%80%9Cboth-of-us-disgusted-in-my-insula%E2%80%9D-mirror-neuron-theory-and-emotional-empathy (accessed 27/10/17).

215

Leys, R. and Goldman, M. (2010) Navigating the genealogies of trauma, guilt, and affect: An interview with Ruth Leys, *University of Toronto Quarterly*, 79 (2): 656–79.

Li, X., Hong, X., Moilanen, A., Huang, X., Pfister, T., Zhao, G. and Pietikäinen, M. (2015) Reading Hidden Emotions: Spontaneous Micro-expression Spotting and Recognition, https://arxiv.org/abs/1511.00423 (accessed 31/10/17).

Li, Y-H., Hu, Y-T., Shen, J., Preda, M., Drexler, A., Sosoiu, C., Stanculescu, F.F., Liu, P. and Ye, J. (2016) 'Ultrafast facial tracker using generic cameras with applications in intelligent lifestyle', in S. Lackey and R. Schumaker (eds), *Virtual, Augmented and Mixed Reality*. Dordrecht: Springer. pp. 234–54.

Lindstrom, M. (2005) *Brand Sense: Sensory Secrets Behind the Stuff We Buy*. London: Kogan Page.

Lindstrom, M. (2009) *Buy-ology: How Everything We Believe about Why We Buy Is Wrong*. London: Kogan Page.

Lindstrom, M. (2011) *Brandwashed: Tricks Companies Use To Manipulate Our Minds and Persuade Us To Buy*. London: Kogan Page.

Lipps, T. (1979 [1903]) 'Empathy, inner imitation and sense-feelings', in M. Rader (ed.), *A Modern Book of Esthetics*. New York: Holt, Rinehart and Winston. pp. 374–82.

Liptrot, A. and Labagnara, P. (2016) A Debrief through a Virtual Reality Window: Using VR to Illuminate the Consumer Like Never Before, *ESOMAR*, www.esomar.org/web/research_papers/Netnography-Analysis-Of-Web-Behaviour_2823_A-Debrief-Through-a-Virtual-Reality-Window.php (accessed 28/10/17).

List, C. and Petit, P. (2011) *Group Agency: The Possibility, Design, and Status of Corporate Agents*. Oxford: Oxford University Press.

Lombardo, E., Guion, C. and Keller, J. (2016) 'Study of a virtual conference in a mirror world with avatars and HMD', in S. Lackey and R. Schumaker (eds), *Virtual, Augmented and Mixed Reality*. Dordrecht: Springer. pp. 330–38.

Lowenstein, G. and Lerner, J.S. (2003) 'The role of affect in decision making', in R. Davidson, K. Scherer and H. Goldsmith (eds), *Handbook of Affective Science*. New York: Oxford University Press. pp. 619–42.

Lupton, D. (2016) *The Quantified Self*. Cambridge: Polity.

Lynskey, O. (2015) *The Foundations of EU Data Protection Law*. Oxford: Oxford University Press.

MacKinnon, C. (1989) *Toward a Feminist Theory of the State*. Cambridge, MA: Harvard University Press.

Margetts, H., John, P., Hale, S. and Yasseri, T. (2016) *Political Turbulence: How Social Media Shape Collective Action*. Princeton, NJ: Princeton University Press.

Marwick, A. (2010) Status Update: Celebrity, Publicity and Self-Branding in Web 2.0., www.tiara.org/blog/wp-content/uploads/2010/09/marwick_dissertation_statusupdate.pdf (accessed 29/10/17).

Matsumoto, D., Yoo, S.H. and Fontaine, J. (2008) Mapping expressive differences around the world: The relationship between emotional display rules and individualism versus collectivism, *Journal of Cross-Cultural Psychology*, 39 (1): 55–74.

Mayer-Schönberger, V. and Cukier, K. (2013) *Big Data: A Revolution That Will Transform How We Live, Work and Think*. London: John Murray.

Mayo, E. (1933) *The Human Problems of an Industrial Civilisation*. New York: Macmillan.

McCarthy, E.D. (1994) 'The social construction of emotions: New direction from culture theory', in W. Wentworth and J. Ryan (eds), *Social Perspective on Emotion*, vol. 2. Greenwich, CT: JAI. pp. 267–79.

McDuff, D. (2014) *Crowdsourcing Affective Responses for Predicting Media Effectiveness*, PhD thesis, http://affect.media.mit.edu/pdfs/14.McDuff-Thesis.pdf (accessed 30/10/17).

McDuff, D. and el Kaliouby, R. (2016) Applications of automated facial coding in media measurement, *Transactions on Affective Computing*, 1–13.

McDuff, D., Girard, J.M. and el Kaliouby, R. (2016) Large-scale observational evidence of cross-cultural differences in facial behavior, *Journal of Nonverbal Behavior* (pre-release): 1–14.

McLure, S.M., Li, J., Tomlin, D., Cypert, K.S. and Montague, L.M. (2004) Neural correlates of behavioral preference for culturally familiar drinks, *Neuron*, 44 (2): 379–87.

McMahan R.P., Lai, C. and Swaroop, K.P. (2016) 'Interaction fidelity: The uncanny valley of virtual reality interactions', in S. Lackey and R. Schumaker (eds), *Virtual, Augmented and Mixed Reality*. Dordrecht: Springer. pp. 59–70.

McStay, A. (2011) *The Mood of Information: A Critique of Online Behavioural Advertising*. New York: Continuum.

McStay, A. (2013) *Creativity and Advertising: Affect, Events and Process*. London: Routledge.

McStay, A. (2014) *Privacy and Philosophy: New Media and Affective Protocol*. New York: Peter Lang.

McStay, A. (2016) Empathic media and advertising: Industry, policy, legal and citizen perspectives (the case for intimacy), *Big Data & Society*, (pre-publication): 1–11.

McStay, A. (2016a) *Digital Advertising*, 2nd edn. Basingstoke: Palgrave Macmillan.

McStay, A. (2016b) The Do's and Don't of Emotion Capture: An Overview of Discussion and Suggestions, https://drive.google.com/file/d/0BzU2NrGCFp7qSldQTmluY2hP-ZEU/view (accessed 05/10/17).

McStay, A. (2017) *Privacy and the Media*. London: Sage.

McStay, A. (2017a) Empathic Media: The Rise of Emotion AI, www.researchgate.net/publication/317616480_EMPATHIC_MEDIA_THE_RISE_OF_EMOTION_AI (accessed 31/10/17).

mediaX (2015) Knowledge Worker Productivity, http://mediax.stanford.edu/themes/kwp (accessed 31/10/17).

mediaX (2015a) The Utility of Calming Technologies in Integrative Productivity, http://mediax.stanford.edu/page/utility-of-calming-technologies (accessed 31/10/17).

Mental Health Foundation (2017) Surviving or Thriving? The State of the UK's Mental Health, www.mentalhealth.org.uk/publications/surviving-or-thriving-state-uks-mental-health (accessed 04/10/17).

Mental Health Foundation (2017a) Mental Health Statistics: The Most Common Mental Health Problems, www.mentalhealth.org.uk/statistics/mental-health-statistics-most-common-mental-health-problems (accessed 04/10/17).

Merleau-Ponty, M. (2002 [1945]) *Phenomenology of Perception*. London: Routledge.

Micu, A.C. and Plummer, J.T. (2010) Measurable emotions: How television ads really work, *Journal of Advertising Research*, 50 (2): 137–53.

Mill, J.S. (1962 [1859]) *'Utilitarianism' and 'On Liberty' and 'Essay on Bentham'*. London: Fontana.

Millett, D. (2001) Hans Berger: From psychic energy to the EEG, *Perspectives in Biology and Medicine*, 44 (4): 522–42.

Minsky, M. (2006) *The Emotion Machine: Commonsense Thinking, Artificial Intelligence and the Future of the Human Mind*. New York: Simon and Schuster.

Mobile Ecosystem Forum (2016) *Mobile Messaging Report 2016*, www.mobileecosystem forum.com/wp-content/uploads/2016/06/Messaging_Report.pdf (accessed 22/03/17).

Morozov, E. (2014) *To Save Everything Click Here*. London: Penguin.

Munyan, B.G., Neer, S.M., Beidel, D.C. and Jentsch, F. (2016) 'Olfactory stimuli increase presence during simulated exposure', in S. Lackey and R. Schumaker (eds), *Virtual, Augmented and Mixed Reality*. Dordrecht: Springer. pp. 164–72.

Nacke, L.E., Kalyn, M., Lough, C. and Mandryk, R.L. (2011) 'Biofeedback game design: using direct and indirect physiological control to enhance game interaction', in *Proceedings of the 2011 Annual Conference on Human Factors in Computing Systems (CHI 2011)*, Vancouver, BC, Canada. pp. 103–12.

Nagel, T. (1970) *The Possibility of Altruism*. New York: Oxford.

Neff, G. and Nafus, D. (2016) *Self-tracking*. Cambridge, MA: MIT.

Nelson, T. (2003 [1974]) 'Computer lib: You can and must understand computers now', in N. Montfort and N. Wardrip-Fruin (eds), *The New Media Reader*. Cambridge, MA: MIT.

Nietzsche, F. (2009 [1882]) *The Gay Science*. Cambridge: Cambridge University Press.

Noelle-Neumann, E. (1974) The spiral of silence: A theory of public opinion, *Journal of Communication*, 24 (2): 43–51.

Nogueira, P.A., Rodrigues, R., Oliveira, E. and Nacke, L.E. (2013) 'Guided emotional state regulation: Understanding and shaping players' affective experiences in digital games', in *Proceedings of the Ninth AAAI Conference on Artificial Intelligence and Interactive Digital Entertainment*. pp. 51–7.

Oatley, K. (1999) Meetings of minds: Dialogue, sympathy, and identification in reading fiction, *Poetics*, 26: 439–54.

Oberman, L. and Ramachandran, V.S. (2009) 'Reflections on the mirror neuron system: Their evolutionary functions beyond motor representation', in J.A. Pineda (ed.), *Mirror Neuron Systems: The Role of Mirroring Processes in Social Cognition*. Totowa, NJ: Humana. pp. 39–62.

Ogilvy (2017) Ogilvy Launches Center for Behavioral Science, www.ogilvy.com/ media-center2017/press-releases/january-26-2017-ogilvy-launches-center-for-behavioral-science/ (accessed 05/10/17).

Ohm, P. (2009) Broken promises of privacy: Responding to the surprising failure of anonymization, *UCLA Law Review*, (57): 1701–77. http://uclalawreview.org/pdf/57-6-3.pdf (accessed 31/10/17).

Oliver, M.B., Dillard, J.P., Bae, K. and Tamul, D.J. (2012) The effects of narrative news format on empathy for stigmatized groups, *Journalism and Mass Communication Quarterly*, 89 (2): 205–24.

O'Reilly, T. (2013) 'Open data and algorithmic regulation', in B. Goldstein and L. Dyson (eds), *Beyond Transparency: Open Data and the Future of Civic Innovation*. San Francisco, CA: Code for America Press. pp. 289–300.

Oyserman, D., Coon, H.M. and Kemmelmeier, M. (2002) Rethinking individualism and collectivism: Evaluation of theoretical assumptions and meta-analyses, *Psychological Bulletin*, 128 (1): 3–72.

Page, G. (2011) 'Increasing our brainpower – using neuroscience effectively', in E. du Plessis (ed.), *The Branded Mind*. London: Kogan Page.

Palti, I. and Bar, M. (2015) A manifesto for conscious cities: Should streets be sensitive to our mental needs? *The Guardian*, https://www.theguardian.com/cities/2015/aug/28/manifesto-conscious-cities-streets-sensitive-mental-needs, accessed 05/06/17.

Panksepp, J. (2007) Neurologizing the psychology of affects: How appraisal-based constructivism and basic emotion theory can coexist, *Perspectives in Psychological Science*, 2 (3): 281–96.

Pantti, M. (2010) The value of emotion: An examination of television journalists' notions on emotionality, *European Journal of Communication*, 25 (2): 168–81.

Papacharissi, Z. (2009) 'The virtual sphere 2.0: The internet, the public sphere, and beyond', in A. Chadwick and P.N. Howard (eds), *Routledge Handbook of Internet Politics*. New York: Routledge. pp. 230–45.

Paré, A. (1649) *The Workes*. London: Richard Coates, https://archive.org/stream/workesofthatfamo00par/workesofthatfamo00par_djvu.txt (accessed 31/10/17).

Perron, B. and Schröter, F. (eds) (2015) 'Video games, cognition, affect and emotion', in B. Perron and F. Schröter (eds), *Video Games and the Mind: Essays on Cognition, Affect and Emotion*. Jefferson, NC: McFarland & Company. pp. 1–14.

PewReseachCenter (2014) Social Media and the 'Spiral of Silence', www.pewinternet.org/2014/08/26/social-media-and-the-spiral-of-silence/ (accessed 31/10/17).

Pfaffenberger, B. (1995) *The USENET Book: Finding, Using, and Surviving Newsgroups on the Internet*. Reading, MA: Addison-Wesley.

Pfister, H.R. and Böhm, G. (2008) The multiplicity of emotions: A framework of emotional functions in decision making, *Judgment and Decision Making*, 3 (1): 5–17.

Phelps, E.A., Ling, S. and Carrasco, M. (2006) Emotion facilitates perception and potentiates the perceptual benefits of attention, *Psychological Science*, 17 (4): 292–99.

Phillips, W. (2015) *This Is Why We Can't Have Nice Things: Mapping the Relationship Between Online Trolling and Mainstream Culture*. Cambridge, MA: MIT.

Picard, R.W. (1995) *Affective Computing*. MIT Media Laboratory Perceptual Computing Section Technical Report No. 321, www.pervasive.jku.at/Teaching/_2009SS/Seminar ausPervasiveComputing/Begleitmaterial/Related%20Work%20(Readings)/1995_Affective%20computing_Picard.pdf (accessed 31/10/17).

Picard, R.W. (1997) *Affective Computing*. Cambridge, MA: MIT.

Picard, R.W. (2007) Toward Machines with Emotional Intelligence, http://affect.media.mit.edu/pdfs/07.picard-EI-chapter.pdf (accessed 31/10/17).

Plato (1993 [360 BC]) *Sophist*. Indianapolis, IN: Hackett.

Popper, B. (2016) This is how Facebook will animate you in VR, *The Verge*, www.theverge.com/2016/10/6/13176906/oculus-connect-3-facebook-social-vr-avatars (accessed 05/10/17).

Privacy International (2013) Who, What, Why, www.privacyinternational.org/ (accessed 31/10/17).

Quattrociocchi, W., Scala, A. and Sunstein, C. (2016) Echo Chambers on Facebook, *SSRN*, https://papers.ssrn.com/sol3/papers.cfm?abstract_id=2795110 (accessed 31/10/17).

Rabiner, L.R. and Juang, B.H. (1993) *Fundamentals of Speech Recognition*. Upper Saddle River, NJ: Prentice Hall.

Rabinow, P. and Rose, N. (2006) Biopower today, *Biosocieties*, 1 (2): 195–217.

Rajan, K.S. (2006) *Biocapital: The Constitution of Postgenomic Life*. Durham, NC: Duke University Press.

RetailDetail (2017) Amazon Enters Top Ten of the World's Largest Retailers, www.retail detail.eu/en/news/algemeen/amazon-enters-top-ten-worlds-largest-retailers (accessed 04/10/17).

Richards, B. (2007) *Emotional Governance: Politics, Media and Terror*. Basingstoke: Palgrave Macmillan.

Richardson, K. (2016) Sex robot matters: Slavery, the prostituted, and the rights of machines, *IEEE Technology and Society Magazine*, 35 (2): 46–53.

Riedl, M., Thue, D. and Bulitko, V. (2011) 'Game AI as Storytelling', in M. Gonzalo and M.O. Gómez-Martín (eds), *Artificial Intelligence for Computer Games*. Heidelberg: Springer. pp. 125–50.

Rose, N. (1999) *Governing the Soul*, 2nd edn. London: Free Association Books.

Rose, N. (2006) *The Politics of Life Itself: Biomedicine, Power, and Subjectivity in the Twenty-first Century*. Princeton, NJ: Princeton University Press.

Rotzoll, K.B., Haefner, J.E. and Hall, S.R. (1996) *Advertising in Contemporary Society*. Urbana, IL: University of Illinois Press.

RUSI (2015) A Democratic License to Operate, https://rusi.org/sites/default/files/20150714_ whr_2-15_a_democratic_licence_to_operate.pdf (accessed 04/10/17).

Russell, J.A. (1980) A circumplex model of affect, *Journal of Personality and Social Psychology*, 39(6): 1161–1178.

Russell, J.A. (1994) Is there universal recognition of emotion from facial expression? A review of the cross-cultural studies, *Psychological Bulletin*, 115 (1): 102–41.

Russell, J.A. and Carroll J.M. (1999) On the bipolarity of positive and negative affect, *Psychology Bulletin*, 125 (1): 3–30.

Russell, S. and Norvig, P. (2010) *Artificial Intelligence: A Modern Approach*. Englewood Cliffs, NJ: Prentice Hall.

Salcedo, J.N., Lackey, S.J. and Maraj, C. (2016) 'Impact of instructional strategies on workload, stress, and flow in simulation-based training for behavior cue analysis', in S. Lackey and R. Schumaker (eds), *Virtual, Augmented and Mixed Reality*. Dordrecht: Springer. pp. 184–95.

Satava, R.M. (1995) Virtual reality and telepresence for military medicine, *Computers in Biology and Medicine*, 25 (2): 229–36.

Satel, S. and and Lilienfeld, S.O. (2013) *Brainwashed: The Seductive Appeal of Mindless Neuroscience*. New York: Basic Books.

Scheler, M. (2009 [1913]) *The Nature of Sympathy*. Piscataway, NJ: Transaction.

Scherer, K.R. and Ekman, P. (1982) *Handbook of Methods in Nonverbal Behavior Research* (Studies in Emotion and Social Interaction). Cambridge: Cambridge University Press.

Scherer, K.R., Shorr, A. and Johnstone, T. (eds) (2001) *Appraisal Processes in Emotion: Theory, Methods, Research*. Cary, NC: Oxford University Press.

Scheve, C. von and Ismer, S. (2013) Towards a theory of collective emotions, *Emotion Review*, 5 (4): 406–13.

Schopenauer, A. (1970 [1851]) *Essays and Aphorisms*. New York: Penguin.

Schreuder, E., Erp, J.van, Toet, A. and Kallen V.L. (2016) Emotional responses to multisensory environmental stimuli: A conceptual framework and literature review, *SAGE Open*, 1–19.

Schwab, K. (2016) *The Fourth Industrial Revolution*. London: Penguin.

Searle, J.R. (1998) *The Mystery of Consciousness*. London: Granta.

Selye, H. (1938) Adaptation energy, *Nature*, 141 (3577): 926.

Selye, H. (1978) *The Stress of Life*. New York: McGraw-Hill.

Shannon, C. and Weaver, W. (1949) *The Mathematical Theory of Communication*. Champaign, IL: University of Illinois Press.

Sharkey, N., Wynsberghe, A. van, Robbins, S. and Hancock, E. (2017) *Our Sexual Future with Robots: A Foundation for Responsible Robotics Consultation Report*, http://responsiblerobotics.org/wp-content/uploads/2017/07/FRR-Consultation-Report-Our-Sexual-Future-with-robots_Final.pdf (accessed 31/10/17).

Simon, H.A. and Newell, A. (1958) Heuristic Problem Solving: The Next Advance in Operations Research, www.u-picardie.fr/~furst/docs/Newell_Simon_Heuristic_Problem_Solving_1958.pdf (accessed 31/10/17).

Skrovan, S. (2017) Why most shoppers still choose brick-and-mortar stores over e-commerce, *RetailDive*, www.retaildive.com/news/why-most-shoppers-still-choose-brick-and-mortar-stores-over-e-commerce/436068/ (accessed 04/10/17).

Slaby, J. (2014) 'Emotions and the extended mind', in C. von Scheve and M. Salmela (eds), *Collective Emotions*. Oxford: Oxford University Press. pp. 32–46.

Smart Dubai (2015) Smart District Guidelines, http://smartdubai.ae/districtguidelines/Smart_Dubai_District_Guidelines_Public_Brief.pdf (accessed 05/10/17).

Smart Dubai (2016) His Highness Sheikh Mohammed Bin Rashid Al Maktoum Adopts Smart Dubai Happiness Agenda Fuelling the City's Transformation with a Globally Unique Focus on Happiness, http://www.smartdubai.ae/story060202.php (accessed 05/10/17).

Smith, A. (1993 [1776]) *An Inquiry into the Nature and Causes of the Wealth of Nations: Inquiry into the Nature and Causes of the Wealth of Nations* [Abridged]. Indianapolis, IN: Hackett.

Smith, A. (2011 [1759]) *The Theory of Moral Sentiments*. Kapaau: Gutenberg.

Smith, T.W. (2015) *The Book of Human Emotions*. London: Profile.

Sorenson, E.R. (1976) *The Edge of the Forest: Land, Childhood and Change in a New Guinea Protoagricultural Society*. Washington, DC: Smithsonian Institution Press.

Spinoza, B. (1996 [1677]) *Ethics*. London: Penguin.

Spire (2017) What Can Spire Track?, http://support.spire.io/customer/en/portal/articles/2335404-what-can-spire-track- (accessed 05/10/17).

Stearns, P.N. (1994) *American Cool: Constructing a Twentieth-century Emotional Style*. New York: NYU Press.

Stern, B. (2004) The importance of being ernest: Commemorating Dichter's contribution to advertising research, *Journal of Advertising Research*, 44 (2): 165–69.

Stiegler, B. (1998) *Technics and Time, 1: The Fault of Epimetheus*. Stanford, CA: Stanford University Press.

Stiegler, B. (2010) *For a New Critique of Political Economy*. Cambridge: Polity.

Sunstein, C.R. (2016) *The Ethics of Influence: Government in the Age of Behavioral Science*. New York: Cambridge University Press.

Suwa, M., Sugie, N. and Fujimora, K. (1978) A preliminary note on pattern recognition of human emotional expression, *Proceedings of the International Joint Conference on Pattern Recognition.* pp. 408–10.

Szczuka, J. and Krämer, N. (2017) Not only the lonely: How men explicitly and implicitly evaluate the attractiveness of sex robots in comparison to the attractiveness of women, and personal characteristics influencing this evaluation, *Multimodal Technologies and Interaction*, 1 (3): 1–18.

Tajfel, H. (1970) Experiments in Intergroup Discrimination, www.box.net/shared/static/ieahzod96e.PDF (accessed 04/10/17).

Tarde, G. (1993 [1890]) *Les lois de l'imitation*. Paris: Kimé.

Tene, O. and Polonetsky, J. (2014) A theory of creepy: Technology, privacy, and shifting social norms, *Yale Journal of Law and Technology*, 16 (1): 59–102.

Thaler, R.H. and Sunstein, C.R. (2003) Libertarian paternalism, *American Economic Review*, 93: 175–79.

Thaler, R.H. and Sunstein, C.R. (2008*) Nudge: Improving Decisions about Health, Wealth and Happiness.* London: Penguin.

The Economist (2016) Against Happiness, www.economist.com/news/business-and-finance/21707502-companies-try-turn-happiness-management-tool-are-overstepping-mark (accessed 30/10/17).

The Intercept (2015) XKEYSCORE: NSA's Google for the World's Private Communications, https://firstlook.org/theintercept/2015/07/01/nsas-google-worlds-private-communications (accessed 05/10/17).

The Supreme Legislation Committee in the Emirate of Dubai (2016) *Law No. (26) of 2015 Regulating Data Dissemination and Exchange in the Emirate of Dubai* (accessed 05/10/17).

Thoits, P.A. (1989) The sociology of emotions, *Annual Review of Sociology*, 15: 317–42.

Titcomb, J. (2017) Mark Zuckerberg Confirms Facebook is Working On Mind-reading Technology, *The Telegraph*, www.telegraph.co.uk/technology/2017/04/19/mark-zuckerberg-confirms-facebook-working-mind-reading-technology (accessed 04/10/17).

Tobii (2017) Tobii Releases Eye Tracking VR Development Kit for HTC Vive, www.tobii.com/group/news-media/press-releases/2017/5/tobii-releases-eye-tracking-vr-development-kit-for-htc-vive/ (accessed 05/10/17).

Tobii (2017a) This Is Eye Tracking, www.tobii.com/group/about/this-is-eye-tracking/ (accessed 05/10/17).

Tomkins, S.S. (1962) *Affect, Imagery, Consciousness, Vol. 1: The Positive Affects*. New York: Springer.

Tomkins, S.S. (1963) *Affect, Imagery, Consciousness, Vol. 2: The Negative Affects*. New York: Springer.

Toscano, A. (2007) Vital strategies: Maurizio Lazzarato and the metaphysics of contemporary capitalism, *Theory, Culture & Society*, 24 (6): 71–91.

Trivers, B. (2011) *Deceit and Self-deception: Fooling Yourself the Better to Fool Others*. New York: Penguin.

True Companion (2017) FAQ (Frequently Asked Questions), www.truecompanion.com/shop/faq (accessed 05/10/17).

Turing, A.M. (1950) Computing machinery and intelligence, *Mind*, 49: 433–60.

Turkle, S. (2005) *The Second Self: Computers and the Human Spirit*. Cambridge, MA: MIT.

Turkle, S. (2007) Authenticity in the age of digital companions, *Interaction Studies: Social Behaviour and Communication in Biological and Artificial Systems*, 8 (3): 501–17.

Turkle, S. (2010) 'In good company? On the threshold of robotic companions', in Y. Wilks (ed.), *Close Engagements with Artificial Companions: Key Social, Psychological, Ethical and Design Issues*. Amsterdam: John Benjamins. pp. 3–10.

Turow J. (2017) *The Aisles Have Eyes: How Retailers Track Your Shopping, Strip Your Privacy, and Define Your Power*. New Haven, CT: Yale University Press.

Unruly (2017) Case Study: How Private Marketplaces Based On Emotions Lead to Movie Success, https://unruly.co/blog/article/2017/02/16/case-study-private-marketplaces-emotions-movie-success (accessed 05/10/17).

Uribe, R. and Gunter, B. (2007) Are 'sensational' news stories more likely to trigger viewers' emotions than non-sensational news stories? A content analysis of British TV news, *European Journal of Communication*, 22: 207–28.

Urry, J. (2000) The Global Media and Cosmopolitanism, www.lancaster.ac.uk/sociology/research/publications/papers/urry-global-media.pdf (accessed 31/10/17).

US Patent and Trademark Office (2015) Technique for Emotion Detection and Content Delivery, http://pdfaiw.uspto.gov/.aiw?docid=20150242679&PageNum=12&IDKey=47BC4614A23D&HomeUrl=http://appft.uspto.gov/netacgi/nph-Parser?Sect1=PTO1 (accessed 31/10/17).

Van der Löwe, I. and Parkinson, B. (2014) Relational emotions and social networks in C. von Scheve and M. Salmela (eds), *Collective Emotions*. Oxford: Oxford University Press. pp. 125–40.

Vischer, R. (1993 [1873]) 'On the optical sense of form: A contribution to aesthetics', in H.F. Mallgrave and E. Ikonomou (eds), *Empathy, Form, and Space: Problems in German Aesthetics, 1873–1893*. Santa Monica, CA: Getty Center for the History of Art. pp. 89–123.

Warren, S. and Brandeis, L. (1984 [1890]) 'The right to privacy [the implicit made explicit]', in F.D. Schoeman (ed.), *Philosophical Dimensions of Privacy: An Anthology*. Cambridge: Cambridge University Press. pp. 75–103.

Weiser, M. (1991) The computer for the 21st century, *Scientific American*, 265 (3): 66–75. www.ubiq.com/hypertext/weiser/SciAmDraft3.html (accessed 20/09/14).

Weizenbaum, J. (1966) A computer program for the study of natural language communication between man and machine, *Communications of the Association of Computing Machinery*, 9 (1): 36–45.

Weizenbaum, J. (1976) *Computer Power and Human Reason*. New York: W.H. Freeman and Company.

Wilkinson, T.M. (2013) Nudging and manipulation, *Political Science*, 61 (2): 341–55.

Williams, S. (2000) *Emotion and Social Theory: Corporeal Reflections on the (Ir) Rational*. London: Sage.

Williams, S. (2001) *Emotion and Social Theory*. London: Sage.

Witmer, B.G. and Singer, M.J. (1998) Measuring presence in virtual environments: A presence questionnaire, *Presence*, 7 (3): 225–40.

Wundt, W. (1902) *Principles of Physiological Psychology*. London: Wilhelm Englemmann.

Yao, M. (2017) Fighting Algorithmic Bias and Homogenous Thinking in A.I., *Forbes*, www.forbes.com/sites/mariyayao/2017/05/01/dangers-algorithmic-bias-homogenous-thinking-ai/#4df997fa70b3 (accessed 04/10/17).

Yearsley, L. (2017) We Need to Talk About the Power of AI to Manipulate Humans, *MIT Technology Review*, www.technologyreview.com/s/608036/we-need-to-talk-about-the-power-of-ai-to-manipulate-humans/ (accessed 04/10/17).

Zelenski, J.M. and Larsen, R.J. (2000) The distribution of basic emotions in everyday life: A state and trait perspective from experience sampling data, *Journal of Research in Personality*, 34 (2): 178–97.

Zhao, S. (2006) Humanoid social robots as a medium of communication, *New Media & Society*, 8 (3): 401.

Zillmann, D. (1991) 'Empathy: Affect from bearing witness to the emotions of others', in J. Bryant and D. Zillmann (eds), *Responding to the Screen: Reception and Reaction Processes*. Hillsdale, NJ: Lawrence Erlbaum. pp. 135–68.

Zimmerman, M.E. (1990) *Heidegger's Confrontation with Modernity: Technology, Politics, Art*. Bloomington, IN: Indiana University Press.

INDEX